# INDUSTRIALISATION, SOCIO-ECÓNOMIC EXTERNALITIES AND STATE POLICY

## About the Editor

**Dr. Abdul Aziz** is Professor of Economics in the Institute for Social and Economic Change, Bangalore and currently directing a project on *Decentralised Governance and Planning*. Besides guiding doctoral students and directing research projects, he has organised many training programmes, and national and international workshops in the area of Decentralisation. Poverty Alleviation and Regional Development. He has published a number of research papers and books in the above areas of his specialization.

Apart from associating himself with the academic bodies of the Universities, Prof. Aziz has served as a member of expert committees of the Government of Karnataka such as the State Finance Commission and the Committee on the fixation of fees in the technical education institutions. He has widely travelled in the East and the West delivering lectures and presenting seminars.

# INDUSTRIALISATION, SOCIO-ECONOMIC EXTERNALITIES AND STATE POLICY

*Editor*

ABDUL AZIZ

Professor
Economic Unit, Institute for Social and Economic Change
Bangalore - 560072

CONCEPT PUBLISHING COMPANY, NEW DELHI - 110059

ISBN 81-7022-629-5

First Published 1997



Abdul **Aziz** (*b*. 1937)

*Published and Printed by*

Ashok Kumar Mittal
**Concept Publishing Company**
A/15-16, Commercial Block,
Mohan Garden,
NEW DELHI - 110059 (India)
Phones: 5554042, 5504042
Fax No. 091-11-5598898

*DEDICATED TO*

*THE MEMORY OF*

*PROF. L.S. VENKATARAMAN*

# PREFACE

This volume is the product of a seminar organised in Bellary city during August 16—18, 1996 on the socio-economic implications of the massive industrial investment expected to flow into Bellary district, Karnataka. The idea of such an exercise came from Shri M.P. Prakash, Minister for Rural Development and Panchayat Raj and Smt. Gouri S. Trivedi, IAS, Deputy Commissioner, Bellary. When our Institute Director, Dr. P.V. Shenoi received a written request from Smt. Gouri Trivedi urging him to take up this assignment, he kindly entrusted this task to me. I, in turn, in consultation with him invited some of my colleagues in ISEC and a few outside scholars to join the research team to carry out this exercise and to prepare papers on themes identified as important.

In a preliminary meeting held in ISEC on November 10, 1995 the proposal dealing with the theme was discussed, topics were identified and assigned to scholars. After collecting secondary data, the team left for Bellary for field work. Three pre-seminar group discussions were held one each with (i) officers and industrialists of Bellary on November 28, 1995, (ii) with citizens of Bellary on November 29, 1995 and (iii) officers, citizens and industrialists of Hospet on December 3, 1995. Smt. Gouri Trivedi very graciously arranged these meetings and provided all facilities to the team for stay at Bellary and visits to industries, Government and municipal offices and some villages.

Based on the first round of field work, preliminary drafts of the papers were prepared and discussed in a one day workshop held in ISEC on January 3, 1996 to clarify concepts, identify data gaps and to link the papers to the main focus of the proposed seminar. To fill the data gaps, a second round of field work was organised. A pre-seminar discussion was hosted in Hospet by Messrs. Tungabhadra Steel Products on January 16, 1996. This was followed by field visits by the team in and around Hospet and Bellary. In Bellary a group discussion was held with the mine owners on January 18, 1996 and took note of their views as was the practice followed in respect of all other groups whom the team met.

On both the occasions, during the field work, apart from holding structured group discussions, we held separate meetings with select industrialists, government functionaries, political leaders and knowledgeable citizens. The field data collected thus formed the database of the papers included here. Maximum care has been taken to ensure that only reliable and authenticated data went into our analysis by subjecting it to thorough scrutiny and discussion at the seminar by a cross-section of industrialists, mine owners, Government and municipal officers, knowledgeable citizens and people's representatives. Further, in the light of the comments and suggestions received from the seminar participants the papers have been appropriately revised and edited.

The seminar was inaugurated by Shri M.P. Prakash, Minister for Rural Development and Panchayati Raj, Government of Karnataka under the chairmanship of Prof. Chandrasekhara Kambara, Vice-chancellor, Kannada University, Hampi, Bellary district. The valedictory address of the seminar was delivered by Dr. P.V. Shenoi, Director, ISEC under the chairmanship of Smt. Gouri Trivedi. Sri Sudhir Krishna presented his thoughts on the operationalisation of the seminar recommendations. The support system for holding the seminar came from Smt. Gouri Trivedi and her colleagues. The technical sessions were chaired by Smt. Gouri Trivedi, Dr. Rajkumar Katri, Mr. R.N. Singh, Mr. Gopal Hosur and Dr. P.V. Shenoi. Dr. M. Prahaladachar, Dr. B.S. Sreekantaradhya, Dr. N. Sivanna, Dr. V.S. Satyapriya, Dr. R.V. Dadibhavi and Dr. K.G. Gayathri Devi acted as rapporteurs.

Dr. P.V. Shenoi, our Director, Dr. M. Venkata Reddy, our past Registrar and Dr. S.N. Sangita, our present Registrar provided administrative and moral support all along. Dr. B. Seshadri and Mr. C. Charles Nelson coordinated field visits. Ms. Lakshmi, Mr. Shivappa and Ms. Padmini Murthy prepared the several drafts of the papers and Mr. T.K. Ganesh took multiple copies of these papers. Dr. Madhushree Sekher checked and rechecked the script for any mistakes. To all of them and to a host of officers, industrialists, mine owners, labour leaders and citizens of Bellary district whose names cannot be mentioned here deserve my grateful thanks. My thanks are also due to Messrs. Concept Publishing Company for bringing the seminar volume as a publication within a short period.

*Bangalore* ABDUL AZIZ

*September 2, 1996*

# CONTENTS

# LIST OF CONTRIBUTORS

**Aziz, Abdul,** Professor, Economic Unit, Institute for Economic Change, Bangalore - 560072

**Chandrasekhara, T.R.**, Reader, Department of Development Studies, Kannada University, Hampi.

**Charles Nelson, C.,** Assistant Director, Decentralisation Project, ISEC, Bangalore.

**Devendra Babu, M.,** Assistant Director, Decentralisation Project, ISEC, Bangalore.

**Gayathri Devi, K.G.,** Assistant Professor, Decentralisation Project, ISEC, Bangalore.

**Jayanna, S.,** Reader, Department of Commerce and Management Studies, Gulbarga University, P.G. Center, Bellary.

**Madhushree Sekher,** Assistant Director, Decentralisation Project, ISEC, Bangalore.

**Prahladachar, M.,** Professor and Head, Rural Economics Unit, ISEC, Bangalore.

**Rao, V.M.,** formerly Professor, ISEC, Bangalore

**Satyapriya, V.S.,** Associate Professor, Agriculture Development and Rural Transformation (ADRT) Unit, ISEC, Bangalore.

**Seshadri, B.,** Professor, Department of Development Studies, Kannada University, Hampi.

**Shenoi, P.V.,** Director, ISEC, Bangalore.

**Shyamala, C.K.,** Training Assistant, Decentralisation Project, ISEC, Bangalore.

**Sivanna, N.,** Deputy Director, Decentralisation Project, ISEC, Bangalore.

**Sudhir Krishna**, IAS, Commissioner for Commercial Taxes, Government of Karnataka, Bangalore.

**Thippaiah, P.,** Assistant Professor, ADRT Unit, ISEC, Bangalore.

**Vasuki, K.G.,** Faculty member, Kannada University, Hampi.

**Vijaykumar, B.,** Assistant Director, Decentralisation Project, ISEC, Bangalore.

**Vittal, T.G.,** an activist based at Bellary.

**Vivekananda, M.,** Assistant Professor, ADRT Unit, ISEC, Bangalore.
**Yadav, Manohar,** Associate Professor, Sociology Unit, ISEC, Bangalore.
**Yeranna**, Senior Lecturer in Economics, Allam Sumangalamma Mahila College, Bellary.

# LIST OF TABLES

# 1

# INTRODUCTION

ABDUL AZIZ

---

Bellary District is likely to attract a massive size of investment in industry during the next 5-6 years. While this will initiate industrial and economic growth and help develop material and human resources in the district, the pumping in of money of this magnitude is likely to cause some major adverse effects on the society, economy and polity unless timely steps are taken to minimise them. These expected adverse effects on *a priory* grounds are listed as follows:

(a) There will be a heavy pressure on basic infrastructure such as power, transport, roads and bridges, and communications. If action is not taken in time to provide as also to expand these infrastructure facilities, the district economy is likely to suffer; particularly industries when starved of these facilities are likely to go red. There will also be a corresponding rise in demand for social infrastructure such as education and health facilities.

(b) There will be a heavy pressure on municipal services such as drinking water supply, housing, sanitation and solid waste management. Since industries are likely to be mostly located in the urban areas, the municipal bodies will be under heavy pressure to provide such services in large quantities in response to heavy demand. In the absence of which the quality of life of the people is likely to suffer.

(c) The huge industrial investment will put pressure on certain resources such as land and manpower resources. It is expected that with the starting of industries there will be heavy demand for land for putting up industrial buildings and housing units for workers. This will cause land prices to go up tremendously. Under these circumstances, land grabbing and other illegal activities which will become profitable might emerge.

The demand for manpower is also likely to go up resulting in shortage of labour particularly the skilled and the managerial workers. As other economic activities will also come up in the district in response to industrial units being set up, demand for unskilled workers will also go up. Since the locally available labour would not be sufficient to meet the manpower requirements there will be in-migration of workers from other districts of Karnataka and even from other States. This may encourage practices such as contract labour system to emerge and the consequent labour exploitation to become rampant. Also, the problem of local *vs.* outside labour will emerge giving rise to building up of social unrest in the region.

Further, industrial labour will come to be organised on a big scale. As initially, working and employment conditions are likely to be less than satisfactory, and if managements tend to be unimaginative, militant unionism may emerge. Under these circumstances, both unions and management may take the help of outsiders giving room for unscrupulous politicians and rowdy elements to control labour movement.

(d) With the increased employment opportunities and income generation, the phenomenon of consumerism may bring in goods of all kinds into market. As a follow-up, activities such as money-lending, liquor trading, gang wars and prostitution may become extensive, putting the administrative machinery under heavy strain.

(e) It is also expected that under all these conditions, there will emerge a nexus among unscrupulous politicians, criminals and unprincipled businessmen leading to erosion of the value system in public life.

(f) The massive investment both in manufacturing and mining of minerals will affect the eco-system causing industrial pollution and creating health hazard to the people.

(g) Finally, some trade off situations are likely to be created by the industrial investment such as the following, for instance:

(i) The drawing up of water from the Tungabhadra irrigation canal for industrial purpose may affect the interest of local agriculture sector.

(ii) The demand for iron ore from the local industries may reduce the quantity of iron ore available to National Mineral Development Corporation for exports causing a drop in foreign exchange earnings.

(iii) Increased incomes by widening income inequalities may create political and social strife in the district.

There could be, of course, other adverse effects too. It will be of interest to identify as also quantify such effects. Given such possibilities, it will be necessary to prepare an action plan in perspective for 1996 - 2011 indicating therein the role of government, industrialists, local self-governments, non-government organisations and conscientious citizens to minimise these adverse effects to the extent possible.

In this process of preparing a perspective plan for the district, two issues are involved : One is substantive and the other is methodological. The substantive issue relates to assessing and quantifying the likely adverse effects of industrial investment by carrying out a futurology exercise. As for the methodological issue is concerned, a question that arises is : How to carry out the futurology exercise? It is a well known fact that an economist who is engaged in predicting the future behaviour of the phenomenon under observation would first understand the past trends in respect of this phenomenon and then project these trends to the future date. But an exercise of this type projecting the past trends will not be just adequate in the present case because here the economist is not dealing with a situation where the parameters are growing at the normal rates, but with a situation where they are likely to grow at a faster rate owing to huge investment that is expected to come in during that period of time. Therefore, the exercise that needs to be carried out is not one of merely projecting the past trends, but rather of working out future trends taking into account what might happen to these parameters during the next 5-6 years consequent to the huge investment that is likely to come in.

In this futurology exercise, therefore, the endeavour has been to identify the basic parameters of the society, economy and polity and to estimate their values based not on past trends but on an estimate of the future behaviour of these parameters consequent to the disturbances created by the increasing investment activities. The methodology followed in this exercise has been as described in the following paragraphs:

Each of the paper writers has prepared a status paper on the theme assigned presenting past trends and stating the present position. In the next stage, growth in demand for a particular commodity or service has been estimated following two different methods: (a) by using the actual growth values and (b) by using the norms accepted by the authorities. For example, when it comes to the question of estimation of demand for municipal services, the futurology exercises estimated the demand for a given service either on the basis of actual ratio arrived at on the basis of the observed trend or by using the norm-based ratio. Obviously, the norm-based result gave a higher value as compared with the result obtained from using the actual ratios. However, it was considered desirable to present the results arrived at using both the ratios and to argue that while the norm-based result could be treated as the maximum the authorities should aim at, the actual ratio-based result should be treated as a minimum the authorities should provide for at different points of time.

Having carried out such exercises, the researchers have then examined as to what extent the adverse effects could be minimised by undertaking planning in advance. In this regard, an attempt has been made to explore the possible roles to be played by three important agencies, namely: (a) industries themselves; (b) government, municipal administration and panchayats; and (c) people at large, their organisations and NGOs. The idea is that while all these agencies will have to play their roles in minimising the adverse impact, each one of them is separately expected to tackle the specific effects of industrial investment. Therefore, the papers have suggested what role these organisations are to be assigned in each of the areas referred to above. Besides, the researchers have suggested not only what quantum of investment needs to be provided for to overcome the adverse effects but also how the available resources have to be efficiently utilised so that there is no wastage. Also, the nature of institutional structures that need to be created in order to minimise the adverse effects more efficiently have been indicated. It is sincerely hoped that these exercises will be of some use to the policy makers. By way of making the results of the seminar easily discernible a separate chapter on recommendations has been drafted and included in the volume.

# 2

# PROFILE OF BELLARY DISTRICT ECONOMY

B. SESHADRI and S. JAYANNA

## INTRODUCTION

This chapter endeavours to present an overview of the physiographic, demographic, administrative, and socio-economic situation obtaining in the district today. The principal objective is to provide background for the seminar whose main focus is on the socio-economic, politico-cultural and eco-environmental challenges, pressures and needs that are likely to emerge owing to the inflow of massive investment into the iron and steel sector and plans and programmes to meet them effectively well in time before they acquire harmful and unmanageable dimensions. The study is based on both secondary and primary sources of data. Depending upon the availability of reliable and comparable data, while identifying the status of the district economy in the division and the State, the status of the various taluks of the district is also identified in respect of iron and steel units. And wherever possible and contextually apt, the past trends in the district economy are also highlighted.

## ADMINISTRATIVE SETUP

Prior to 1953, Bellary District was a part of the then State of Madras. The district (excluding the taluks of Adoni, Alur and Rayadurga) was transferred to Karnataka (erstwhile State of Mysore) in October 1953 under the Andhra Act, 1953.

Bellary district is situated in the mid-eastern border of Karnataka, and is surrounded by Raichur district in the north, Chitradurga district in the south, Dharwad district in the west, and Anantapur and Kurnool districts of Andhra Pradesh in the east. By and large, the bilingual culture of Karnataka and Andhra Pradesh flourishes in the eastern parts of the district.

Bellary district comes under the administrative jurisdiction of Gulbarga division and under the developmental jurisdiction of HKADB (Hyderabad Karnataka Area Development Board) Gulbarga. There are two revenue sub-divisions in the district. It has 8 taluks, 11 towns, 9 municipalities, and 591 inhabited and 26 uninhabited villages. On the rural side, under the new three-tier Panchayati Raj System, the Bellary Zilla Parishad has 8 Taluk Panchayats and 222 Gram Panchayats in it.

The emerging industrial scenario, *inter alia*, is sure to pose some problems and challenges to the district administration. The development administration which is evolving out of the 73rd and 74th amendments to the Constitution, *per se*, may not be able to face the emerging situation. Keeping in view the nature and extent of the administrative and law and order problems which are likely to be engendered by massive industrialisation, the district administration, to be effective, needs restructuring.

## AREA AND POPULATION

The district occupies 9900 sq. kms. of area and accommodates 18,90,000 people of the State; it is the eleventh biggest district in terms of area and the thirteenth biggest district in terms of area and the thirteenth biggest district in terms of population in the State. With reference to both the characteristics, it occupies the third position at the Division. To be precise, it occupies 5.16 per cent of the area and accommodates 4.2 per cent of the population in the State context, and 21.76 per cent of the area and 23.51 per cent of the population at the divisional level.

The density of population, of all the districts has been increasing, as it should be, in view of the invariant geographical size and the positive growth of population. Its present density of population (191) is higher than the division's (177), but markedly lower than the State's (235). Not only that, its density of population has been lower than the State's right from 1961 down to 1991.

Its decennial growth rates of population have been positive, but there are inter-temporal variations in growth rates: the decennial growth rates for 1961-71 (22.66%), 1971-81 (32.65%) and 1981-91 (27.09%) if projected on a graph, trace an inverted U-shaped curve; between 1961-71 and 1971-81, we notice a substantial increase, but between 1971-81 and

1981-91 a considerable decline. A similar trend is also noticed at the State level. But, it is disheartening to note that the district's growth rates have been significantly higher than those of the State's : 1971-81 (26.75%) and 1981-91(20.69%). For the decade 1981-91, the district's growth rate is slightly higher than the division's (26%).

The trends in rural urban population ratios of the district reveal not only that rural population continues to be predominant but also the implied fact that the process of urbanisation, industrialisation and modernisation has been slow; the urbanisation trend has received a set-back in the latest decade of 1981-91. The ratio of rural population to total population declines from 77.4 per cent in 1961 to 72.8 per cent in 1971, and to 66.9 per cent in 1981, but records a rise to 70.1 per cent in 1991. This is not a sign of progress. We observe continuous decline in the ratio at the State level for the same reference points of time : 1961 (77.7%), 1971 (75.7%), 1981 (75.1%) and 1991 (69.1%). For 1991 the district's ratio of rural population is lower than the division's (76.36%).

The district has been experiencing favourable trends in sex ratio; it is moving towards achieving sex parity in the total population. Except for 1961, its sex ratio has been higher than that of the State; as against the State's ratio of 959 (1961), 957 (1971), 963 (1981) and 960 (1991), it claims 917, 967, 973 and 965 for the same reference points of time. For 1991, its sex ratio is slightly higher than the division's (964).

## STRUCTURE OF THE DISTRICT ECONOMY: SECTORAL COMPOSITION OF INCOME AND WORKFORCE

The claims of three broad sectors—primary, secondary and tertiary—in any given region's income and workforce are important indicators of the degree of industrialisation and modernisation, and also of the relative importance of the sectors and their productivity. General development through deliberate industrialisation initiates that pattern of sectoral transformation which is characterised by progressive decline in the importance of the primary sector and of the increase in the importance of the non-primary sectors. At the State and District levels, the sectoral behaviour is not uniform with reference to both income and workforce. We observe significant decline in the primary sector's share in income both at the State level and district level; its share in Net State Domestic Product (NSDP) falls from 61.25 per cent (1960-61) to 36.3 per cent (1991-92) and in Net District Domestic Product (NDDP) from 60.58 per cent (1960-61) to 49 per cent (1991-92). It is disturbing to note that the decline in primary sector's share is made good more by the income earning tertiary sector than by the income producing secondary sector at both the levels: for the same reference points, at the State level, the tertiary sector's share increases from 23.59 per cent to 39.7 per cent, whereas that of the secondary sector's from 15.16 per cent to 24 per cent; and at the district level, tertiary sector's share increases from 24.63 per cent to 34.6 per cent, whereas that of the secondary sector's from 14.79 per cent to 16.4 per cent.

It is intriguing to observe a different kind of trend with reference to the sectoral shares in workforce. The changes in this area do not match the changes that we observe in NSDP and NDDP : at the State level, the decline in primary sector's share in workforce is not as significant as in NSDP; it declines from 75.14 per cent (1961) and 69.2 per cent (1991), and it continues to be the most predominant sector. But this predominance indicates lower productivity in the primary sector. At the district level the situation is more disturbing : its share in workforce, instead of recording a fall, has actually gone up from 74.26 per cent (1961) to 78.02 per cent (1991) and this increasing predominance viewed in the background of its declining importance in NDDP speaks of the progressively falling productivity in the sector. Again, in the case of workforce also, it is distressing to note that at the State level, the fall in primary sector's share is made good more by the tertiary sector than by the secondary sector: the tertiary sector's share increases from 14.13 per cent (1961) to 18.15 per cent (1991), whereas that of the secondary sector from 10.73 per cent (1961) to 12.15 per cent (1991). At the district level, the situation is altogether different because of the increase in the share of the primary sector mainly owing to the increasing importance of mining activity : the increase in primary sector's share has caused decline in the non-primary sectors' shares; the secondary sector records a decline from 9.09 per cent (1961) to 7.2 per cent (1991) and the tertiary sector from 16.65 per cent (1961) to 14.76 per cent (1991).

In brief, we can say that at the district level, the primary sector is the most dominant sector in terms of its share in income and workforce, but its dominance is more pronounced in workforce than in income. And amongst the non-primary sectors, the tertiary sector is more dominant than the secondary sector. The primary sector's dominance is more pronounced in workforce than in income whereas that of the non-primary sectors' is more pronounced in their shares in income than in workforce, indicating thereby the fact that they are more productive than the primary sector. With the massive investment in Jindal Vijayanagar Steel Ltd. (JVSL), and other six capital intensive plants which are in the offing, the secondary sector is going to gain higher degree of importance.

## MINERAL RESOURCES

The district's distinction and potential for industrialisation and economic development, among other things, lie in its mineral resources (of course, it should not be forgotten that they are non-renewable resources). The minerals have been a major source of foreign exchange and also a significant source of employment to thousands of unskilled and semi-skilled persons. The district has both metallic and non-metallic minerals: the former include iron ore, manganese ore, red oxide, gold, copper and lead; and the latter include andalusite, asbestos, corundum, clay, dolomite, lime stone, lime kankar, moulding sand, quartz, soap stone, granite and red ochre. Here, we focus only on the principal metallic mineral resources which have bearing on the iron and steel sector. Iron ore and manganese ore are the two principal mineral ores of the district. The iron ore deposits of the district are essentially hematite and are grouped into eight ranges. The range-wise estimated reserves of iron ore and block-wise estimated reserves of manganese ore are given in Table 2.1(a) and 2.1(b). The details of production and value of the major minerals in the districts are given in Table 2.1(c). As per the latest estimates, we have 1032.40 million tonnes of iron ore and 18.81 million tonnes of manganese ore though the lease-wise estimates of iron ore reserves provided by MMTC of India Ltd., are 1713.31 million tonnes. In all there are 98 lease holders.

It is important to note that the mineral resources and mining activity are not spread over all the taluks of the district. Both in terms of production and value of four minerals mentioned, with a few minor exceptions, Sandur

TABLE 2.1(a): **Range-wise Estimation of Iron Ore Deposits in Bellary District**

| Sl. No. | Name of the Range | Strike length in Kms | Estimated Reserves in million tonnes |
|---|---|---|---|
| 1. | Ramadurga Range | 10.3 | 212.7 |
| 2. | Copper Mountain Range | 16 | 33 |
| 3. | Yetkinahatti Range | 3.2 | 55 |
| 4. | Thimmappanagudi Range | NA | 47 |
| 5. | Donimalai Range | 12 Sq. Kms | 156 |
| 6. | Devadari Range | 5 | 7.9 |
| 7. | Kumaraswamy Range | 3.5 | 210.8 |
| 8. | NEB Range | NA | 310 |
| | Total | — | 1032.4 |

TABLE 2.1(b): **Block-wise Estimation of Manganese Ore Deposition in Bellary District**

| Sl. No. | Name of the Block | Extent in Kms. | Estimated Reserves in million tonnes |
|---|---|---|---|
| 1. | Deogire Block | 3 | 5.4 |
| 2. | Swamy Halli Block | 3.2 | 8.4 |
| 3. | Subbarayana Halli Block | 4 | 3.58 |
| 4. | Sunderbench Block | 0.5 | 0.38 |
| 5. | Ramgad Block | 1 | 0.09 |
| 6. | Seshagiri Block | NA | 0.72 |
| 7. | Donikolla Block | 0.5 | 0.15 |
| 8. | Tumberguddi Block | NA | 0.09 |
| | Total | — | 18.81 |

TABLE 2.1(c): **Production and Value of Major Minerals in Bellary District**

| Sl. No. | Mineral | 1989 Production | 1989 Value | 1990 Production | 1990 Value | 1991 Production | 1991 Value |
|---|---|---|---|---|---|---|---|
| 1. | Iron Ore | 4113096 | 8226120 | 4519133 | NA | 3825140 | NA |
| 2. | Manganese Ore | 1813834 | 27207510 | 1857519 | NA | 2151210 | NA |
| 3. | Iron Ore fines | 192621 | 11557260 | 283802 | NA | 257430 | NA |
| 4. | Red Oxide | 39709 | 595605 | 26635 | NA | 11670 | NA |
| | Total | 6159260 | 47586495 | 66877089 | NA | 6245450 | NA |

taluk occupies the first position, the second place goes to Hospet, and the third place to Bellary. Hadagali, Kudligi, Hagaribommanahalli, and Siruguppa do not have any mining activity and Harapanahalli claims only a negligible proportion of manganese ore only.

The annual production of iron ore ranges from 2.75 to 4.5 million tonnes, and of manganese ore from 0.13 million tonnes to 0.32 million tonnes (between 1976 and 1991). A major portion of these ores has been exported in the raw state. As per the projections made by Kalyani Steels Ltd., for 1995-96, 49 lakh tonnes will be exported and 24 lakh tonnes will be used for internal consumption. Of the total export of 49 lakh tonnes, the private mine owners claim 21 lakh tonnes and the public sector units claim 28 lakh tonnes. Over 25,000 workers are said to be directly employed in the mining activity of the district.

## LEVELS OF DEVELOPMENT

Social scientists use a variety of indicators to measure the socio-economic development of any given region. In the present study, we use Composite Index of Development (CID) and indicators of Physical Quality of Life (PQL) to identify the position of Bellary in the division as well as in the State.

Bellary attracts the first position in the division with its CID of 91.05 per cent, whereas, it gets the twelfth rank in the State. The inter-temporal trends are not indicative of linear growth: the district slides down from the fourteenth rank (89.23) in 1960-61 to the fifteenth rank (83.90) in 1971-72, but scales up to the tenth rank (100.09) in 1976-77, but thereafter it slips down to the eleventh rank (94.98) in 1979-80, and further to the twelfth rank (91.05) in 1985-86 (Table 2.2).

To get further insights into the level of development of the district, the three principal indicators of the physical quality of life of the people in the region and also the per capita income are used in the present analysis. Viewed in terms of all the four indicators, Bellary is far below the State's socio-economic performance : its literacy rate is 45.57 per cent as against the State's (56.04%); its infant mortality rate is 87 as against the State's (69); its life expectancy at birth is 53.17 as against the State's (57.71); and its per capita income at constant prices (1980-81 prices) for 1990-91 is Rs. 1936 as against the State's Rs 2048 (Table 2.3).

The indicators of physical quality of life of the district such as literacy rate, infant mortality rate and life expectancy at birth do speak of the inadequate access to health and educational facilities. In the given situation, unless the local people get better access to such facilities, they may not be able to take advantage of the emerging employment opportunities.

## LEVELS OF INDUSTRIAL DEVELOPMENT

Bellary, besides being industrially active, has great potential for the development of mineral-based and agro-based industries. Under the new dispensation of liberalisation and privatisation, it has been attracting a number of mega industrial units into its iron and steel sector. And, from the units which have begun their work and from the project clearance records of the Government, one can visualise that in 4-5 years, Bellary is likely to scale up to the top most position in the State in terms of industrial investment.

TABLE 2.2: **Composite Index of Development of Karnataka: 1960-61, 1985-86**

| Sl. No. | Districts | 1960 - 61 | | 1971 - 72 | | 1976 - 77 | | 1979 - 80 | | 1985 - 86 | |
|---|---|---|---|---|---|---|---|---|---|---|---|
| | | Index | Rank | Index | Rank | Index | Rank | Index | Rank | Index | Rank |
| 1. | Bangalore | 218 | 2 | 206.26 | 1 | 206.42 | 1 | 198.7 | 1 | 172.73 | 1 |
| 2. | Chitradurga | 100.24 | 11 | 104 | 9 | 107.02 | 7 | 101.36 | 9 | 99.33 | 7 |
| 3. | Kolar | 136.53 | 4 | 129.65 | 4 | 107.55 | 6 | 103.81 | 8 | 97.77 | 8 |
| 4. | Shimoga | 108.15 | 3 | 141.07 | 3 | 118.05 | 3 | 120.44 | 4 | 113.47 | 3 |
| 5. | Tumkur | 84.52 | 15 | 83.47 | 16 | 88.64 | 13 | 85.91 | 16 | 83.66 | 15 |
| 6. | Belgaum | 91.12 | 12 | 95.06 | 11 | 91.89 | 12 | 91.7 | 12 | 103.16 | 5 |
| 7. | Bijapur | 71.66 | 16 | 77.38 | 18 | 79.99 | 17 | 87.2 | 15 | 79.6 | 17 |
| 8. | Dharwad | 118.54 | 8 | 103.19 | 10 | 98.74 | 11 | 96.23 | 10 | 94.83 | 9 |
| 9. | Uttara Kannada | 118.24 | 9 | 106.17 | 8 | 102.05 | 9 | 106 | 6 | 92.43 | 11 |
| 10. | Bellary | 89.23 | 14 | 83.90 | 15 | 100.09 | 10 | 94.98 | 11 | 91.05 | 12 |
| 11. | Bidar | 64.28 | 17 | 86.85 | 14 | 85.46 | 15 | 82.11 | 17 | 83.62 | 16 |
| 12. | Gulbarga | 60.1 | 19 | 63.19 | 19 | 66.83 | 19 | 65.77 | 19 | 67.79 | 19 |
| 13. | Raichur | 63.04 | 18 | 80.53 | 17 | 76.34 | 18 | 80.72 | 18 | 77.12 | 18 |

| | | | | | | | | | | | |
|---|---|---|---|---|---|---|---|---|---|---|---|
| 14. | Chikmagalur | 123.74 | 7 | 92.66 | 12 | 84.56 | 16 | 90.16 | 14 | 84.43 | 14 |
| 15. | Dakshina Kannada | 230.21 | 1 | 187.04 | 2 | 172.86 | 2 | 176.69 | 2 | 153.84 | 2 |
| 16. | Hassan | 90.03 | 13 | 87.21 | 13 | 86.22 | 14 | 91.91 | 13 | 87.82 | 13 |
| 17. | Kodagu | 124.15 | 6 | 107.79 | 7 | 103.44 | 8 | 105.84 | 7 | 94.73 | 10 |
| 18. | Mandya | 114.7 | 10 | 111.96 | 6 | 112.94 | 4 | 118.87 | 5 | 112.38 | 4 |
| 19. | Mysore | 124.6 | 5 | 123.35 | 5 | 112.09 | 5 | 124.45 | 3 | 103 | 6 |
| | State | 100 | | 100 | | 100 | | 100 | | 100 | |

*Source*: (1) Planning Department, *Draft Eighth Five Year Plan 1990-95*, Vol.1, Government of Karnataka, Bangalore
(2) Planning Department, *Karnataka Draft Annual Plan 1987-88*, Government of Karnataka, Bangalore, 1986

TABLE 2.3: Indicators of Physical Quality of Life in Karnataka: 1981 and 1991

| Sl. No. | District | Literacy Rate | | Infant Mortality Rate | | Life Expectancy at Birth | | Per Capita Income at Constant Prices (1980 - 81) | |
|---|---|---|---|---|---|---|---|---|---|
| | | 1981 | 1991 | 1981 | 1991 | 1981 | 1991 | 1980-81 | 1990-91 |
| 1. | Bangalore (U) | | 76.27 | | | | | | |
| | | 51.32 | | 54 | NA | 61.64 | NA | 2114 | 3297 |
| 2. | Bangalore (R) | | 50.17 | | | | | | |
| 3. | Chitradurga | 38.25 | 55.48 | 75 | NA | 57.09 | NA | 1628 | 1783 |
| 4. | Kolar | 33.57 | 50.45 | 65 | NA | 58.67 | NA | 862 | 1335 |
| 5. | Shimoga | 44.44 | 61.53 | 69 | NA | 57.71 | NA | 1808 | 2128 |
| 6. | Tumkur | 36.92 | 54.48 | 74 | NA | 57.25 | NA | 1179 | 1570 |
| 7. | Belgaum | 36.64 | 53 | 67 | NA | 58.35 | NA | 1407 | 2088 |
| 8. | Bijapur | 31.96 | 55.13 | 80 | NA | 57.75 | NA | 977 | 1595 |
| 9. | Dharwad | 42.36 | 58.68 | 75 | NA | 57.09 | NA | 1289 | 1597 |
| 10. | Uttara Kannada | 48.35 | 66.73 | 62 | NA | 59.64 | NA | 1665 | 1979 |
| 11. | Bellary | 30.64 | 45.57 | 87 | NA | 53.17 | NA | 1586 | 1936 |
| 12. | Bidar | 26.44 | 45.11 | 70 | NA | 57.4 | NA | 1335 | 1588 |
| 13. | Gulbarga | 24.94 | 38.54 | 71 | NA | 57.09 | NA | 1386 | 1758 |

| | | | | | | | | | |
|---|---|---|---|---|---|---|---|---|---|
| 14. | Raichur | 24.72 | 35.96 | 77 | NA | 57.57 | NA | 1452 | 1549 |
| 15. | Chikmagalur | 43.5 | 61.05 | 70 | NA | 57.56 | NA | 1865 | 2290 |
| 16. | Dakshina Kannada | 53.47 | 75.86 | 40 | NA | 65.63 | NA | 1704 | 2471 |
| 17. | Hassan | 37.49 | 56.85 | 67 | NA | 58.35 | NA | 1385 | 1665 |
| 18. | Kodagu | 50.15 | 68.35 | 57 | NA | 60.97 | NA | 3071 | 3582 |
| 19. | Mandya | 30.4 | 48.15 | 69 | NA | 57.71 | NA | 1599 | 1837 |
| 20. | Mysore | 31.34 | 47.32 | 66 | NA | 58.51 | NA | 1466 | 1840 |
| | State | 36.46 | 56.04 | 67 | 77 | 57.71 | 63.3 | 1527 | 2048 |

*Source:* 1. Vinod K. Mishra, James A. Palmore and Sunil K. Sinha, Indirect Estimates of Fertility and Mortality at the District level, 1981, Occasional Paper No. 4 of 1994, Office of the Registrar General, India, Ministry of Home Affairs, New Delhi, 1995, p. 73.

2. Directorate of Economics and Statistics, District Socio-Economic Indicators, 1994, Government of Karnataka, Bangalore, 1995.

So far, we had only two major mineral-based industries, namely, the Sandur Manganese and Iron Ore Ltd., producing pig iron, ferro-manganese and ferro-silicon, and Bellary Steels and Alloys Ltd., producing sponge iron. There are two more units which draw their ore and water requirements from Bellary district, namely, Shathavahana Ispat Ltd., (located in Anantapur district of Andhra Pradesh), and Kirloskar Ferrous Industries Ltd., (located in Raichur district). As on date, the district has 20 large and medium scale units, including the mega steel plant, Jindal Vijayanagar Steel Limited (JVSL), which came into being in August 1994. The JVSL has already invested Rs. 1200 crores, and is expected to invest another Rs. 4800 crores in 2-3 years from now. The 20 units put together have been employing over 10,673 workers and claim an investment of Rs. 1,41,184.13 lakhs. Further, the resultant ancillarisation is likely to involve an investment of Rs. 1000 crores. At present, the district attracts the eighth position in terms of units, the third position in terms of investment, and the seventh position in terms of industrial employment in the State by claiming 2.69 per cent of the units, 16.56 per cent of the investment, and 3.78 per cent of the industrial employment in the State. In addition to the above, 6 Steel plants, 1 float glass unit, and 1 quartz unit are awaiting government's clearance to enter the industrial arena of the district. They are, Mukund Vijayanagar Steel Ltd., (with an investment of Rs. 8000 crore), Dalton Steel Ltd., (Rs. 438 crore), Bellary Steels & Alloys Ltd., (Rs. 657 crore), Bhuwalaka Steel Industries (Rs. 315 crore), Mittal Steel Ltd., (Rs.1310 crore), Elkay Steels Ltd., (Rs. 84 crore), Karnataka Float Glass (N.A) and Overseas Quartz (N.A). With the exception of the last two units, which are getting located in Harapanahalli taluk, the rest of the 6 steel plants will be located in Bellary-Sandur-Hospet belt.

It is of importance to know that the large and medium scale industrial activity is not found in all the taluks of the district. Of the 8 taluks, 3 taluks namely Hadagali, Hagaribommanahalli and Kudligi do not have any units. A substantial proportion of the activity is concentrated in 3 taluks namely Sandur, Hospet and Bellary. Of the 20 units, Bellary claims 4, Sandur 5, Hospet 8, Siruguppa 2 and Harapanahalli 1. In terms of industrial employment, Sandur gets the first place by claiming 50.13 per cent of the workers, and it is followed by Hospet (26.51%), Bellary (14.42%), Siruguppa (8.34%) and Harapanahalli (0.60%). Viewed in terms of investment too, Sandur gets the first place by claiming 87.39%, and is followed by Bellary (5.53%), Siruguppa (4.12%), Hospet (2.34%), and Harapanahalli (0.62%). The industrial activity is dominated by mining and mineral based iron and steel sector, and the second place goes to the agro-based industries (Table 2.4).

TABLE 2.4: **Large and Medium Scale Industries in Bellary District: 1995**

| Sl. No. | Taluk | Name of the Unit | Investment Rs. in lakhs | Employment Nos. |
|---|---|---|---|---|
| 1. | Bellary | (1) Bellary Steels and Alloys Ltd | 4500 | 585 |
| | | (2) Navakarnataka Steels Ltd | 900 | 385 |
| | | (3) Panyam Cement & Mineral Industries Ltd., Hagari | 970 | 520 |
| | | (4) Sarada Vegetable Oils Ltd | 348 | 49 |
| 2. | Sandur | (1) Jindal Vijayanagar Steel Ltd | 120000 | 3000 |
| | | (2) Sandur Laminates Ltd | 602.05 | 130 |
| | | (3) National Minerals Development Corporation | 4200 | 1500 |
| | | (4) Tungabhadra Minerals Ltd | 320 | 620 |
| | | (5) Sandur Micro Circuit Ltd | 780 | 100 |
| 3. | Hospet | (1) Fishnet Making Factory | 80 | 80 |
| | | (2) India Sugars & Refineries Ltd | 133 | 750 |
| | | (3) Pampasar Distilleries Ltd | 200 | 207 |
| | | (4) Kampli Co-op. Sugar Factory Ltd | 680 | 446 |
| | | (5) Tungabhadra Steel Products Ltd | NA | NA |
| | | (6) Karnataka Oil Federation | 900 | 123 |
| | | (7) Sandur Manganese Iron Ore Ltd | 600 | 800 |
| | | (8) Mineral Sales (P) Ltd | 244 | 423 |
| 4. | Siruguppa | (1) Kothari Sugars & Chemicals | 497 | 490 |
| | | (2) Uni Metals Ispat Ltd | 4500 | 400 |
| 5. | Harapana-halli | (1) Samson Distilleries | 750 | 65 |
| 6. | Hadagali | NIL | 0 | 0 |
| 7. | H.B. Halli | NIL | 0 | 0 |
| 8. | Kudligi | NIL | 0 | 0 |

*Source:* Information pertaining to Medium and Large Scale Industry in Bellary District, District Industries Center, Bellary.

As far as small scale industrial activity is concerned, Bellary's position in the State and in the division, is not so comfortable at present. By claiming 3.85 per cent of the units, 2.29 per cent of the investment, and 2.80 per cent of the employment, it secures the 9th, 15th and 13th ranks respectively in the State. However, the situation is likely to improve significantly with reference to all the three characteristics in 3 to 4 years. The spin off ancillarisation effect of Jindal Vijayanagar Steel Ltd., alone is expected to attract around Rs. 1000 crores into the SSI sector which is, by and large, labour intensive.

The emerging changes may engender and accelerate the forces that promote inter-taluk disparities at the district level, and inter-district disparities in industrial development and economic development at the State level.

**Levels of Infrastructure Development**

Notwithstanding perceptible improvement in infrastructure facilities in terms of transport, communication, power, finance, education and health, Bellary district has not been improving at the rates at which some of the developed districts have been progressing. Here, an attempt is made to identify Bellary's position with reference to an infrastructure development index, and also with specific reference to the select indicators of development of the physical, financial and human infrastructure.

**Infrastructure Development Index**

The district has also been lagging behind the State's average performance in the area of infrastructure development measured in terms of railway route length, broad gauge length, road length, national highways, surface metalled roads, number of goods vehicles, number of post offices, telephone exchanges, telephone lines, and electricity consumption by industry. In fact, it has been scaling down : this is evident from the overall infrastructure development indices for the districts of Karnataka for the years 1976 and 1990 computed by Dr. M. Prahladachar (ISEC, Bangalore); Bellary which occupies the eighth rank at the State level and the first rank at the division level in 1976, drops down to the twelfth rank at the State level and the second rank at the division level in 1990.

**Select Indicators of Infrastructure Development**

In the present inquiry, the indicators of infrastructure development are broadly classified into three broad categories : the physical infrastructure, which includes transport, communication and power consumption; the financial infrastructure, which includes commercial banks, gramina banks and co-operative banks; and the human infrastructure which includes education and health.

*Physical Infrastructure*

The district's road length for 100 sq. kms. of geographical area has been increasing from decade to decade between 1970-71 and 1992-93. But the road length has been far below the State average for all the reference points. As at 1992-93, the district has 49.36 kms for 100 sq. kms. of area as against the State's road length of 70.17 kms and the division's road length of 44.61 kms. With that road length it gets the sixteenth rank at the State level and the second rank at division level.

Bellary emerges as the middle order district when we view the number of motor vehicles per lakh of persons. Despite increase in the number of motor vehicles between 1970-71 and 1992-93, it continues to lag far behind the State; in 1992-93, it claims only 2676.5 motor vehicles per lakh of persons as against the State's figure of 4028.93 and the division's figure of 1990.80. And with that number of vehicles, the district attracts the tenth rank at the State level and the first rank at the division level. The situation is not that encouraging when we see the physical infrastructure in terms of the number of goods vehicles for lakh of persons; in 1992 - 93, the district claims 88.14 goods vehicles per lakh of persons, as against the State average of 181.63 and the division average of 82.49. In this case the district attracts the sixteenth position in the State and the second position in the division.

Bellary district claims to have reasonable development in terms of railways and railway stations when compared to other districts in the division and State. As per the data for 1992-93, the district has 3.34 kms. of railway route length per 100 sq.kms. of geographical area as against the State average of 1.61 kms. and the division average of 1.59 kms. It attracts the second rank at the State level and the first rank at the division level. And it claims the first position at both the levels, if we view the railway route length per lakh of persons; it has 17.51 as against the State average of 16.85 kms and the division average of 8.99 kms. The situation is equally encouraging when we measure the development of railway transport in terms of the number of railway stations per lakh of persons. As per 1992-93 data, it claims 1.43 railway stations, whereas the State average comes only to 0.85 and the division's comes to only 0.90 railway stations per lakh of persons. With that number of railway stations, the district occupies the second place in the State and the first place in the division.

The number of post offices, telephones and telephone exchanges per lakh of persons, are the three important indicators of communication development. The available data are indicative of the district's backwardness when compared to other developed districts in the State, though its position is comfortable in the division. As at 1992-93, the district claims 24.07 post offices, 629.63 telephones, and 4.40 telephone exchanges per lakh of persons as against the State's average of 21.75 post offices, 1129.47 telephones, and 4.15 telephone exchanges, and the division's average of 24.07 post offices, 531.23 telephones, and 4.28 telephone exchanges per lakh of persons. With these figures, the district attracts the tenth rank in the State in the case of post offices and telephone exchanges, and the 13th rank in the case of telephones, whereas it attracts the second rank in the division in the case of post offices and telephone exchanges, and the first rank in the case of telephones.

With reference to the per capita consumption of power, Bellary district claims the highest position in the division: its per capita consumption in all the uses taken together in 177 KwH as against the division's figure of 112 KwH; its per capita domestic consumption is 29 KwH as against the division's (22 KwH); its per capita consumption in agriculture is 8 KwH as against the division's (5 KwH); its per capita consumption in industries is 130 KwH as against the division's (79 KwH); and its per capita consumption in other sectors is 10 KwH as against the division's (6 KwH). But it lags behind the State's per capita consumption of power except in the case of consumption in industries; the State's per capita consumption figures are 313, 48, 137, 90 and 39 KwH respectively in the said uses.

*Financial Infrastructure*

The district is relatively better placed in the division when we view the banking services rendered by commercial banks, gramina banks, co-operative banks and co-operative credit societies. The district has 9.05 commercial banks per lakh of persons and 1.73 commercial banks per 100 sq. kms. of area, as against the division's average of 7.4 and 1.31 respectively. However, it lags behind the State's averages of 9.7 commercial banks per lakh of population, and 2.28 commercial banks per 100 sq. kms. of area. Both in terms of the number of commercial banks per lakh of persons and per 100 sq. kms of area, the district occupies the first rank in the division whereas it gets the ninth and the twelfth ranks respectively at the State level. With reference to the banking activity of the co-operative sector, the district and the division are close to each other, but somewhat away from the State average: the district has 13.39 co-operative banks per lakh of population and 2.56 co-operative banks per 100 sq. kms. of area, as against the division's average of 13.51 and 2.39 respectively; whereas the State averages for the same indicators are 15.74 and 3.69 respectively. Both in terms of the number of co-operative banks per lakh of persons and per 100 sq. kms. of area, the district gets the second position in the division, whereas, it gets the fourteenth and the seventeenth positions respectively in the State.

*Human Infrastructure*

The quality of human factor/human capital, among other things, is governed by the access that people have to education and health facilities. As far as educational facilities are concerned, the district lags behind both the division and the State, with the exception of medical colleges per lakh of population where it excels the division: the district with 72.86 primary schools per lakh of persons as against the division's average of 86.90 and the State's average of 93.12, occupies the fourth position (last position) in the division and the seventeenth position in the State; with 8.99 high schools per lakh of persons as against the division's average of 9.50 and the State's average of 12.74, it attracts the third rank in the division and the nineteenth rank in the State; with 2.22 pre-university colleges per lakh of persons as against the division's average of 2.80 and the State's average of 3.24, it gets the third place in the division and the sixteenth place in the State; with 0.90 general education colleges per lakh of persons as against the division's average of 1.13 and the State's average of 1.37, it gets the third place in the division and the seventeenth place in the State; with 0.37 institutions of technical education per lakh of persons as against the division's average of 0.39 and State's average of 0.51, it attracts the third rank in the division and the sixteenth rank in the State; and with 0.16 medical colleges per lakh of population as against the division's average of 0.14 and the State's average of 0.22, it gets the 2.5th rank in the division and the 9.5th rank in the State. These data do provide conclusive evidence to the relative backwardness of Bellary in terms of education infrastructure.

The health facilities available in Bellary district are better than those of the average health facilities of the division. But it is yet to go a long way to catch up with the State average. The district with 6.46 hospitals and 97.40 beds per lakh of persons, as against the division's average of 6.00 and 69.70, and the State's average of 6.66 and 115.57, claims the second and the first positions in the division, and the fourteenth and the tenth positions in the State with reference to hospitals and beds respectively.

The massive investment in the industrial sector of the district is bound to exert unprecedented pressure on all the infrastructure facilities; not only in terms of their quantity and quality but also in structure.

## TRADE UNIONS AND INDUSTRIAL RELATIONS

The emerging industrial activity has implications for labour organisations and industrial relations. Automation and contract labour could give new turns and twists to the attitudes and approaches of the trade unions in reconciling the interest of the employees and employers.

A recent study shows that industrial relations in Karnataka are relatively better than those obtaining in the neighbouring States. Another ongoing inquiry into the trade union activity and industrial relations reveals that a similar situation prevails in Bellary district, particularly in the iron and steel sector, and also in its feeder industry of iron ore and manganese.

In all these 182 labour unions in the district, of which, 27 unions are found in the mining and steel sectors. The 27 unions put together have a membership of 10,360 workers, and a major portion of the workers are found in the unions affiliated to AITUC (6000 workers) and INTUC (3700 workers) and the rest are in CITU (160), HMS (200) and others (300).

With the entry of seven steel plants including Jindal Vijayanagar Steel Limited and Mukund Vijayanagar Steels Limited, and the resultant emergence of a number of labour intensive ancillary units in and around the plants, the labour union activity is likely to acquire new directions and dimensions. And the change in the offing cannot but influence industrial relations in a big way.

## SUMMARY AND CONCLUSIONS

The foregoing analysis gives us an overview of the socio-economic situation obtaining in the district of Bellary today. Of course, the write-up cannot claim either exhaustiveness or finality for the views expressed.

The assessment of the district economy is done keeping in view the socio-economic, politico-cultural, and eco-environmental implications of the massive industrial investment which has already begun to flow into the iron and steel sector and into the resultant ancillary industrial activity.

The mining activity and the iron and steel industry based on it are concentrated in the Bellary-Sandur-Hospet belt. The area is likely to undergo metamorphosis in its overall natural and socio-economic life with the entry of mega steel plants like Jindals and Mukunds.

The present structure of the district economy reveals the dominance of the primary sector over the non-primary sectors taken separately. The emerging hyper industrial activity is likely to augment the share of the secondary sector in the Net District Domestic Product (NDDP) and workforce of the district's tri-sectoral economy. As a consequence, the process of urbanisation and modernisation will gain momentum.

The composite index of development, per capita income, and all the indicators of Physical Quality of Life show that Bellary is a moderately developed district. However, it is better placed in Gulbarga division/ Hyderabad Karnataka Region.

As to the levels of industrial development, the district's position is more comfortable in the large and medium scale industries than in the small scale industrial activity. But, hereafter, both the segments are going to get significant momentum.

The moderately developed nature of the district economy is also reflected in the levels of development of infrastructure. Of course, its position in physical and financial infrastructure facilities is somewhat comfortable at the division level, but not so in the case of human infrastructure, particularly in terms of educational facilities.

The trade union activity in the district, which is not so militant today, is going to acquire new directions and dimensions with the emerging phenomenon of automation and contract labour practice. The change will have significant bearing on industrial relations, a decisive factor in sustaining industrial production etc.

The aforesaid status background of the district economy among other things, may be of some help in preparing the perspective plan, policies and programmes to face the emerging challenges, pressures and needs well in time to minimise the impact of negative externalities and maximise the impact of positive externalities of the massive industrial investment.

# 3

# INDUSTRIAL DEVELOPMENT PATTERN AND LOCATION

M. PRAHLADACHAR

Despite endowed richly with mineral resources (iron ore and manganese in particular), Bellary district continues to be industrially backward for want of exploitation of these for the purposes of industrial development. A synoptic view of the status, pattern and location of industry in the district would help appreciate the problems and constraints that hinder the full realisation of its industrial potential. In what follows is an attempt to provide such a synoptic view within the limitations of data on industry at our disposal.

An analysis of time series data on industry across types of industry and across taluks within the district is rendered difficult due to changes over time in the general definitions (large, medium, small) and coverage of sub-sectors (census, factory) and due to differences in data (both in qualitative and quantitative terms) furnished by various sources (e.g. Annual Survey of Industries, Directorate of Industries and Commerce, Khadi and Village Industries Commission). Nevertheless an effort in this direction in the case of the manufacturing sector at least was attempted in a study brought out by the Institute for Social and Economic Change (ISEC), Bangalore.[1] According to this study, in respect of the census sub-sector of manufacturing, the growth rates of number of units, fixed capital, employment and value added in Bellary during the period 1960-80 were 5.62, 2.79, 6.91 and 5.6 per cent per annum respectively. Except the growth rate of fixed capital, the growth rates of other industry parameters (No. of units, employment and value added) were broadly in tune with the respective growth rates at the State level. However closeness in growth rates between the district and the State need not give rise to complacency about the district's performance in industry, during the reference period cited above or perhaps even in the years thereafter, once it is noted that the share of Bellary in the State total in regard to industry parameters persist to be unimpressive even as late as 1995. This is evident from the discussion that follows.

**Large and Medium Industries**

By the end of March 1995, there were 21 large and medium industries in the district with an investment of Rs.19333.58 lakhs providing employment to 8421 persons (Table 3.1). The relative ranks of Bellary in the State in respect of per unit investment and per unit employment were 9 and 10 respectively. To view it differently, the shares of Bellary in the State in respect of number of units, investment and employment were meagre with 2.8 per cent, 3.1 per cent and 3 per cent respectively.

**Small Scale Industries**

By the end of March 1995, there were about 6300 Small Scale Industrial (SSI) units in the district, with an investment of Rs. 4428.98 providing employment to 30,118 persons (Table 3.2). As in the case of large and medium industries, the shares of Bellary in the State in regard to number of units, investment and employment were of very low order. It also belonged to the category of districts where per unit employment and investment respectively were quite meagre.

**Location of Industries**

Distribution of industries: large, medium and small across taluks indicates that three taluks viz., Bellary, Hospet and Sandur dominate the scene (Table 3.3). Availability of mineral resources in their neighbourhood, better access to infrastructure facilities, in a relative sense, within the district, a legacy of local entrepreneurship may be deemed to be the important factors for the relative concentration of industrial units in these three taluks.

Summing up, it is clear from the brief synoptic account of the status of industry in Bellary, that it has not been successful in getting a place of recognition in the industrial map of the State. Whatever 'status' that the district has struggled over the years to attain, shrinks further, if it is juxtaposed with the problem of "industrial sickness" affecting the industrial

TABLE 3.1: **Large and Medium Scale Industries in Karnataka**

*(As on March 1995)*

| Districts | No. of Units | Percentage to the State total | Investment (Rs. lakhs) | Percentage to the State total | Employment Nos. | Percentage to the State total | Per unit investment (Rs. lakhs) | Rank | Per unit employment | Rank |
|---|---|---|---|---|---|---|---|---|---|---|
| 1. Bangalore (Rural) | 337 | 45.17 | 129158.2 | 20.51 | 124192 | 44.32 | 383.26 | 13 | 368 | 11 |
| 2. Bangalore (Urban) | | | | | | | | | | |
| 3. Belgaum | 30 | 4.02 | 21885.32 | 3.47 | 16960 | 6.05 | 920.64 | 7 | 565 | 4 |
| 4. Bellary | 21 | 2.82 | 19333.58 | 3.07 | 8421 | 3 | 729.51 | 9 | 410 | 10 |
| 5. Bidar | 17 | 2.28 | 4972.45 | 0.79 | 2697 | 0.96 | 292.5 | 15 | 159 | 17 |
| 6. Bijapur | 10 | 1.34 | 4519.23 | 0.73 | 4697 | 1.68 | 451.92 | 11 | 470 | 8 |
| 7. Chickmagalur | 5 | 3.48 | 67743.23 | 10.76 | 2638 | 1.16 | 13548.64 | 2 | 528 | 6 |
| 8. Chitradurga | 26 | 0.67 | 2346.49 | 0.37 | 3211 | 0.94 | 89.86 | 17 | 123 | 19 |
| 9. Dakshina Kannada | 34 | 4.56 | 23893.69 | 3.79 | 7106 | 2.54 | 702.76 | 10 | 209 | 14 |
| 10. Dharwad | 68 | 9.11 | 16019.27 | 2.54 | 10380 | 3.7 | 235.58 | 16 | 153 | 18 |
| 11. Gulbarga | 14 | 1.88 | 193502.9 | 30.75 | 10508 | 3.75 | 13821.63 | 1 | 751 | 3 |
| 12. Hassan | 5 | 0.67 | 1497.61 | 0.24 | 1027 | 0.37 | 299.52 | 14 | 205 | 15 |
| 13. Kodagu | 2 | 0.27 | 174 | 0.04 | 375 | 0.13 | 87 | 18 | 188 | 16 |
| 14. Kolar | 13 | 1.74 | 14078.82 | 2.23 | 27680 | 9.86 | 1082.6 | 5 | 2125 | 1 |

| | | | | | | | | | | |
|---|---|---|---|---|---|---|---|---|---|---|
| 15. Mandya | 9 | 1.21 | 6570.45 | 1.04 | 5015 | 1.79 | 730.05 | 8 | 557 | 5 |
| 16. Mysore | 88 | 11.80 | 34442.08 | 5.47 | 20020 | 7.14 | 391.39 | 12 | 228 | 13 |
| 17. Raichur | 22 | 2.95 | 28162.86 | 4.47 | 9576 | 3.42 | 1280.13 | 4 | 435 | 9 |
| 18. Shimoga | 15 | 2.01 | 39330.63 | 6.24 | 14864 | 5.3 | 2622.04 | 3 | 991 | 2 |
| 19. Tumkur | 19 | 2.55 | 10612.07 | 1.68 | 5199 | 1.86 | 558.53 | 9 | 274 | 12 |
| 20. Uttara Kannada | 11 | 1.47 | 11564.58 | 1.84 | 5689 | 2.03 | 1051.33 | 6 | 517 | 7 |
| STATE | 746 | 100 | 629802.4 | 100 | 280205 | 100 | | | | |

*Source* : Department of Industries and Commerce, Government of Karnataka, Bangalore.

TABLE 3.2: **District-wise Small-Scale Industries in Karnataka**

*(As on March 1995)*

| District | No. of units | Investment (Rs. lakhs) | Employment | Per unit Investment in Rs. | Rank | Per unit Employment |
|---|---|---|---|---|---|---|
| Bangalore (Rural) | 6489 | 5644.82 | 33704 | 87298.81 | 16 | 5 |
| Bangalore (Urban) | 323538 | 54492.95 | 288656 | 167474.3 | 2 | 9 |
| Belgaum | 14168 | 13024.87 | 63118 | 91931.61 | 13 | 4 |
| Bellary | 6300 | 4428.98 | 30118 | 70301.27 | 19 | 5 |
| Bidar | 3578 | 5242.34 | 21451 | 146516.93 | 3 | 6 |
| Bijapur | 6033 | 4535.76 | 34597 | 75182.5 | 18 | 6 |
| Chitradurga | 5988 | 8560.15 | 33275 | 142977.62 | 5 | 6 |
| Chickmagalur | 2921 | 2287.61 | 13287 | 78315.99 | 20 | 5 |
| Dakshina Kannada | 11115 | 20404.15 | 73903 | 183573.1 | 1 | 7 |
| Dharwad | 13940 | 13770.41 | 121093 | 98703.43 | 10 | 9 |
| Gulbarga | 5240 | 4711.66 | 29304 | 89917.17 | 14 | 6 |
| Hassan | 3554 | 3166.92 | 18143 | 89108.61 | 15 | 5 |
| Kolar | 5895 | 8032.95 | 42440 | 136267.18 | 6 | 7 |
| Kodagu | 1733 | 1759.81 | 16145 | 101547.03 | 9 | 9 |
| Mandya | 3590 | 3363.4 | 19448 | 93688.02 | 12 | 5 |
| Mysore | 14060 | 10620.59 | 80889 | 75537.62 | 17 | 6 |
| Raichur | 5327 | 7762.77 | 39542 | 145724.99 | 4 | 7 |
| Shimoga | 7926 | 7513.71 | 35695 | 94798.26 | 11 | 5 |
| Tumkur | 10152 | 11024.59 | 59971 | 108595.25 | 8 | 6 |
| Uttara Kannada | 2977 | 3248.34 | 21194 | 109114.54 | 7 | 7 |

*Source*: Department of Industries and Commerce, Government of Karnataka, Bangalore

units. Data on industrial sickness available at the State level from the Report on the Second All India Census of Small Scale Industrial Units : Karnataka, though somewhat dated in so far as it relates to 1988, is still worth noting to obtain useful insights into the nagging problems of industry. According to this report, there were 89 non-SSI sick units and 10,982 Small Scale Industries (SSI) sick units in the State. Besides 14,628 SIDO units were closed down for various reasons.

TABLE 3.3: **Distribution of Large, Medium and Small Scale Industries in Bellary District—Taluk-wise 1994-95 (cumulative)**

| Taluks | Large & Medium Scale Industries | Small-Scale Industries |
|---|---|---|
| Bellary | 4 | 1609 |
| Siruguppa | 2 | 408 |
| Sandur | 5 | 379 |
| Hospet | 8 | 1494 |
| Kudligi | 0 | 387 |
| H B Halli | 0 | 449 |
| H P Hally | 1 | 292 |
| Hadagali | 0 | 277 |
| Total | 20 | 5295 |

*Note*: Total Number of units differ from the corresponding totals in Table 3.1 and 3.2 respectively.

*Source*: District Industries Centre, Bellary.

The factors/reasons responsible for industrial sickness have been listed in various studies on this subject as follows:

(i) financial indiscipline;
(ii) management deficiency;
(iii) shortage of raw materials;
(iv) obsolete machinery;
(v) labour trouble;
(vi) surplus manpower; and
(vii) power shortage.

It may not be unreasonable to guess that some of these reasons/ factors, if not all, apply to the units in Bellary with an added vengeance!

It is presumable that several problems and constraints operate inhibiting the full realisation of industrial potential of the district. It is necessary to examine various parameters: resources, infrastructure, finance and government policy, as these help to understand the ramifications in regard to the full realisation of industrial potential within a given time frame. We take up the examination of these parameters in succession.

**Resources**

*Mineral Resources*

Mineral resources found in the district are:

| 'A' Principal Mineral Resources | | 'B' Minor Minerals |
|---|---|---|
| Metallic | Non-Metallic | |
| Iron ore | Moulding Sand | Ornamental stone |
| Iron ore fine | Quartz | Ordinary Sand |
| Manganese | Red Ochre | Brick Earth |
| Gold | Red Oxide | Building stone |
| Silver | | |

Special attention may be drawn to the fact that Bellary enjoys the prime place in respect of iron ore deposits/mines and manganese ore deposits/mines in the State. Donimalai Iron Ore Project located near Sandur operated by NMDC (a public sector enterprise) and the Sandur Manganese and Iron Ore Ltd, Sandur (a private sector enterprise) are the main producers. Besides there are about 63 licensed private iron ore mine operators, and about 11manganese ore operators who are sub-classified into large, medium and small, depending on their levels of productions. At present the annual average production of iron ore and manganese ore are 46.58 lakh tonnes and 2.42 lakh tonnes respectively (*Source*: Department of Mines and Zoology, Bellary). It is incumbent upon the private mine operators to sell the produce to MMTC.

Huge untapped stocks of iron ore deposits in the district may be gauged from the assertion in the knowledgeable circles that at the present levels of tapping, the stocks would last for another 150-200 years!

Iron ore extracts are exported mainly through the Madras Port. Importani railway stations for exporting iron ore extracts are as follows:

Bellary Cantonment
Hospet
Kariganuru
Papinayakanahalli
Toranagallu
Ranajitpura
Vyasanakere

**The above description brings forth the physical aspects regarding the major mineral resources and touches on the vital dimension of the huge untapped potential in the district.**

### *Agricultural Resources*

With as high as 75 per cent of the total labour force dependent on agriculture for its livelihood and a major part of the district's income originating from the primary sector, agriculture is the mainstay of the district's economy. About 30 per cent of net cropped area is irrigated. Bellary, Hagaribommanahalli, Hospet and Siraguppa are better endowed with irrigation facilities compared to the remaining taluks. Jowar, cotton, groundnut, pulses, paddy, maize are the major crops of the district.

Major agro-based industries viz., rice mills, oil mills, cotton ginning hold evidence to the fact that primary processing forms the core of industrial activities and no adequate attention is given to secondary and tertiary processing activities which essentially enhance the value addition.

It is clear that there is vast scope for tapping the under-exploited resources: both minerals and agricultural for industrial production. The experience of Bellary is a telling evidence to the fact that sheer existence or availability of resources locally does not ensure or facilitate location of industries, unless other objective conditions such as infrastructure facilities, market, finance and so on are fulfilled. An exercise in industrial planning based on local availability of resources may at best be indicative, but to translate it into reality requires to be supplemented with other crucial parameters of industrial production.

## Infrastructure

Without going into the details of individual industrial infrastructure items: railway route length, road length, number of goods vehicles, number of post offices, telephone exchanges, telephone lines and electricity consumption by the industry, but making a forceful plea for overhauling and improving (both in qualitative and quantitative terms) the access of industry to these crucial inputs, we move on to construct an Industrial Infrastructure Index for Bellary and the remaining districts in the State at two points of time 1976 and 1991 in order to demonstrate the worsening of the situation in Bellary.

The relative rank of Bellary with respect to Infrastructure Development Index deteriorated from 8th to 12th rank over the period 1976 to 1991 (Table 3.4). Also the differentials in the levels of infrastructure development between Bellary on the one hand and industrially developed districts like Bangalore, Mysore, Dakshina Kannada, Belgaum, Dharwad on the other are too marked to be missed out for their implications on the growth of industry.

TABLE 3.4: **Infrastructure Development Index for districts in Karnataka**

| Districts | 1976 Index | Rank | 1991 Index | Rank |
|---|---|---|---|---|
| Bangalore | 44812 | 1 | 33140 | 1 |
| Belgaum | 8143 | 3 | 6860 | 3 |
| Bellary | 3338 | 8 | 2616 | 12 |
| Bidar | 1000 | 19 | 1306 | 19 |
| Bijapur | 4686 | 6 | 3186 | 8 |
| Chickmagalur | 2292 | 17 | 2310 | 15 |
| Chitradurga | 3802 | 7 | 3384 | 6 |
| Dharwad | 7291 | 4 | 6045 | 5 |
| Dakshina Kannada | 9460 | 2 | 10226 | 2 |
| Gulbarga | 2533 | 11 | 2660 | 10 |
| Hassan | 2416 | 16 | 2502 | 14 |
| Kodagu | 1471 | 18 | 1748 | 18 |
| Kolar | 2509 | 13 | 2659 | 11 |
| Mandya | 2519 | 12 | 2081 | 16 |
| Mysore | 6391 | 5 | 6151 | 4 |
| Raichur | 2471 | 15 | 2058 | 17 |
| Shimoga | 3287 | 9 | 3202 | 7 |
| Tumkur | 2560 | 10 | 2531 | 13 |
| Uttara Kannada | 2480 | 14 | 2668 | 9 |

*Source*: M. Prahladachar, *et al.*, *Industrial Potential in Karnataka*, ISEC, 1994 (Mimeo).

The crucial role that infrastructure plays in creating industry-friendly-environment and in determining the pace and pattern of industrial development of a region is too obvious to be overstressed. If so, questions arise as who should discharge these responsibilities: Public and/or private sector. As building up of infrastructure facilities is a cost-intensive process with long gestation, the private sector may not be expected to take up this responsibility unless of course it is assured of a profit margin for its investment. In such a contingency, individual constituent items of infrastructure which are in the nature of intermediate inputs become relatively costly adding to the overall manufacturing cost of the products for final use. If so, it sounds reasonable to argue that on considerations of discharging the social responsibility, public sector should assume the primary role in building up the infrastructure facilities. This argument, however, should not be mistaken to suggest that private sector has no role or is devoid of social responsibility considerations in building up the infrastructure facilities. In fact many areas within the infrastructure sector may be identified for private firms' participation both at individual and/or consortium level. Nevertheless the essential point that needs to be stressed is that for the development of this sector the lead and major sharing of the burden should rest on the government.

It is unrealistic to plead for a uniform and simultaneous development of infrastructure facilities across the district. Instead it would be sensible to map out the potential growth centres of industry within the district and try to fill up the gaps in their infrastructure requirements. Recalling the reference made earlier that the belt comprising of three taluks: Bellary, Hospet and Sandur constitutes the hub of industrial activity and has also rich untapped potential, its infrastructure base deserves to be strengthened on a top priority.

**Industrial Finance**

Taking the cue from Schumpeter's view that financial services promote economic development in general and industrial development in particular, an attempt is made to examine, in brief, the network of financial institutions and the role played by them in facilitating the industrial development in the district. Relevant data are presented in Tables 3.5 and 3.6. In view of the fact that Karnataka State Industrial Investment Development Corporation and Karnataka State Finance Corporation are the only two major institutions extending industrial finance, the reference is restricted to them alone.

It is indeed intriguing to observe that while presenting the details of industrial finance, these two major institutions include Bellary in the classification of "other than backward districts". Apparently dimensions other than industry have gone into this consideration.

The total finance sanctioned by KSFC and KSIIDC since inception upto March 1992 to Bellary amounted to Rs. 2851.44 lakhs and Rs.649.01 lakhs respectively accounting for 3 per cent and 1.4 per cent in the corresponding State totals. If one were to exclude Bangalore district which by virtue of its pre-eminent industrial status has been able to corner

TABLE 3.5: **District-wise Sanctions and Disbursements for Small-scale Sector by KSFC since Inception upto March 1992**

| Districts | SANCTIONS | | | | DISBURSEMENTS | | | |
|---|---|---|---|---|---|---|---|---|
| | No. | Per cent | Amount | Per cent | No. | Per cent | Amount | Per cent |
| I.BACKWARD DISTRICTS | | | | | | | | |
| 1. Bidar | 1167 | 2.61 | 3631.99 | 3.68 | 1125 | 2.88 | 3483.65 | 4.22 |
| 2. Mysore | 3264 | 7.29 | 7356.13 | 7.45 | 2742 | 7.03 | 6239.8 | 7.56 |
| 3. Dharwad | 3871 | 8.65 | 6677.47 | 6.76 | 3000 | 7.69 | 5625.58 | 6.82 |
| 4. Raichur | 995 | 2.22 | 2444.19 | 2.47 | 910 | 2.33 | 1815.54 | 2.2 |
| 5. Belgaum | 3734 | 8.34 | 5224.33 | 5.29 | 3564 | 9.14 | 4719.17 | 5.72 |
| 6. Bijapur | 3637 | 8.13 | 2231.36 | 2.26 | 3142 | 8.06 | 1632.07 | 1.98 |
| 7. Dakshina Kannada | 2396 | 5.35 | 5468.34 | 5.54 | 1949 | 5 | 4624.47 | 5.61 |
| 8. Tumkur | 3223 | 7.2 | 5279.41 | 5.35 | 2923 | 7.49 | 4581.26 | 5.55 |
| 9. Gulbarga | 1464 | 3.27 | 2198.04 | 2.23 | 1218 | 3.12 | 1947.65 | 2.36 |
| 10. Uttara Kannada | 788 | 1.76 | 1157.69 | 1.17 | 721 | 1.85 | 924.64 | 1.12 |
| 11. Hassan | 1114 | 2.49 | 1773.43 | 1.8 | 907 | 2.33 | 1340.11 | 1.62 |
| TOTAL : I | 25653 | 57.32 | 43442.38 | 43.98 | 22201 | 56.93 | 36633.94 | 44.4 |

| | | | | | | | |
|---|---|---|---|---|---|---|---|
| **II. OTHER DISTRICTS** | | | | | | | |
| 1. Bangalore | 8147 | 18.21 | 39046.5 | 39.53 | 7014 | 17.93 | 32135.67 | 38.95 |
| 2. Shimoga | 4519 | 10.1 | 2767.23 | 2.8 | 3937 | 10.09 | 2465.99 | 2.99 |
| 3. Kolar | 1058 | 2.36 | 3402.96 | 3.45 | 1020 | 2.62 | 2837.81 | 3.44 |
| 4. Chitradurga | 1789 | 4 | 4075.23 | 4.13 | 1637 | 4.2 | 3351.65 | 4.06 |
| 5. Mandya | 1096 | 2.45 | 2036.32 | 2.06 | 1065 | 2.73 | 1851.69 | 2.24 |
| 6. Chickmagalur | 700 | 1.56 | 709.59 | 0.72 | 574 | 1.47 | 707.59 | 0.86 |
| 7. Bellary | 1329 | 2.97 | 3851.44 | 2.89 | 1132 | 2.9 | 2209.14 | 2.68 |
| 8. Kodagu | 460 | 1.03 | 437.08 | 0.44 | 420 | 1.08 | 306.8 | 0.37 |
| TOTAL : II | 19098 | 42.68 | 55326.35 | 56.02 | 16799 | 43.07 | 45866.34 | 55.6 |
| STATE TOTAL | 44751 | 100 | 93768.73 | 100 | 39000 | 100 | 82500.28 | 100 |

*Source*: KSFC Annual Reports, Various issues.

TABLE 3.6: **District-wise Analysis of Assistance (in Rs. lakhs) by KSIIDC since Inception upto March 1992**

| | Districts | Total No. | Per cent | Amount sanctioned | Per cent | Amount disbursed | Per cent |
|---|---|---|---|---|---|---|---|
| BACKWARD DISTRICTS | | | | | | | |
| CATEGORY 'A' | Bidar | 23 | 3.17 | 1548.79 | 3.28 | 1447.19 | 3.98 |
| CATEGORY 'B' | Raichur | 26 | 3.58 | 1352.47 | 2.86 | 693.19 | 1.91 |
| | Dharwad | 37 | 5.1 | 2225.82 | 4.71 | 1957.15 | 5.39 |
| | Mysore | 115 | 15.84 | 9290.46 | 19.89 | 7091.71 | 19.52 |
| CATEGORY 'C' | Belgaum | 19 | 2.62 | 1233.22 | 2.61 | 837.42 | 2.8 |
| | Bijapur | 10 | 1.38 | 490.99 | 1.04 | 396.56 | 1.09 |
| | Gulbarga | 6 | 0.83 | 325.28 | 0.69 | 324.28 | 0.89 |
| | Hassan | 8 | 1.1 | 388.1 | 0.82 | 363.85 | 1 |
| | Kolar | 18 | 2.48 | 1105.34 | 2.34 | 799.28 | 2.2 |
| | Uttara Kannada | 11 | 1.52 | 906.75 | 1.92 | 715.75 | 1.97 |
| | Dakshina Kannada | 37 | 5.1 | 2211.5 | 4.68 | 1796.49 | 4.94 |
| | Tumkur | 19 | 2.62 | 1162.33 | 2.46 | 1036.33 | 2.85 |
| | Coorg | 1 | 0.14 | 27 | 0.06 | 26.5 | 0.07 |
| | SUB-TOTAL | 330 | 45.45 | 22368.05 | 47.38 | 17485.98 | 48.12 |

| | | | | | | |
|---|---|---|---|---|---|---|
| OTHER DISTRICTS | | | | | | |
| Bangalore | 354 | 48.76 | 20458.29 | 43.4 | 16147.8 | 44.44 |
| Bellary | 9 | 1.24 | 649.01 | 1.37 | 336.41 | 0.93 |
| Chitradurga | 24 | 3.31 | 2029.62 | 4.8 | 1325.37 | 3.65 |
| Chickmagalur | -32765 | 0.41 | 111.22 | 0.24 | 102.97 | 0.28 |
| Mandya | 10 | 1.38 | 591.7 | 1.25 | 341.7 | 0.94 |
| Shimoga | 13 | 1.79 | 970.21 | 2.06 | 598.33 | 1.65 |
| SUB-TOTAL | 413 | 56.89 | 24840.1 | 58.62 | 18852.58 | 51.88 |
| TOTAL | 726 | | 47208.1 | | 36338.56 | |

*Source:* Calculated from KSIIDC Reports.

roughly 1/6th of the finance extended by these two institutions and rework out the shares of remaining districts in the residual State total the position of Bellary does not register any conspicuous change.

**Government Industrial Policy**

Under the Industrial Policy announced in 1993, Government of Karnataka has come out with a package of incentives with a view to, among others, attracting entrepreneurs to industrially backward districts in the State. Without going into the details of these specific incentives, suffice it to mention that these incentives by themselves do not bring the expected results unless crucial pre-conditions required for industrial development such as infrastructure, rational tax regime and so on are not fulfilled. In this context one may also mention bureaucratic hurdles, inter-departmental non-coordination (both vertical and horizontal), resulting in the disillusionment of prospective entrepreneurs. Despite the functioning of 'single window agency' which is initiated with a view to expediting and smoothening the setting up of new enterprises, the fact that entrepreneurs are condemned to run from pillar to post for obtaining various already cleared (!) factors of production, such as land, water and power calls for a politico-administrative introspection and correction.

In summing up the discussion undertaken so far, it may be highlighted that the exploitation of rich mineral resources with which the district is endowed promises to inject industrial dynamism and thereby act as a prime mover for the all-round development of this backward district. For this to happen, as Leibenstein rightly theorises elsewhere, there is need for a 'big push' and for improving the level, quality and time element in creating a congenial environment for industrial development.

Thanks to the new economic policy which lays emphasis on liberalisation, privatisation and so on, the district seems to be set for a breakthrough in the industrial sector. The opening up of the economy in general and the steel industry in particular which has traditionally been the strong citadel of the public sector, to private sector seems to beacon a new era in the industrial development of the district. It is gathered from the DIC, Bellary that in all 16 fresh projects in medium and large scale industries have been already cleared by the State Level High Power Committee, and are at various stages of implementation. The total expected investment of these projects is Rs.10146.71 crores. (This is nearly 55 times more than the present level of investment!). The belt comprising of 3 taluks: Bellary, Hospet and Sandur constitutes the hub of this activity. It may be observed that the list includes 4 projects proposed to be set up in the neighbouring

Raichur district. In so far as these projects depend for their raw material supplies on mines in Bellary district and because of their geographical proximity need to be included in our discussion frame.

It may sound tautological if one points out that pattern and pace of industrial growth of this region is inextricably interlinked with the status, performance and growth of several related sectors and also with the sincerity of efforts in creating an 'enabling environment' for realising the intended results.

It is to be recognised that the proposed medium and large scale steel projects both in the pre- and post-stages of their establishment disturb the district's low level equilibrium, if not stagnation, and set in motion a new wave of expectations (employment prospects, technology options), demands (factors of production: land, labour and capital, power, transport, raw materials, etc.) and opportunities (ancillary and downstream industries, interlinkages between agriculture and industry, service activities) thereby exerting extra pressures on various dimensions of the district's economy before moving to a high level of equilibrium.

To illustrate, the district has already started to witness the pressures of increased demand for factors of production like land and water. So will be the case sooner with the demand for raw material supplies. The increased momentum of industrial activity is already exerting its pressures on the existing institutional arrangements and weak infrastructure network of the district, and also on housing, municipal services and so on. In order to address these emerging problems effectively, a well coordinated and integrated plan is imperative and urgent. In this context it is commendable that the District Industry Centre has already made an exercise to identify a host of ancillary and downstream industries (in the wake of new steel industries coming up in the district) with their possible locations. So also must be mentioned the comprehensive development plan prepared by BUDA. If such examples of forethought and perspective planning are multiplied by several other official and non-official agencies, the future development scenario will be quite bright and reassuring. In order to implement a well conceived and designed perspective plan, a nodal agency may be constituted. Participation and cooperation of public and private sectors, local institutions and NGOs in this endeavour of taking the economy to new heights will make the journeying smoother and quicker.

## REFERENCE

1. M. Prahladachar *et al.*, *Industrial Potential in Karnataka*, (Mimeo) ISEC, 1994.

# 4

# PHYSICAL INFRASTRUCTURE
## Present Status and Future Prospects

ABDUL AZIZ and M. DEVENDRA BABU

### Introduction

In the previous chapters it has been brought out that Bellary district has a high potential for developing as an industrial region considering the availability of high quality iron ore (estimated at over 1,000 million tonnes with 60-70 per cent iron content) and the prospect of related economic activities coming up as backward and forward linkages to the steel mills. As of now, the Bellary-Thornagal-Sandur-Hospet region is emerging as a major industrial belt of the district. In the next few years, this belt including the surrounding areas, will perhaps be bubbling with industrial activity. That is good news indeed. But the bad news is, the industrialisation process will demand certain facilities and put heavy pressure particularly on the infrastructure facilities which are basic to the sustenance of industries once they are established. The basic infrastructure facilities needed for the sustained growth of industries, albeit even for their survival, are electric power, transport and communications. Power shortages and transport bottlenecks can adversely affect the day-to-day working of the industries and thereby throttle industrial growth. It is proposed here to review the position regarding the availability of these infrastructure facilities *vis-a-vis* the requirements of the industry, identify gaps in them, if any, and suggest ways and means of augmenting those facilities.

The problem that we faced is lack of hard statistical data.This was further compounded by the non-availability of systematic official studies on the theme. Though as far back as 1968 an attempt was made to assess the infrastructure needs of this region in response to the coming up of the

Tungabhadra irrigation project, this attempt did not cover certain items of infrastructure especially power and communications.[1] Similarly, an attempt was made recently (1993) by the Bellary Urban Development Authority (BUDA) to prepare a development plan for the Vijayanagar Steel Planning area.[2] But as the title itself suggests, this plan, though quite useful in terms of its focus on area development, did not look at the broad socio-economic implications of a large number of steel mills and other types of industries getting established in future. Hence, the present note had to draw mainly from the data collected from the field by holding discussions with local officials, industrialists and knowledgeable persons and from whatever published material that was available at the time of writing it.

**Power Supply**

Power is the most important and crucial requirement of industry. As such, power shortage, power shutdown and power cuts could paralyse industrial activity, throw thousands of workers out of job and cause inconvenience to consumers. This problem is further compounded by the fact that the steel industry is power intensive and requires large quantities of power, and that, power generation is capital intensive and natural resource-specific. Therefore, power cannot be generated everywhere and by everyone. Only those who have large capital resources can venture into taking up generation of power. It is, therefore, not surprising that power generation as an economic activity has been in the public sector though in recent years private initiative is forthcoming in some places in a small way.

As Bellary district is experiencing rapid industrialisation, demand for power has been increasing day-by-day. What is the power supply position and how far is it in conformity with the local needs? It is generally held that Bellary district, particularly its industrial belt, is well-served by a network of power generating stations and power lines.[3] Thus, the three power generating stations of this region viz., the Tungabhadra Right Bank Power House, the Hampi Power House and the Munirabad Power House have an installed capacity of 99 MW. These power systems on the other hand are interconnected with the Sharavathi generating station and with the Kali power system making it possible for this region to draw power from different sources. However, this does not ensure that all the power requirements of this region will be met. For, with the establishment of all the proposed six steel mills and townships in the region the demand for power is likely to increase by manifolds. Thus, power is required for industries right from the construction stage to final production stage in different quantities. For instance, in the case of the contemplated Vijayanagar Steel plant at Toranagallu the estimated power requirement is 6 MW at the construction stage and 160 MW at the production stage. Obviously, power generated at present in the region would not be sufficient to meet the requirements of even one steel mill! So, the region will have to draw power from the State grid notwithstanding what is being locally generated.

A rough estimate of power requirement of the steel mills proposed to be set up may give an indication of the magnitude of the problem. It is stated that the power requirement norm of an integrated steel plant of one million tonne capacity is 400 to 450 KwH per tonne of steel produced.[4] Assuming that the final capacity of all the proposed steel mills is 6.6 million tonnes of steel and that the minimum of power required per tonne of steel produced is 400 KwH, the final demand for power from the steel mills alone will be 2640 million KwH. To this has to be added the demand (i) from the downstream industries that are likely to come up in the region both as backward and forward linkages and (ii) from the residents of the townships that are likely to come up in the vicinity of the steel mills. Since data on the number of downstream mills and the expected number of residential units in the townships on the one hand and the norms of electricity consumption by them are not available it is not possible to estimate the precise quantum of power required for this purpose. However, if the power required by the steel mills, the downstream industries and the residents of industrial townships is roughly assumed to be of the order of 3000 KwH, even this will be a fantastic figure. The least that can be said here is that it may be difficult, if not impossible, to meet the electric power requirement of Bellary district when it finally reaches its potential as an industrial centre. This is because, as it is, there is a general shortage of power in the State and that, as a result, power cuts and shut-downs have been common. This is more so in recent months owing to serious shortages that have developed in power generation. The impact of these shortages is very much likely to be felt in Bellary district too. As it is, the level of power use in this district is not comparable. Table 4.1, which presents data about indicators of electricity consumption in Bellary in relation to State averages gives not so encouraging picture. Though the per capita power consumption in industries is higher than the State average, in respect of other indicators like percentage of village and towns electrified, electric connections per 1000 population and distribution lines per 1000 sq. km and per capita power consumption by all users the situation is not favourable compared to the State average position. Therefore, attempts should be made to plan for power generation from all possible sources in the region so that power availability is augmented for all uses in the district.

TABLE 4.1: **Indicators of Levels of Development in Electricity Use in Bellary District and Karnataka State**

| Indicators | Bellary District | Karnataka State |
|---|---|---|
| 1. Percent of villages and Towns Electrified (March 1989) | 96.50 | 97.09 |
| 2. Electric connections per 1000 population (1993-94) | 124.00 | 160.00 |
| 3. Distribution line (LT & HT combined) per 1000 Sq. Km (length in Km in 1993-94) | 1714 | 2120 |
| 4. Per capita power consumption in industries (KwH, 1993-94) | 130 | 90 |
| 5. Per capita power consumption—all uses (KwH, 1993-94) | 177 | 313 |

*Source*: Johnson Samuel (1996), "Infrastructure for Regional Development" in Abdul Aziz and Sudhir Krishna (Eds.), *Regional Development : Problems and Policy Measures*, Concept, New Delhi, p. 67.

An important source of energy that can be tapped in the district is solar energy. The district has sunny days throughout the year and that will provide opportunities for tapping solar energy on a big scale. Perhaps, we can learn from the experience in Rajasthan where the Government has issued letters of intent to three companies to generate solar power in what is proposed to be called the Solar Energy Enterprise Zone (SEEZ) comprising the districts of Jodhpur, Barmer and Jaisalmer. These companies are expected to generate 300 MW of solar power in the next five years on a Build, Own, Operate and Maintain (BOOM) basis.[5] The Government of Karnataka should encourage private initiative to generate solar energy on the BOOM basis either for sale or for own use. Before that, of course, the economics of solar energy generation should be worked out to find out if the cost of energy from this source is comparable and well within the reach, and if it can be stored and transmitted to the consuming points.

The other possibility is to ask industries to establish captive power plants. In fact, one of the pre-conditions to permitting any entrepreneur to start a steel industry should be, as it seems so, to insist on installing a captive power plant of his own to generate power for his use. In view of the high capital cost of establishing and also operating the captive power plants, the local industrialists feel that this is not a practical proposition considering their weak financial position[6]. This is understandable when one looks at the financial capacity of small and medium scale industries. But, if a consortium of such industries is formed to establish a captive power plant the proposition of generating power on their own should be feasible. Perhaps, feasibility of such a proposition may be examined by the local industries and their association. However, it should be well-within the financial ability of the steel mills to establish their own captive power plants and to generate power required for their use. Therefore, in their case captive power generation should become a precondition to the clearance of their project.

## Transport Facilities

While power is the life-blood of industry, transport is its arterial system. Industry depends on this system for transporting both raw materials and the finished products. An extensive and efficient system of transport will be a basic support system to industrial growth. For a district like Bellary with the kind of industries that are likely to come up roadways and railways will be of crucial importance though the importance of airways cannot be played down when in the near future Bellary district becomes a highly industrialised centre. When actually the need arises, the Bellary airport which at present can accommodate the Vayudoot aircraft may be upgraded to operate bigger aircrafts. If the bigger industries desire to operate helicopters of their own, as is being done by the Kudremukh Iron Ore Company, a helipad may also be built for their use.

### *Roads*

In Bellary district, where steel industry is going to dominate the industrial scene and since this industry's major raw material is iron ore, the transport system should be specific to transporting this raw material which is heavy and available in areas that cannot be reached easily by railways. Road transport in that case assumes crucial importance. For an efficient road transport system to develop, the basic requirement is a good surface road network. This network should be adequate to take in the growing number of vehicles, their carrying capacity and the trips they need to make in a given time period. What is the present status of the road network in Bellary district?

The data presented in Appendix I indicates that the position on the road transport front is not satisfactory in the district. For, the number of vehicles registered per lakh population in the district compared with the State average is less. The position regarding the goods vehicles registered per lakh population is even less (50%) than the State average (it is possible that vehicles registered outside the district are operating to take care of the increasing transport needs). Also, the road length in Bellary district is far less than the State average. This is true of the National highways, State highways and district roads, though the district appears to be well-endowed with what are called the "other roads". In regard to major bridges too the position is not comparable. All these point out to the underdeveloped nature of the road transport system in the district. The low level of road development in Bellary district is due to lack of a good and adequate network of national and State highways. No doubt, the national highway No. 13 passes through the district but as only a portion of its length (90 Km) passes through the district this is of no great help. The State highways such as Bellary-Hospet-Harihar and Bellary-Guntakal do provide some relief. So are the district roads which connect Bellary with the taluk headquarters—chiefly Sandur and Hospet.

Considering that these roads are used for carrying iron ore from the sites of deposits such as the Donimalai, Kumaraswamy, Ramghad and Jambunatha Hills range to the factory sites and to railway heads for export by rail upto Madras port two main problems can be noted about them. One, the length, width and the weight-bearing capacities of the roads are totally inadequate as they were planned and laid some three decades ago. Thus, the existing narrow seven-metre roads would be woefully inadequate to bear, among other things, 6.6 million tonnes of steel per annum and several million tonnes of coal and iron ore. Therefore, there is need to widen the roads (ranging from 10-12 metres) as also to develop multi-lane roads from the raw material point to the steel mill site. The multi-lane roads, apart from facilitating the smooth movement of traffic will also, minimise accidents. Simultaneously, culverts also should be widened. Besides, State highways need to be converted into national highways, at least the ones between Bellary and Guthi, and Bellary and Karwar.

Secondly, as these roads run through towns and cities not only do they cause the problem of congested traffic in a big way but also impose a health hazard on the people by kicking up dust and spilling iron particles into air. Particularly, the present practice of carrying ore from mining areas to railway stations at Hospet, Bellary, Papinayakanahalli, Kariganur and Torangallu has resulted in traffic congestion along this route. To ease the traffic congestion, truck terminals should be developed at Bellary, Tornagallu and Hospet. In Hospet, particularly, the citizens are angry that the ore-carrying lorries which spill dust and obstruct normal traffic are allowed to pass through the city roads to reach the railway station. In this regard two alternative solutions are suggested : (a) either the Hospet railway goods yard be closed and ore carrying lorry traffic diverted to the neighbouring Kariganur goods yard, (b) or a ring road (or even a bypass road via the high level canal) be formed such that the lorry traffic is connected to Hospet railway goods yard such that the lorries do not pass through the city at all, (c) or, bifurcate the railway track just before the Kariganur railway station, take the new track upto NH 13—a distance of 3.5 Kms—and build a railway goods yard on the plenty of Government land that is available over there. May be the bridges along the route, if any, need to be strengthened to allow for heavy traffic movement.

The first alternative does not appear to be a feasible solution considering the low capacity of the Kariganur railway goods yard to take on the additional load of 1.5 million tonnes apart from its own load of one million tonnes. So, a proposal for laying a ring road has been submitted and it is being examined. But the constraint that has come in the way is the problem of land acquisition because the private land owners are resisting acquisition of land by the Government. The third alternative does not appear to pose the problem of any such resistance from private land owners as the land all along the route is said to be Government land. The additional advantage claimed is (i) the bulk load of Hospet and Kariganur railway station can be taken care of by creating larger load capacity here and (ii) the lorries can speed away after loading and unloading to any destination without touching Hospet city. However, a technical committee should examine the economic feasibility of these alternative proposals.

*Railways*

In respect of railways, however, the situation appears to be somewhat better when compared with the State average position. Bellary district has a larger number of railway stations, longer rail route and a longer broad guage route when compared with the State average (Appendix I).

But the basic question is whether even this liberal availability of the railway network system will meet the future needs of the industry. There are a few deficiencies to which a reference may be made. While today the railways appear to be adequate to handle the current traffic of the export-oriented iron ore, the rising demand for rail service particularly in respect of coal, and limestone from their source to the factory site and from the factory site to major cities (for transporting the finished product) there is need for a multi-lane rail track, particularly, from Hospet to Guntakal. Also, the wagon capacity should be increased from the current level to the level needed in future. One more suggestion is, at least at three points viz., Hospet, Tornagallu and Sandur, goods stations should be separated from the passenger stations keeping a distance of 5 Kms between them to avoid congestion and to facilitate free movement of passenger and goods trains. Secondly, while transport of iron ore is served by road and rail, there is need to have some rail links with the neighbouring districts to have other raw materials transported to the factory site. One such case relates to the transport of limestone which is available in the neighbouring districts of Chitradurga, Shimoga and Dharwar, and manganese in Chitradurga and Shimoga (apart from Bellary itself). A railway line linking Kottur with Davangere or Harihar will facilitate transport of these raw materials to the factory site at lower cost as Kottur is linked now by rail with Hospet.

At present, a large part of the iron ore is being exported. The transport route is by rail upto Madras and from there by ship. With the steel mills starting production in Bellary district, the relative proportion of the ore exported may decline, but in absolute terms its magnitude may not decline. Hence, ore will continue to be exported as before. But there are two problems here : One is inadequate wagon capacity and the other is the long rail route by which ore is conveyed to the Madras port which is already crowded. To beat the rail transport cost of ore, it is suggested that it may be routed through the west coast ports preferably Mangalore and Karwar ports. If this is economically feasible, then there is a need to develop and expand the West coast port facilities to accommodate the Bellary district-based ore exports.

As the Bellary region will shortly develop into an industrial area, shortages will be felt in regard to passenger traffic. At present, Bellary is, no doubt, linked to major cities of India via. Hubli and Guntakal. What needs to be done is to introduce more number of passenger trains and more number of A.C. coaches in them to meet the needs of tourists and business executives.

## Communication System

Modern industry depends heavily on the electronic communication system. Telephone, Telex, E-mail and Fax facilities are a *sine qua non* of industrial culture. These facilities should, therefore, be available in the required scale and at competitive prices to industry.

How is Bellary district served with communication facilities? Appendix I which presents this information shows that in regard to the number of post offices and telephone exchanges per lakh of population the district appears to be better served compared with the overall position in the State. But the same cannot be said about the telephones because the number of telephones per lakh of population is dismally lower when compared with the State average. This is disturbing considering the fact that the situation will worsen in future with industries coming in. As the Department of Communication states, the types of communications that are in great demand from the industrial community are Fax facility, PABX lines, Data circuits, Speech circuits and wireless systems. The Department is not in a position to indicate the extent of demand for these facilities as of now though it expects that in future there will be heavy pressure for such facilities. As for the telephones, the estimates put out by the Department is that the demand per annum for the district will be 3500 lines. The break up for the taluks is as follows : Bellary 1500, Hospet 1000, H. B. Halli, Harapanahalli and Siruguppa 200 each, Kudligi and Sandur 150 each and Hadagali 100. It is not clear if the future demand from the industrial community is taken into account in this estimate. Assuming that the demand from the industrial community will be 500 lines per annum from next year, the Department will have to make provision for 4000 lines in all per annum.

Keeping the demand for these services in view, we have to examine whether there is extra capacity available in regard to these facilities so that when demand goes up for these services with the acceleration of industrialisation, the communications department would be able to meet it without straining itself. Considering the present experience of the users, the existing capacity seems to be quite inadequate. There are complaints that at present users have to wait for hours to get STD calls. This calls for automising the STD call system and increasing the capacity of telephone exchanges. Also, in an industrially developed area demand for telephones and telegraphic services will naturally go up. To meet such growing demand the number of telephone exchanges and telegraph offices should be increased commensurately. The general feeling of the industrialists is that the capacity of the communication system should be at least doubled particularly telephones by 2001 AD when all the proposed industries would have been established. With the establishment of industries and worker townships demand for both industrial and residential telephone connections would have gone up. Therefore, a doubling of telephone connections as also telephone exchanges will have to be envisaged by the turn of the present century.

**Industrial Area Development**

Apart from providing the basic infrastructure such as power, transport and communications, it will be necessary for the Government to provide other infrastructure particularly for the small and ancillary industries that might come up in due course. The Government should acquire land for industrial purpose and develop it into small plots of varying sizes for allotment to small entrepreneurs on lease basis. Possibly, this work may be assigned to private builders. They can also be assigned the task of planning and building townships with all facilities provided to the resident population. Schools, hospitals, housing, recreation, hotels and restaurants, shopping centres may be built by the private entrepreneurs. That will lighten the burden on the industrialists.

Besides, to meet the requirements of some specialised industries, the State should develop industrial parks. Also a technology bank to assist investors who seek technology from within and outside the country and commercial banking and financial institutions which specialize in handling the financial requirements of industry may also be established in the region.

**Some Policy Issues**

While emphasising on the need for providing adequate physical infrastructure facilities keeping the growing demand for it in future some points for discussion may be stated before we conclude this chapter. In the first place, it is not enough if quantitative targets are set for reaching; there should be an equal emphasis on the quality aspects too. On this point, it would be helpful to quote the World Development Report here:

> "But....., the *quantity* of investment cannot be the exclusive focus of policy. Improving the *quality* of infrastructure service is also vital. Low operating efficiency, inadequate maintenance and

lack of attention to the needs of users have all played a part in reducing the development impact of infrastructure investments in the past. Both quantity and quality improvements are essential to modernise and diversify production, help countries compete internationally and accommodate rapid urbanisation".[7]

Secondly, it is not enough if the infrastructure facilities are provided in required quantities and qualities; provision should also be made for their proper maintenance. It is a well-known fact that inadequate maintenance, which is common everywhere, could reduce the life of the asset created for providing such facilities. For example, as the World Development Report opines, "a well-maintained paved road surface should last for ten to fifteen years before needing resurfacing, but lack of maintenance can lead to severe deterioration in half that time..... inadequate maintenance means that power systems in developing countries have only 60 per cent of their generating capacity available at a given time, whereas best practice would achieve levels over 80 per cent".[8] Therefore, special attention to the maintenance of these facilities should be paid by the concerned authorities. It is a well-known fact that lorries which carry iron-ore of the order of 10 tonnes in general cause damage to the roads at a much quicker pace than otherwise. Hence, these roads need greater and frequent attention of the maintenance staff in the absence of which the long run cost of road maintenance will be much larger and at the same time the traffic will have the prospect of using inefficient road service.

The provision of physical infrastructure in the required qualities and quantities and its proper maintenance will raise the question of financing and managing these projects. Here we may consider some views on this issue. As for management, one view is that to promote a more efficient and responsive service delivery we should:

(i) manage infrastructure like business and not as a bureaucracy meaning that these services should be run as an industry that respond to consumer demand;
(ii) introduce competition by liberalising entry into activities so that consumer has better choices and suppliers are pressurised to be efficient and accountable to users; and
(iii) give users a strong voice by giving access at planning, designing and regulation of infrastructure services.

In the context of liberalisation policy in our country, there appears to be some logic in the above perspective presented by the World Development Report. There is obviously a need now to consider these options by those who are responsible for providing the infrastructure facilities. Financial requirement of these projects are of enormous magnitude. Funding them has to be taken care of. A major share of the burden has to be borne by the Government itself. In this connection, a two-tier analysis may be carried out one is the infrastructure which is of national importance such as airways, railways, ports, telephones, telegraphs and to some extent power and national highways. The other which is of local importance such as State and district roads, power and lorry terminals. The former is the responsibility of the Central Government and the latter is that of the State Government. There are, however, some areas where the industrialists should/can participate. For instance, in regard to captive power plants, solar energy generating plants, approach roads to factories, worker townships and so on the participation of industrialists in their supply will be more economical and, therefore, they should be made responsible for providing them.

## NOTES

1. See Government of Mysore, *An Outline Project Report on the Investment for Infrastructure in the Tungabhadra Project Ayacut*, Directorate of Evaluation and Manpower, Bangalore 1969.
2. Bellary Urban Development Authority, *Comprehensive Development Plan of Vijayanagar Steel Planning Area*, BUDA, Bellary.
3. K.S. Rame Gowda, "Integrated Development of Tungabhadra Valley Region", a paper submitted to the *National Workshop on Hospet and its Environs—2001 AD*. Organised jointly by the Institute for Social and Economic Change, Bangalore and the National Society of Urban Development, Hospet.
4. This is the figure given by Bellary Steels and Alloys Limited, Bellary.
5. "Rajasthan Surges Ahead", *The Hindu*, Dec. 25, 1995, p. 26.
6. Pre-seminar discussion held in Bellary with the district industrialists and administrators on 28.11.1995.
7. World Bank, Foreword, *The World Development Report, 1994: Infrastructure for Development*, Oxford University Press, New York, 1994, p. iii.
8. *Ibid.*, p.4.

## APPENDIX—I

### LEVEL OF BASIC INFRASTRUCTURE IN BELLARY DISTRICT VIS-A-VIS KARNATAKA, 1993-94

| | | Item | Bellary District | Karnataka State |
|---|---|---|---|---|
| 1. | | Total No. of Motor Vehicles | 51343 | 1812092 |
| | | (Per lakh Population) | (2720.88) | (3625.85) |
| | (i) | Goods vehicles | 2149 | 81695 |
| | | (Per lakh population) | (113.88) | (163.47) |
| 2. a. | | Road Length (in Kms) | 4887 | 134592 |
| | | (Per 100 Sq. Kms.) | (49.44) | (70.17) |
| | (i) | National Highways | 90 | 1997 |
| | | (Per 100 Sq. Kms.) | (0.91) | (1.04) |
| | (ii) | State Highways | 471 | 11288 |
| | | (Per 100 Sq. Kms.) | (4.76) | (5.89) |
| | (iii) | Major district Roads | 1279 | 28169 |
| | | (Per 100 Sq. Kms.) | (12.94) | (14.69) |
| | (iv) | Others | 3047 | 41454 |
| | | (Per 100 Sq. Kms.) | (30.82) | (21.61) |
| 2. b. | | Major bridges | 15 | 466 |
| | | (Per 1000 Sq. Kms.) | (1.52) | (2.43) |
| 3. a. | | Railway Route (in Kms) | 331 | 3079 |
| | | (Per 100 Sq. Kms.) | (3.35) | (1.61) |
| | (i) | Broad Gauge | 127 | 1195 |
| | | (Per 100 Sq. Kms.) | (1.28) | (0.62) |
| | (ii) | Metre Gauge | 204 | 1735 |
| | | (Per 100 Sq. Kms.) | (2.06) | (0.90) |
| | (iii) | Narrow Gauge | 0 | 149 |
| | (iv) | Railway Stations | 27 | 381 |
| | | (Per 1000 Sq. Kms.) | (2.73) | (1.99) |
| 4. | | Communication Facilities | | |
| | (i) | No. of Post Offices | 455 | 9781 |
| | | (Per lakh Population) | (24.11) | (19.57) |

*(Contd.)*

| Item | Bellary District | Karnataka State |
|---|---|---|
| (ii) No. of Telephone Exchanges | 84 | 1866 |
| (Per lakh Population) | (4.45) | (3.73) |
| (iii) No. of Telephones | 13344 | 508000 |
| (Per lakh Population) | (707.15) | (1016.47) |

*Note:* Figures in brackets are standardised to population or area as the case may be.

*Source*: 1. District Statistical Office, *District at a Glance, 1993-94*, Bellary.

2. Directorate of Economics and Statistics, *Karnataka at a Glance, 1993-94*, Bangalore.

# APPENDIX II

## TALUKWISE DATA ON INFRASTRUCTURE

### A: Taluk-wise Position of Transport and Roads in Bellary District

| Taluk | Trucks | Trucks Per lakh Pop | Total Vehicles | Vehicles Per lakh Pop | National High-way (In Kms.) | N H per 100 Sq. Kms. | State High-ways (In Kms.) | S.H. per 100 Sq. Kms. | Main Roads | M. R. per 100 Sq. Kms. | District Roads | Others | Total Road Length | T R per 100 Sq. Kms. | No. of Heavy Bridges |
|---|---|---|---|---|---|---|---|---|---|---|---|---|---|---|---|
| Bellary | 940 | 190.28 | 28234 | 5715.38 | 0 | 0 | 109 | 6.45 | 301 | 17.84 | 4 | 908 | 1322 | 78.27 | 5 |
| Hadagali | 20 | 13.61 | 909 | 618.37 | 0 | 0 | 26 | 2.74 | 184 | 19.41 | 16 | 194 | 420 | 44.30 | 1 |
| H.B.Halli | 36 | 26.67 | 1273 | 942.96 | 0 | 0 | 31 | 3.27 | 112 | 11.83 | 25 | 146 | 314 | 33.16 | 1 |
| H.P.Hally | 42 | 18.03 | 1570 | 673.82 | 0 | 0 | 80 | 5.56 | 124 | 8.62 | 17 | 356 | 577 | 40.13 | 0 |
| Hospet | 629 | 200.96 | 12781 | 4083.39 | 21 | 2.25 | 61 | 6.53 | 130 | 13.92 | 0 | 362 | 574 | 61.46 | 1 |
| Kudligi | 38 | 17.35 | 1196 | 546.12 | 69 | 4.31 | 71 | 4.43 | 161 | 10.05 | 47 | 286 | 634 | 39.58 | 1 |
| Sandur | 345 | 221.15 | 2912 | 1866.67 | 0 | 0 | 49 | 3.90 | 125 | 9.94 | 19 | 320 | 513 | 40.78 | 2 |
| Siruguppa | 99 | 52.38 | 2468 | 1305.82 | 0 | 0 | 34 | 3.26 | 142 | 13.63 | 0 | 357 | 533 | 51.15 | 4 |
| Total | 2149 | 113.88 | 513043 | 27188.29 | 90 | 0.91 | 471 | 4.78 | 1279 | 12.97 | 128 | 2919 | 4887 | 49.57 | 15 |

*Note*: N H = National Highway
S H = State Highway
M R = Main road
T R L = Total Road Length

*Source*: District Statistical Office, *District at a Glance, 1993-94*, Bellary.

**B : Taluk-wise Railway Route Length in Bellary District (in KMs.)**

| Taluk | Broad Gauge | B G Per 100 Sq. Kms. | Metre Gauge | M G Per 100 Sq. Kms. | Total Railway length | T R L per 100 Sq. Kms | Railway Stations (No.) | R S per 100 Sq. Kms |
|---|---|---|---|---|---|---|---|---|
| Bellary | 53 | 3.14 | 41 | 2.43 | 94 | 5.57 | 9 | 0.53 |
| Hadagali | 0 | 0 | 0 | 0 | 0 | 0 | 0 | 0 |
| H.B. Halli | 0 | 0 | 30 | 3.17 | 30 | 3.17 | 4 | 0.42 |
| H.P. Hally | 0 | 0 | 0 | 0 | 0 | 0 | 0 | 0 |
| Hospet | 36 | 3.85 | 60 | 6.42 | 96 | 10.20 | 7 | 0.75 |
| Kudligi | 0 | 0 | 20 | 1.25 | 20 | 1.25 | 2 | 0.12 |
| Sandur | 38 | 3.02 | 53 | 4.21 | 91 | 7.23 | 5 | 0.40 |
| Siruguppa | 0 | 0 | 0 | 0 | 0 | 0 | 0 | 0 |
| Total | 127 | 1.29 | 204 | 2.07 | 331 | 3.36 | 27 | 0.27 |

*Note*: R S = Railway Station
B G = Broad Guage
M G = Metre Guage
T R L = Total Railway Length

*Source*: District Statistical Office, *District at a Glance, 1993-94.*

**C: Taluk-wise Position of Communications in Bellary District**

| Taluk | Post Offices | P O per Lakh Pop | Tele-graph Offices | T G O per Lakh Pop | Tele-phones Exchanges | T E per Lakh Pop | Tele-phones in use | Telephones Per Lakh Pop |
|---|---|---|---|---|---|---|---|---|
| Bellary | 97 | 19.64 | 52 | 10.53 | 32 | 6.48 | 6975 | 1411.94 |
| Hadagali | 41 | 27.89 | 10 | 6.80 | 6 | 4.08 | 346 | 235.37 |
| H.B. Halli | 34 | 25.19 | 17 | 12.59 | 9 | 6.67 | 501 | 371.11 |
| H.P. Hally | 63 | 27.04 | 18 | 7.73 | 10 | 4.29 | 584 | 250.64 |
| Hospet | 55 | 17.57 | 21 | 6.71 | 9 | 2.88 | 3168 | 1012.14 |
| Kudligi | 76 | 34.70 | 34 | 15.53 | 6 | 2.74 | 456 | 208.22 |
| Sandur | 36 | 23.08 | 9 | 5.77 | 11 | 7.05 | 781 | 500.64 |
| Siruguppa | 53 | 28.04 | 19 | 10.05 | 10 | 5.29 | 533 | 282.01 |
| Total | 455 | 24.11 | 180 | 9.54 | 84 | 4.45 | 13344 | 707.15 |

*Note*: P O = Post Office

T G O = Telegraph Office

T E = Telephone Exchange

*Source*: District Statistical Offices, *District at a Glance, 1993-94*, Bellary.

# 5

# SOCIAL INFRASTRUCTURE
## Education and Health Facilities

T.R. CHANDRASEKHARA

### Introduction

Industrial investment in Bellary district is going to take a quantum jump in the next 10 to 15 years. This kind of massive direct investment, will bring about a good measure of indirect investment also in the ancillary industry and commercial sector. We are told that as of now 20 to 25 applications of industrialists requesting clearance are waiting with the Karnataka Pollution Control Board (KPCB). We can expect a very big increase in indirect investment.

This kind of massive investment and the resultant industrial revolution, ancillarisation will in the first instance bring about a rapid growth of the district's economy in terms of income, output and employment. At the same time, they will have also lot of bearing on resource base of the district. The effects of industrial investment will be felt in physical and social infrastructure. Hence an attempt is made to discern the impact of massive industrial investment on social infrastructure in Bellary district. For the purpose of our study, we have taken two important components of social infrastructure namely educational infrastructure and health infrastructure. What kind of pressure this massive investment would create so far as education and health sectors are concerned? Whether or not the education and health sectors are capable of bearing this pressure? What will be the disease structure in the district after the advent of industrial revolution? Whether or not the district's educational infrastructure is capable of supplying the kind of manpower-skilled, semi-skilled, technically trained, women etc., required by the industries? Do these changes involve any trade-off between economic development and social development? These are the questions we intend to probe into. More specifically, we propose to:

(i) Review the existing educational and health infrastructure both in the public and private sectors in the districts;
(ii) Analyse the nature and adequacy of the educational and health services;
(iii) Study the impact of massive industrial investment on disease structure, quality of the population, the composition of the demand for manpower etc.; and
(iv) Finally, indicate the requirements of educational and health facilities in the next 15 years and to project the needs of the district so far as education and health are concerned in the next 15 years against the backdrop of massive investment.

We have adopted a simple method of indicating the gaps between the supply of education and health facilities and the demand for such facilities in the light of the expected increase in industrial investment. Simple statistical methods were used to calculate the supply and demand position in education and health sectors. The data required for this study were collected basically from two offices. They are the Office of Deputy Director of Public Instruction and the Office of the District Health and Family Welfare, Bellary. We have supplemented this data with the additional information collected from technical institutions, physicians, industrialists etc. We have also used the data published by the State and the central governments.

**A Review of the Present State of Health Infrastructure**

Tables 5.1 and 5.2 give a bird's eye view of the state of health sector in Bellary district. In Appendix-A, we have given the taluk-wise location of PHCs in the district.

If we put all the categories of medical institutions together (public sector), we find that the total number of beds available in 1993-94 were 1841 (Table 5.1). Approximately we have 91.25 beds per lakh population (population-18,92,715, 1991 census). There are 24 medical institutions per lakh population and there are 5.6 physicians (public) per lakh population (Table 5.2).

TABLE 5.1: **Selected Indicators on Health Infrastructure in Bellary District: 1993-94 (Public Sector)**

| Sl. No. | Indicators | Number | Number of beds |
|---|---|---|---|
| 1. | Number of hospitals | 14 | 1401 |
| 2. | Number of dispensaries | 11 | — |
| 3. | Number of primary health centres (PHCs) | 52 | 339 |
| 4. | Number of primary health units (PHUs) | 28 | 04 |
| 5. | Number of family welfare centres | 17 | — |
| 6. | Number of sub-centres | 330 | — |
| 7. | Number of Indian system of Medicines Hospitals | 05 | 97 |
| 8. | Total | 457 | 1841 |
| 9. | Number of doctors (MD+AS+LMO) | 106<br>(77 regular<br>29 contract) | — |
| 10. | Sanctioned numbers of junior health assistants (Male) | 268 | — |
| 11. | Actual working | 124 | — |
| 12. | Vacant position as a per cent of sanctioned posts | 42.54 | — |
| 13. | Sanctioned number of junior health assistants (Female) | 380 | — |
| 14. | Actual working | 335 | — |
| 15. | Vacant position as a per cent of sanctioned posts | 11.85 | — |
| 16. | Sanctioned number of senior health assistants (Male) | 43 | — |
| 17. | Actual Working | 38 | — |
| 18. | Vacant position as a per cent of sanctioned posts | 11.63 | — |
| 19. | Sanctioned number of senior health assistants (Female) | 43 | — |
| 20. | Actual Working | 38 | — |
| 21. | Vacant position as a per cent of sanctioned posts | 15.10 | — |
| 22. | Number of paramedical workers (leprosy) | 31 | — |

*Source*: ASO, DHFW, Bellary.

TABLE 5.2: **Basic Health Infrastructure Ratios**

| | |
|---|---|
| 1. No. of medical institution per lakh population | 24.14 |
| 2. No. of PHCs per lakh population | 2.74 |
| 3. No. of subcentres per lakh population | 17.43 |
| 4. No. of beds per lakh population | 97.26 |
| 5. No. of Physicians (public sector) per lakh population | 5.60 |

*Source*: In Table 5.1 (Ratios were calculated by this scholar).

So far as health personnel is concerned we find gaps between the sanctioned posts and the actual working persons in all categories. This gap is very wide so far as junior health assistants (Male) is concerned. The vacant position as a per cent of sanctioned posts in this case was 42.54 per cent. We find this kind of gaps also between sanctioned posts and actually working in case of junior health assistant (Female), senior health assistant (male and female) by 11.85 per cent, 11.63 per cent and 15.10 per cent respectively.

## Number of PHCs and Sub-centres

According to the norms laid down by the Government, there should be one PHC per 30,000 population and also one sub-centre per 5000 population. As per this norm and the population of 1991 census (18,92,715), Bellary district needs 63 PHCs and 378 sub-centres. But actually there are only 52 PHCs and 330 sub-centres in 1995-96. So there is a gap between the number of PHCs and sub-centres required as per the norm and the number actually obtains by about 21.22 per cent and 22.70 per cent respectively.

We should also consider another problem regarding health infrastructure and that refers to the concentration of PHCs in some parts of the district. Of the 52 PHCs existing, 40.38 per cent i.e., 2/5th are located in Bellary and Hospet taluk (Appendix-A). The western taluks of the district, namely, Hadagali, Harapanahalli, H.B. Halli and Kudligi taluks account for 38.46 per cent of PHCs. This intra-district inequality in the distribution of the number of PHCs is a matter of great concern. First because Bellary and Hospet taluks have other kind of health facilities such as ESI dispensaries, labour welfare hospital (central government: Kariganur) and medical units maintained by industries such as Sandur Maganese and Iron Ores Ltd. (SMIORE), Tungabhadra Steel Products,

(TSP), Dalmia, National Minerals Development Corporation (NMDC) etc. Secondly, the apprehension is that the existing imbalance in the distribution of PHCs will get aggravated because increased industrial activity is going to take place mostly in Bellary and Hospet taluks and to some extent in Sandur taluk which may attract more of these facilities. The western taluks are not going to benefit much from massive industrial investment. Therefore, they may not attract such facilities.

Another important area in the health sector that is a matter of great concern is the lack of specialised medical institutions and well equipped diagnostic centres. There are small and simple pathological laboratories owned privately where facilities are available for simple tests of blood, CSF, malaria etc. We don't have a well developed, sophisticated and well equipped diagnostic centre in this district.

**Impact of Massive Investment on Disease Structure**

The existing disease structure will undergo a metamorphosis as a result of intensified industrial activities. In our field work and discussions we had with physicians, industrialists, social workers and NGO activists, we have come to know that the menace of prostitution will get expanded and assume a diabolic proportion. The reasons given for this apprehension were the in-migration of labour and the existing institution of prostitution in this district. This kind of flesh trade will give rise to the acceleration of the incidence of STDs. There will be nothing surprising if AIDS also enter the district. The physicians and doctors running private nursing homes and maternity homes have told us that the rate of the termination of pregnancies among both married and unmarried young girls has been increasing alarmingly.

As a fallout of air and water pollution and scarcity of drinking water, we can expect an increase in the respiratory diseases, all kinds of fevers, psychiatric disorders, neurologic diseases etc. Apart from these changes in the disease structure, there will be rapid increase in the number of accidents both inside the factories and outside.

It is possible to speculate over the location pattern of these diseases. Accidents will take place mostly on highways and inside the factories. The incidents of STDs and termination of pregnancies will be found mostly in slum areas. The incidence of psychiatric disorders, neurological diseases will be more in the case of middle income and high income families. The general diseases like respiratory diseases, fevers, malaria, diarrhoea etc., could be found everywhere.

## A Projection of Health Needs of the District by 2010 AD

So the massive industrial investment will have two kinds of bearing on health infrastructure.

1. As it is, there is so much gap between the supply of and demand for health services. The demand for health services will increase due to the natural increase in population. So there is a need to expand health infrastructure in proportion to the increase in population.
2. Massive industrial investment would give rise to increase in industrial activities, immigration, mushrooming of slums, environmental pollution, water scarcity etc. All these developments will bring about a metamorphosis in disease structure. So there is a need to expand and improve health infrastructure to meet these changes and challenges.

Our calculations, based on the norms laid down by the Government, have shown that the district as a whole needs 89 PHCs and 535 sub-centres by 2010 AD. The population of this district would be 23,07,205 by 2001 AD and 26,77,600 by 2010 AD (Table 5.3). This calculation has taken

TABLE 5.3: **A Projection of the Number of PHCs and Sub-centres Required in Bellary District as per the Norm: 2010 AD**

| | | |
|---|---|---|
| 1. | Number of PHCs required as per the norm based on 1991 population: 18,92,715 | 63 |
| 2. | Actual number of PHCs in 1996 | 52 |
| 3. | The gap between the number required as per the norm and the number exist | 21.22% |
| 4. | Number of PHCs required as per the norm by 2010 AD. Projected population by 2010 AD—26,77,600 | 89 |
| 5. | Number of sub-centres required as per the norm based on 1991 population: 18,92,715 | 378 |
| 6. | Actual number of sub-centres in 1996 | 330 |
| 7. | The gap between the number required as per the norm and the number exist | 22.70 |
| 8. | Number of sub-centres required as per the norm by 2010 AD. Projected population by 2010 AD—26,77,600 | 535 |

*Source*: ASO, DHFW, Bellary.

*Note*: The projection of population for 2010 AD has been made by assuming an annual rate of growth of population at 2 per cent for 1991 to 2001 AD and 1.5 per cent for 2001 AD to 2010 AD. The annual rate of growth for 1981 to 1991 was 2.79 per cent.

only natural growth of population into account. We have not considered increase in population on account of immigration.

**Location Pattern of Medical Institutions**

In the above pages we have shown the location pattern of the diseases. This is very important because such information is useful to plan the location pattern of new medical institutions. Our study has shown the necessity of expanding the medical and health services in the district in general and Bellary-Hospet-Sandur belt in particular. Accidents and emergency treatment centres will have to be set up with well-developed and sophisticated communication network and transport facilities in Hospet and Bellary. These centres will have to work in coordination with Police and Fire Brigade department. There will be tremendous increase in the demand for blood. So blood bank network has to be developed in the district.

**Need of Specialised Medical Institutions**

In the light of the expected increase in industrial investment and its impact on people's health condition (PHC), Bellary district needs specialised medical institutions such as diagnostic centres, centres for the treatment of psychiatric and neurological disorders etc. There is a need for setting up of as many dispensaries as possible in slum areas to treat particularly industrial diseases, STD and termination of pregnancies.

Greater attention has to be paid for meeting the health needs of the rural sector. The PHCs and sub centres have to be set up mostly in villages. Incidentally, we would like to bring the fact to the notice of the people that Bellary district is one among the 100-150 worst districts in the country, so far as infant mortality rate is concerned. So special attention should be given for child and mother health care in the district.

**The State of Education Infrastructure in Bellary District**

Tables 5.4 to 5.7 show the state of education in Bellary district. Our analysis of educational infrastructure has to start with the incidental reference to literacy rates in the district. It is admitted that literacy has no direct bearing on industrial investment. However, for the sake of reference we have given the literacy rate in the district over the last three decades in Appendix-B. From literacy figures it is very clear that Bellary district even in 1991 has a very low rate of literacy and particularly in rural areas and among women, it is abysmally low (rural women 19.36 per cent). So we have to consider the impact of massive industrial investment on education in particular and employment in general against this background.

TABLE 5.4: **Educational Infrastructure in Bellary District, 1993-94**

| Sl. No. | Particulars | Number of schools | Number of students | Number of teachers |
|---|---|---|---|---|
| 1. | Primary School | 1431 | 3,34,297 | 5863 |
| 2. | High School | 173 | 49,000 | 1437 |
| 3. | Composite Junior College | 42 | 16,000 | — |
| 4. | General Education | 17 | 10,500 | — |
| 5. | Polytechnic | 6 | 1,800 | — |
| 6. | Professional Education | | | |
| | (i) Engineering | 1 | 1,300 | — |
| | (ii) Medical (Allopathy) | 1 | 977 | — |
| | (iii) Indian System of Medicine | 2 | 172 | — |
| | (iv) Teacher Training Institutes | 3 | 240 | — |
| | (v) Colleges of Education | 2 | 220 | — |
| | Sub Total | 9 | 2909 | — |

*Source*: Karnataka at a Glance, 1993-94. DES, Bangalore. ASO, DDPI, Bellary.

We have worked out the school-student ratio and also teacher-school ratio. We have found that there are on an average 4 teachers per primary and 8 teachers per secondary school in the district. The work pressure on teachers is very high in primary school. So far as school-student ratio is concerned we have a peculiar trend of ascending order of this ratio as shown in Table 5.7. At the primary school level there are 233 students on an average per school. As we move upwards to secondary, pre-university and university, the ratio goes up to 283, 380 and 617, respectively. In fact, as we move upwards school-student ratio should have declined. But the exact reverse is the case in Bellary district. Table 5.5 shows the increasing pupil-teacher ratio over the period both at primary and secondary school levels. This is not desirable from the point of view of the quality of education.

It is heartening to note that the proportion of girl students to total enrolment has been increasing over the period as shown in Table 5.6 so far as primary schools are concerned. But if we observe keenly it can be noticed that the proportion of girl students to total enrolment declines as

TABLE 5.5: **Pupil-Teacher Ratio**

| Particulars | 1970-71 | 1980-81 | 1990-91 | 1993-94 |
|---|---|---|---|---|
| Primary School | 37 | 48 | 55 | 63 |
| Secondary School | — | 27 | 46 | 43 |

*Source*: Socio-Economic Indicators, DES, Bangalore.

TABLE 5.6: **Proportion of Girl Students to Total Enrolment (Primary)**

| Years | I | II | III | IV | V | VI | VII |
|---|---|---|---|---|---|---|---|
| 1992-93 | 45.37 | 44.08 | 43.62 | 44.17 | 39.34 | 38.46 | 36.36 |
| 1995-96 | 46.82 | 45.38 | 45.44 | 43.94 | 41.39 | 40.03 | 38.10 |

*Source*: ASO, DDPI, Bellary.

TABLE 5.7: **Number of Students Per School (Institutions)**

| Particulars | Number of Students |
|---|---|
| 1. Primary | 233 |
| 2. Secondary | 283 |
| 3. Pre-university | 380 |
| 4. General Education (college) | 617 |
| 5. Polytechnic | 300 |

*Source*: As in Table 5.6.

we move from I to VII standards. At VII standard in 1995-96 girls constituted only 38.10 per cent of total enrolment. Whereas, they accounted for as much as 46.82 per cent in the first standard.

## Impact of Industrial Development on Education

In our discussions with industrialists in particular and public in general, we have come to know that the nature of manpower required by the new industries cannot be met by our education system. Industrialists hold the view that the highly technical manpower will be selected at all India level. Preference will be given to locals only in the lower level jobs such as skilled, semi-skilled and unskilled roles. So Bellary district needs a few more polytechnic institutions and ITIs to train students keeping an eye on the nature of manpower required by the industries. Any way, we cannot expect any great increase in the demand for labour, particularly skilled and semi-skilled labour and service labour for the simple reason that all the industries coming up in the district have chosen high capital intensity and machanisation processes.

We were told that Jindal Vijayanagar Steel Limited (JVSL) Company's ultimate employment potential is 4500. The estimated investment is Rs.5000 crores. This gives us a capital-labour ratio of Rs.1 crore : 1.11 labour. Similarly, in Kalyani Steels the job potential is 1400 and the estimated investment is Rs.700 crores. So in general we can assume that the capital-labour ratio will be Rs.1 crore: 1.5 jobs. So we can expect that Rs.15,000 crore investment would generate 22,500 jobs directly in this district. These jobs include technical, managerial as well as administrative positions.

The polytechnics, numbering 6 in the district, will produce 600 diploma holders every year. This output may not be sufficient to meet the increased demand for technical manpower. So it is necessary to increase the number of polytechnics and, more than this, the quality of education and training must be improved. To encourage women's employment, it is essential to set up separate polytechnics for girl students.

## The Impact of Industrial Investment on Indirect Employment

The massive industrial investment will bring about an ancillarisation of the industrial sector. So direct investment will give rise to a good measure of indirect investment. This indirect investment has a lot a bearing on job-potential. It is not possible to estimate the manpower required by indirect investment. There will be lot of indirect investment not only on ancillary units but also on mining, transport, housing, service activities etc. The capital-labour ratio in the case of indirect investment will be lower than that of the capital-labour ratio in direct investment. It is also not possible to find out what kind of manpower is needed by this indirect investment. So to meet the increased demand for manpower by direct investment it is necessary to undertake a special programme to impart all kinds of training to the youth of this district and put them into the labour market. All these training programmes should not be certificate-based. Training like how to run a *kirana* shop, a small hotel, training for driving vehicles of all kinds, training in repairing small domestic electronic gadgets, training in secretarial practice etc., should be given to youth irrespective of their educational qualifications.

**A Note on Science Education in the District**

The status of science education in the district is very poor. Of the 15 colleges in the district, only 6 colleges have science section. This means that 40 per cent of the colleges have facilities to teach science subjects. At the pre-university college level, the situation of science education is far from satisfactory. More than 70-80 per cent of the pre-university colleges do not have science sections at all. Therefore, with a view to appropriating the benefits of massive industrial investment, both direct and indirect, we recommend the opening of science sections in all the existing composite junior colleges. The quality of teaching science subject must be improved. For this, well-equipped laboratory facilities must be provided to students and teachers at secondary and pre-university level.

**Economic Development and Social Development—The Trade-off**

The massive industrial investment which we are speaking about, involves an element of trade-off between economic development and social development. The industrial revolution will definitely bring about an acceleration in the growth of income, output and employment. But this development has its own cost in terms of deterioration of the health of the people and the quality of the environment. Further, the benefits of economic development will accrue mostly to socially and economically forward groups of the society while the socially and economically backward groups will have to bear the cost of this development. It seems that the most important impact of the massive industrial investment will be this trade-off. We are not saying that the trade-off was not there before the advent of heavy industrial investment. But industrial revolution will accentuate this trade-off.

So we have to think in advance of what measures could be initiated to take care of this trade-off. Here, the development of health and educational infrastructure could play a crucial role in keeping the trade-off within the tolerable level. In fact, there is no competition as between economic development and social development, both are in a way complementary. The deterioration of the health of the people and the degradation of the environment will have adverse consequences on the economic efficiency. The management of this trade-off is necessary not from the point of view of equality principle but from the point of view of efficiency principle. So we have to take suitable measures for investment on social infrastructure.

## Conclusion

This chapter has tried to take stock of the present state of social infrastructure consisting of health and education in Bellary district. It has analysed the expected impact of massive industrial investment on the social infrastructure. As part of this exercise, we have tried to examine the economic implications interfacing the social implications of the industrial investment. This chapter has shown the gaps between the existing capacity of social infrastructure and the expected increase in the demand for educational and health services. This chapter calls for greater investment on social infrastructure and greater expansion of health and education sectors in the district.

Specifically, this chapter pleads for the setting up of more number of polytechnic institutions, ITIs, opening of science courses in all the existing composite pre-university colleges, a polytechnic for women, special programmes to train youth so that they could undertake self-employment ventures. In the health sector, we have pleaded for the setting up of diagnostic centres, accident treatment units, STDs and termination of pregnancy treatment units, psychiatric and neurological centres in Bellary and Hospet towns. More number of PHCs and subcentres must be opened in rural parts of the district.

Finally, this chapter earnestly urges the authorities to commission a special study to find out the reasons for the abysmally low rates of literacy in general and the rural women in particular in Bellary district and also to embark upon a massive literacy programme to raise the literacy rates of this district at least to the level equivalent to the State average literacy level by the end of the century. Otherwise, Bellary will have to enter the 21st century with three-fourths of illiterate rural women folk.

Unless these measures are initiated at the earliest, it would be very difficult to avoid and to arrest the accentuation of the trade-off between economic development and social development caused by the massive industrial investment.

*APPENDIX—A*

LOCATION OF PHCs, UFWCs AND PPCs IN BELLARY DISTRICT, 1994

BELLARY SUBDIVISION

| Name of the Place | Nature of medical institution |
|---|---|
| 1. Kurugodu | Primary Health Centre |
| 2. Kuduthini | -do- |
| 3. Voravayu | -do- |
| 4. Sidhiginamala | -do- |
| 5. Chellagurki | -do- |
| 6. Rupanagudi | -do- |
| 7. Koslagundi | -do- |
| 8. Moka | -do- |
| 9. M. Gonal | -do- |
| 10. Bellary | Family Planning Association of India |
| 11. Bellary | Post Partum centre |
| 12. Bellary | Urban Family Welfare Centre (UFWC) (Medical College Hospital) |
| 13. Bellary Caul Bazar | UFWC |
| 14. Bellary | UWFC, FPAI |
| SAUNDUR TALUK | |
| 1. Choranur | Primary Health Centre |
| 2. Bandri | -do- |
| 3. Toranagal | -do- |
| 4. Metriki | -do- |
| SIRIGUPPA | |
| 1. Siriguppa | Primary Health Centre |
| 2. Raravi | -do- |
| 3. Ravihal | -do- |
| 4. Sirigeri | -do- |
| 5. Tekkalakoti | -do- |
| 6. Karuru | -do- |
| 7. Sirigupa | Post Partum Centre |
| Total 25 | |

*(Contd.)*

HOSPET SUBDIVISION

HADAGALI TALUK

| Name of the Place | Nature of medical institution |
|---|---|
| 1. Holalu | Primary Health Centre |
| 2. Ittigi | -do- |
| 3. M.M. Voda | -do- |
| 4. Hire Hadagali | -do- |
| HARAPANAHALLI TALUK | |
| 1. Arisikere | Primary Health Centre |
| 2. Huchangidurga | -do- |
| 3. Chigateri | -do- |
| 4. Halavagalu | -do- |
| 5. Parakahalu | -do- |
| 6. Teligi | -do- |
| HOSPET TALUK | |
| 1. Mariyammana Halli | Primary Health Centre |
| 2. Gadhiganur | -do- |
| 3. Kampli | -do- |
| 4. Hospet | PPC |
| 5. Hospet | UFWC |
| 6. Kampli | UFWC |
| 7. Kamalapura | Primary Health Centre |
| HAGARIBOMMANAHALLI TALUK | |
| 1. Hampasagar | Primary Health Centre |
| 2. Tambrahalli | -do- |
| 3. B.G. Halli | -do- |
| 4. Kogali | -do- |
| 5. Morageri | -do- |
| KUDLIGI TALUK | |
| 1. Gudekote | Primary Health Centre |
| 2. Bellighatto | -do- |
| 3. Hosahalli | -do- |
| 4. Kottur | -do- |
| 5. Ujjini | -do- |
| Total 27 | |
| Grand Total 25+27 = 52 | |

*Source*: ASO, DHFW, Bellary

## APPENDIX—B

LITERACY RATES IN BELLARY DISTRICT BY SEX AND RESIDENCE, 1961 to 1991

| Residence | 1961 | | | 1971 | | | 1981 | | | 1991 | | |
|---|---|---|---|---|---|---|---|---|---|---|---|---|
| Sex | P | M | F | P | M | F | P | M | F | P | M | F |
| Total | 20.91 | 32.16 | 9.19 | 25.12 | 35.31 | 14.58 | 30.64 | 41.61 | 19.32 | 45.57 | 58.71 | 31.97 |
| Rural | 16.98 | 28.09 | 5.56 | 19.74 | 29.67 | 9.61 | 24.06 | 35.32 | 12.61 | 38.71 | 41.79 | 19.36 |
| Urban | 34.41 | 45.76 | 22.05 | 39.55 | 50.07 | 28.26 | 43.97 | 54.27 | 33.14 | 60.93 | 59.91 | 41.05 |

*Source*: Socio-Economic Indicators, DES, Bangalore.

P-person, M-male, F-female.

# 6

# MUNICIPAL SERVICES
## Present Status and Future Prospects

ABDUL AZIZ and M. DEVENDRA BABU

### Introduction

Next only to basic infrastructure, municipal services occupy an important place as a requirement for industrial growth. It may be noted that industrialisation is taken roughly as synonymous with urbanisation. And urban growth, seen in terms of growth of urban population and expansion of urban area, will demand more of municipal services such as housing, sanitation, drinking water and solid waste disposal services. In the present context of limited availability of these services any further increase in demand will put a heavy pressure on these services. Unless these services are expanded, the quality of life of people living in urban areas will deteriorate. Under such circumstances, industries will find it difficult to attract the required labour and manpower and many a time will be obliged to incur extra expenditure themselves on providing these services to their workers. Therefore, what is primarily a responsibility of the municipal bodies will be passed on to industries—a clear case of public failures raising private costs! It is proposed in this chapter to take a look at the available municipal services in Bellary district, examine the implications of the massive industrial investment to the availability and distribution of these services and identify areas where action on a priority basis needs to be taken in advance.

### Urbanisation

Bellary district with a total population of 18.87 lakh (1991) has 5.65 lakh people living in the urban areas. That means the urban population of Bellary district works out to 29.84 per cent of the district population coming close to the State average of 30.92 per cent. But there are variations across taluks. Thus, while Sandur (6.3%), Kudligi (8.7%), H. B. Halli (0.0%), Hadagali (12.8%) and Harapanahalli (14.6%) are on the lower side, Siruguppa (26.6%) is close to the district average; Bellary (49.6%) and Hospet (59.8%) taluks are on the higher side. It is clear that the inter-taluk variation in urbanisation is rather high—varying from zero to nearly 60 per cent. As a large number of taluks have urbanisation levels of 6 per cent to 14 per cent it can be said that Bellary district is basically rural. But it may be noted that the low levels of urbanisation of some taluks is more than compensated for by a very high level of urbanisation in Bellary and Hospet taluks. As we shall shortly see notwithstanding these disparities across taluks the district emerges as a highly urbanised unit.

As for the growth of urban population in Bellary district (Table 6.1) two main points may be noted. One is, the decennial growth has uniformly recorded a high rate across taluks during 1971-81 as for instance in Bellary (61%), Siruguppa (48%), Hospet (44%) and Kudligi (surprisingly 129%)—giving an average of 61 per cent for the district as a whole. But during the following decade i.e., 1981-91, this rate has unbelievably come down to 15 per cent. Even the traditional high growth taluks like Bellary (22%), Hospet (17%) and Siruguppa (32%) have recorded a slow growth of urban population. Kudligi which had recorded an exceptionally high growth rate during 1971-1981 now shows a negative growth of 35 per cent and so does Sandur (56%). Secondly, H. B. Halli continues to be in the rural category. And Sandur has moved into the urban category from 1981 onwards. It is true that the decennial growth rate of the State urban population too has come down from 50.65 per cent during 1971-81 to 29.62 per cent during 1981-91 indicating that the urbanisation process has slowed down in recent years. But the decline noticed in respect of Bellary district (15%) is far more than the case with the State. This is quite surprising. But there is an explanation for this. What were rural settlements in 1971 were upgraded into urban settlements in 1981. This was the case with Kudligi and Sandur which as a result showed extraordinary urban growth in 1981. But subsequently where parts of these settlements were declared rural and panchayats were formed, they showed a negative urban growth ! Obviously, 1981 and the 1991 urban growth rates of the district were found to be either abnormally high or abnormally low.

Notwithstanding the volatile nature of urbanisation rate, Bellary district ranks third in this regard next only to Bangalore Urban (86.15%)

TABLE 6.1: **Taluk-wise Urban Population in Bellary District, 1971 to 1991**

| Taluk | 1971 | 1981 | 1991 | Growth Rate (%) | |
|---|---|---|---|---|---|
| | | | | 1971 to 81 | 1981 to 91 |
| Bellary | 125183 | 201579 | 245758 | 61 | 22 |
| Hadagali | 10455 | 13724 | 18713 | 31 | 36 |
| H. B. Halli | 0 | 0 | 0 | 0 | 0 |
| Harapanahalli | 19694 | 27308 | 34139 | 39 | 25 |
| Hospet | 110741 | 159935 | 187176 | 44 | 17 |
| Kudligi | 12873 | 29426 | 19107 | 129 | −35 |
| Sandur | 0 | 22084 | 9774 | infinite | −56 |
| Siruguppa | 25826 | 38104 | 50116 | 48 | 32 |
| Total | 304772 | 492160 | 564783 | 61 | 15 |

*Source*: (i) Various Census Reports.

(ii) Growth rates were calculated by us.

and Dharwar (34.94%) districts. Besides, two of the district urban centres viz, Bellary and Hospet, are experiencing heavy pressure of population. Thus, Bellary's population (2.45 lakh in 1991) recorded a growth rate of 22 per cent during the last decade. Though the growth rate of population during the same period was 17 per cent in respect of Hospet, its density was 12,575 per sq km which is one of the highest in the State barring, of course, Bangalore city. The other important urban centres of the district such as Siruguppa with a population of 50 thousand, Harapanhalli (34 thousand) recorded a growth rate of 32 per cent and 25 per cent respectively.

Though the urban centres (barring Bellary and Hospet) as of now are well within the manageable size, it is expected that they will grow rapidly with industries coming up in large numbers shortly. That apart, the new industrial units—especially the steel mills—are likely to set up town complexes of large population much of which will be the immigrant population causing a sudden spurt in the urban population growth. Much of the expected population growth will be the product of inmigration of workers and their families in response to a heavy demand for manpower. There was already one bout of such inmigration especially from the neighbouring State viz., Andhra Pradesh, when the Tungabhadra dam was constructed. It is reasonable to expect that there will be a second bout of inmigration from Andhra Pradesh following industrialisation of the district. For, the first generation inmigrants will now serve as a "facilitating" factor in the second bout of inmigrants by providing to the latter information, lodging facilities and links with the recruitment agencies. Of course, people from neighbouring districts of Karnataka and other parts of India will also come in search of work and settle down here. These two streams of inmigration along with the natural growth, and the growth on account of upgradation of villages will push the urban population growth in Bellary district making it the highest urbanised district in Karnataka next perhaps only to the Bangalore Urban district.

What will be the rate of growth of urban population in the next 15 years? This calls for an exercise of projecting the urban population growth to 2011 A.D. We have carried out an exercise using the past growth rate of urban population, and compounding it for the next 15 years we have presented the results in Table 6.2. The results show that the urban population of Bellary district which was 5.65 lakh would have gone upto 6.68 lakh by now (1996). By 2001 A.D. it will rise to the level of 7.90 lakh and to 11.04 lakh by 2011 A.D. In other words, our estimate is that the urban population of Bellary district will almost double between the period 1991 and 2011.

Growth of urban population at this rate in future and of this magnitude will have its own socio-economic implications. As stated earlier, among other things, it will accelerate the demand for municipal services such as housing, drinking water, sanitation, city/town roads, solid waste disposal and so on. We may now examine the present status of these services and the future requirements.

TABLE 6.2: **Annual Compound Growth Rate of Population in Bellary District—Past and Projected**

| I. Past Growth Rate (per cent) | 1961-71 | 1971-81 | 1981-91 | 1961-91 |
|---|---|---|---|---|
| Total | 2.064 | 2.866 | 2.394 | 2.441 |
| Rural | 1.443 | 2.000 | 2.860 | 2.100 |
| Urban | 3.968 | 4.909 | 1.386 | 3.410 |
| II. Projected Growth | 1991 (Actual) | 1996 | 2001 | 2011 |
| Urban | 5,64,783 | 6,67,876 | 7,89,786 | 11,04,428 |

## Housing and Slum Improvement

After food and clothing, shelter is the most important need of the population which is felt more intensively by the urban population due to scarcity of housing and high rates of rent that prevail there. In the Indian context, since the responsibility for shelter has all along been that of the individual in the past when industrial workers moved into urban areas, either they looked around for rented shelter or made their own arrangement to build shelters. The latter course resulted in slum formation as workers tended to build shelters close to the work place where land was scarce. To beat the problem of scarcity of land, as it were, they threw over board the housing norms which a civilized society would consider necessary, and built dwelling units on whatever surface was available and in whatever form it was available.

As Bellary district population was no exception to this general rule, a large number of slums have already come up all over. From Table 6.3 it can be seen that there are in all 93 slums in the district covering an area of 281 acres and having a population of over 65.6 thousand living in them. In this respect, Bellary city leads with 30 slums having about 32 thousand people living there followed by Hospet (30 slums with about 22 thousand people). One estimate is that the slum population of Bellary city accounts for 3.56 per cent of the State slum population taking a third rank next to Bangalore city (21.00%) and Raichur (5.17%). Hospet accounts for 1.94% of State slum population. Even the small towns have slums in them as can be seen from Table 6.3. These slums will certainly provide a base for further slumming of the towns and cities particularly in Bellary and Hospet where more and more employment opportunities are likely to be generated both in the formal and the informal sectors.

What will be the magnitude of the slum population by 2011 A D? One way of arriving at this figure is to take the present proportion of the slum population and project it to future applying that ratio. Thus, the present proportion of slum population to the estimated urban population of the district is 9.84 per cent. Of course, this figure will be much higher in respect of Bellary and Hospet cities where the district slum population is concentrated. Taking the average proportion of the district slum population, if we apply it to the projected urban population of the district to 2001 A.D. and 2011 A.D. the figures relating to the projected slum population will be respectively 78,714 and 1,08,674. In other words, by this estimate Bellary district will have about 1.1 lakh slum population by 2011 A.D. But that will be an underestimate because much of the future growth of urban population

TABLE 6.3: **Number, Area and Population of Slums in Bellary District**

| Taluk | No. of Slums | Ownership | | Area (in acres) | No. of Huts | Category of Population | | | Total |
|---|---|---|---|---|---|---|---|---|---|
| | | Public* | Private | | | SC | S T | Others | |
| Bellary | 30 | 24 | 6 | 98.96 | 5574 | 10126 | 7772 | 13700 | 31598 |
| Hospet | 30 | 21 | 9 | 111.85 | 4102 | 5521 | 4074 | 12083 | 21678 |
| Kamalapur | 8 | 6 | 2 | 24.77 | 948 | 2295 | 1404 | 1016 | 4715 |
| Amaravathi | 5 | 5 | 0 | Data not available | | | | | |
| Harapanahalli | 6 | 5 | 1 | 8.31 | 302 | 20 | 229 | 1383 | 1632 |
| Hadagali | 7 | 5 | 2 | 16.07 | 321 | 880+ | 265+ | 545+ | 1599+ |
| Sandur | 2 | 2 | 0 | 5.85 | 236 | 727 | 425 | 13 | 1165 |
| Siruguppa | 5 | 5 | 0 | 0.19 | 629 | 2199 | 317 | 678 | 3194 |
| Total | 93 | 73 | 20 | 281.15 | 12112 | 21768 | 14486 | 29327 | 65581 |

*Note*: * Includes Town Municipality and Z.P. area.

+ Data not included for two slums.

*Source*: Statistical Division, Karnataka Slum Clearance Board, Bangalore.

will be on account of immigrant workers who in all probability, for want of proper accommodation, will get into slums or raise new slums. Therefore, it will be reasonable to argue that a large proportion of the immigrant work force will live in the slums in the absence of accommodation made available by the industrialists. Granting that out of the 11 lakh projected urban population if one lakh happens to be the immigrant population then the total slum population will add upto 2.1 lakh by 2011 A.D. Out of this if the present slum population of 65.6 thousand is taken out, the addition by 2011 A.D. will be 1.44 lakh. Assuming that the present population has some form of accommodation or other we have to find shelter for 1.44 lakh slum population by 2011 A.D. Taking an average size of slum family to be six members, the number of housing units required will be 24,000.

This is as for the requirement of the new housing units is concerned. But there is also this need for improving the living conditions of the slum dwellers. The wretched conditions in which the slum population is living should be seen to be believed. The box size houses, narrow lanes, insanitary surroundings, lack of lavatories, drinking water connections, street lights and other amenities make the life of people living there quite miserable. To improve the living conditions of the slum dwellers the Slum Clearance Board has been implementing three schemes :

1. Under the Slum improvement scheme the Board provides basic amenities like roads, drains, street lights, drinking water, community halls and latrines and sewerage.
2. Under the slum clearance scheme, the Board clears the huts in the slum areas and rehabilitates them by providing alternative housing units.
3. Sites and essential services are provided to the slum dwellers under a separate scheme.

What is the progress under these various schemes? From the data that are available, it seems that only a little less than Rupees one crore has been spent for providing amenities in six of the district town slums and Rs.17.55 lakh on houses constructed in Bellary city slums (Table 6.4). Considering the magnitude of the housing problem this amount seems to be too inadequate. This is attributed to the inadequate resources made available to the Slum Clearance Board which in turn is said to be the product of Government policy of providing a fixed amount to the Board on per capita basis—the latest upgraded figure being Rs. 525 per head of slum population. Even here the problem is, this is a one-time grant and secondly,

TABLE 6.4: **Amenities/Rehabilitation and Expenditure incurred in Slums in Bellary District**

| Taluk | No of Slums where Amenities provided | Expenditure incurred for providing amenities (in lakhs) | No of New Houses cons-tructed | Expenditure on House construction (in lakhs of Rs.) | Outlay for 1995-96 (Rupees in lakhs) |
|---|---|---|---|---|---|
| Bellary | 23 (30) | 40.29 | 280 | 17.55 | 3.75 |
| Hospet | 23 (30) | 38.09 | 0 | 0 | 0 |
| Kamalapur | 0 (8) | 0 | 0 | 0 | 0 |
| Amaravathi | 0 (5) | 0 | 0 | 0 | 0 |
| Harapanahalli | 6 (6) | 5.43 | 0 | 0 | 0 |
| Hadagali | 5 (7) | 6.67 | 0 | 0 | 0 |
| Sandur | 2 (2) | 1.29 | 0 | 0 | 0 |
| Siruguppa | 5 (5) | 4.69 | 0 | 0 | 0 |
| Total | 64 (93) | 96.48 | 280 | 17.55 | 3.75 |

*Note*: 1. Figures in brackets are total number of slums
2. Amenities include Roads, Streetlights, Tube Well, Drainage

*Source*: Statistical Division, Karnataka Slum Clearance Board, Bangalore.

a large portion of this grant goes towards salaries and office maintenance leaving a small proportion for actual development works.

Housing in slums apart, demand for housing units in general will also go up in future with new industries coming up in the district. By 2011 the urban population will go up from 6.68 lakh in 1996 to 11.04 lakh in 2011—a net addition of 4.36 lakh in 15 years. If the estimated 2.1 lakh slum population is taken out of this, the addition to the non-slum urban population will be 2.26 lakh. On the basis of six members per unit, the housing units required for this population will be about 37,700. Of course, private effort is going to play a major role in supplying the required housing units in their case. But the government agencies too will be expected to do their best to cushion the problem of housing shortage experienced by the non-slum population. There are several urban housing schemes: One which is meant for weaker sections is being implemented by the Karnataka Housing Board. Under another scheme house sites are distributed by the urban development authorities. The Karnataka Slum Clearance Board has a scheme of construction of houses for the economically weaker sections. Under the Nehru Rozgar Yojana housing and shelter upgradation scheme is implemented. Finally, Government constructs quarters for its employees in all places.

What is the progress recorded under these various schemes in Bellary district? From Table 6.5 which presents data on houses constructed under various schemes in urban areas the progress achieved does not appear to be satisfactory considering the targets set. So, given the track record in the past of these agencies it is frightening indeed to imagine what might happen to housing facilities when actually the urban population will increase to the estimated level.

**Drinking Water Supply**

Drinking water is one of the most important necessities that is in demand from the urban population. Generally speaking, the drying up of wells and ponds, and the underground water level going down every year makes this commodity scarcer and imposes heavier sacrifices on the common man. The provision of this service has been the responsibility of the municipal bodies. But because of lack of water sources, and inadequate financial resources at their command these bodies found it difficult to meet the growing requirements of drinking water. Therefore, since 1975 the responsibility of planning, designing and executing water supply and drainage schemes has been entrusted to the Karnataka Urban Water Supply and Drainage Board (KUWSDB). The two schemes which at present are being executed are (i) the piped water supply scheme to towns with a population of less than 20,000 and (ii) the urban water supply scheme to urban areas having a population of over 20,000. Under these schemes, normally while KUWSDB is responsible for tapping and making bulk water supply available to the municipal bodies, the latter are responsible for distribution of water and collection of water rates.

What is the position relating to water availability in the Bellary Urban areas? There are two ways of answering this question: One, by comparing the water availability with demand for water. Two, by comparing water availability with the standards or norms laid down by international agencies. According to an estimate put out by the Housing and Urban Development Board, Government of Karnataka, the demand for water in urban areas is of the order of 124 litres per capita per day (LPCPD). Similarly, the WHO norm of minimum water required is somewhat more conservative and suggests an average figure of 70-100 LPCPD[1]. Table 6.6 which presents the per capita availability of water in Bellary district towns brings out the gravity of the situation as it obtains now. As against the

TABLE 6.5: **Details of Houses Constructed and Distributed in Bellary District since Inception by the KHB**

| Place | Category of Houses | | | | | | | | | Total |
|---|---|---|---|---|---|---|---|---|---|---|
| | EWS | LIG | MIG | MIG | SRMS | SIHS | MOH | T Q | OTHERS | |
| Bellary | 281 | 951 | 445 | 12 | 24 | — | — | 12 | 26 | 1753 |
| Hospet | — | 36 | 4 | — | 312 | 11 | 14 | — | — | 377 |
| H. B. Halli | — | 94 | 36 | — | 10 | — | — | 8 | — | 148 |
| Harapanahalli | 13 | 24 | — | — | 16 | — | — | 4 | — | 57 |
| Hadagali | — | 38 | 22 | — | — | — | 6 | 12 | — | 78 |
| Kudligi | — | 53 | 36 | — | — | — | 21 | 8 | — | 118 |
| Sandur | 70 | 128 | 16 | — | 24 | — | — | 20 | — | 258 |
| Siruguppa | 143 | 134 | 15 | — | 12 | — | — | 8 | — | 312 |
| Total | 507 | 1458 | 574 | 12 | 398 | 11 | 41 | 72 | 26 | 3101 |

*Source*: Karnataka Housing Board, Bellary.

norm of 70-100 litres per day per capita the availability of water is much lower. The average works out to 42 LPCPD in the district. In none of the cities and towns this norm has been reached. What is worse, in some towns like Amaravati and Tekkalakota the per capita availability of water is unimaginably low—as low as a fifth of the norm.

TABLE 6.6: **Municipality/Town-wise Availability of Drinking Water in Bellary district, 1995**

| Town/Taluk | Population | | Total Supply from all sources (Gallons) | Per Capita litre per day |
|---|---|---|---|---|
| | 1991 Census | Present (estimated) | | |
| Bellary | 245391 | 300000 | 5724000 | 86 |
| Siruguppa | 31364 | 35000 | 488000 | 61 |
| Tekkalakota | 18792 | 22000 | 125000 | 25.73 |
| Hospet | 96322 | 125000 | 1234000 | 44 |
| Amaravathi | 20645 | 24000 | 129000 | 14 |
| Kampli | 31788 | 35000 | 340000 | 45 |
| Kamalapur | 20451 | 24000 | 218000 | 41 |
| Kottur | 19174 | 21000 | 136200 | 32.5 |
| Harapanahalli | 34139 | 42000 | 325000 | 35 |
| Hadagalli | 18113 | 20000 | 150000 | 34.05 |

*Source*: Karnataka Urban Water Supply and Drainage Board, Bellary.

Drinking purpose apart, water is required for industrial purpose too. The water requirement of a basic industry like iron and steel plant is very high. It is stated that water requirement per one million tonne capacity steel plant is of the order of 36 million litres a day.[2] If the capacity of steel production is about 6.6 million tonnes per annum the water requirement of the steel industry alone will be at the minimum 237.6 million litres per day! Of course, water can be drawn from the canals of the Tungabhadra dam to meet the needs of industry. But in that case, what will be its implications to the availability of water for irrigation purpose? As it is, there are protests from farmers on allowing Jindal Steels to draw 3 TMC of water from the TB canal. Any way, that is a problem which does not concern the municipal governments. But what concerns them is the question of how to meet the growing needs of drinking water by the citizens.

The KUWSDB is planning to augment drinking water supply by implementing various schemes. The estimated total supply of water to

Bellary under various schemes is 59.74 lakh gallons or 270 lakh litres (Table 6.7). The KUWSDB claims that with the "completion of this scheme, Bellary city will have a permanent solution for the perennial drinking water problem for the coming 20 years".[3] This is some solace. But a careful examination suggests that there is no reason to be optimistic. For, the roughly 60 lakh gallons of final capacity for an estimated population of 3 lakh today would give a daily per capita supply of 20 gallons or 90 litres. At the current level of population this is well over the norm of 80 litres per capita per day fixed for city municipal councils. But with the population of Bellary going up to 5 lakh by 2015 AD if the water supply capacity remains at 60 lakh gallons the per capita availability would have drastically come down to 12 gallons or 54 litres. Therefore, 20 years hence the situation on drinking water front would be worse than obtains now!

TABLE 6.7: **Water Availability to Bellary City from Various Sources**

| Sources | Availability in lakh gallons |
|---|---|
| 1. Moka Head Works | 22.50 |
| 2. Hagari Infiltration Wells | 4.01 |
| 3. Power Run Borewells | 3.24* |
| 4. Allipur Scheme | 30.00 |
| Total | 59.74 |

* In addition 514 hand pump borewells are in use in different parts of the city.

In the towns of Bellary district too the situation does not appear to be different. The KUWSDB has been planning to augment drinking water supply to these towns by formulating and implementing various schemes. According to its estimates, when these schemes are implemented the projected water availability by 2006 A.D. will be 100 LPCD in towns other than Bellary and Hospet. In our view considering what obtained in respect of Bellary city after scrutinising the projected water availability figures, the figures put out in respect of these towns, to say the least, are quite optimistic.

## Sanitation

Sanitation is a closely associated amenity with water supply. Its importance lies in flushing out dirt and dust and making way for a hygienic environment in the residential area. The households are the producers of dirt and they do so under different conditions such as in a lavatory attached to homes, or in community lavatories or in the open space. But the responsibility of disposing such waste rests with the municipal bodies. In tune with this responsibility and also to ensure to citizens a good sanitation condition, the Government has an underground drainage scheme which is operated by KUWSDB. All urban areas irrespective of their population size are eligible for this scheme which is financed by LIC and HUDCO. At present, Bellary and Hospet have partial underground drainage i.e. 60 per cent. The other towns have surface drainage and sceptic tank/soak pit system. But when the new townships are laid perhaps underground drainage system will be the preferred system. Further, as for sanitation at the household level, the Government has recently introduced two different schemes—one for the rural areas and one for the urban areas. Thus, there is a scheme of "Sulabh Souchalayas" in the urban areas and the scheme of "Nirmala Karnataka" in rural areas which are targeted to providing better sanitary facilities.

This is what is being done as far as liquid waste disposal is concerned. There is also the problem of solid waste disposal. The households, offices and enterprises every day produce solid wastes such as vegetable wastes, left over foods, dust and discarded materials like waste paper, broken glasses, plastic, wood and metal, used household articles, dug up earth and stones, fallen trees/plants. The municipal bodies are engaged in disposing such wastes by employing pourakarmikas. To illustrate, as on March 31, 1995 there were 437 pourakarmikas on the rolls of Bellary City Municipal Council who under the supervision of six Health Inspectors and one Health Officer were engaged in removing garbage using four vehicles. But yet, they do not collect the entire amount of solid waste and this becomes clear when we see the piling up of wastes along roads, in street corners and in dust bins. They have also failed to achieve environmentally safe disposal of such waste. Is the number of pourakarmikas short of the number required? According to a Government circular dated June 1977 the norm specified is one pourakarmika for 700 people. By this norm for a population of 2,45,758 (1991) the number of pourakarmikas required is 351 against 437 on rolls. And for the current estimated population of about three lakh the number required is 429 which is still lower than the actual. So the problem is not the inadequacy of the personnel but their full capacity utilisation. The situation is reported to be even worse in Hospet; it is so bad that Hospet city has earned the title of *Holasupet* (dirty city)! Accumulation of dirt along streets and street corners, spilling of iron-ore dust, spoilt fruits and vegetables make the city roads unhygienic to even to step on. At present there are 221 pourakarmikas for a population estimated to be 114.3 thousand. At the rate of one pourakarmika for 700 people gives the number of 163 which is much less than the actual number. Therefore, lack of personnel cannot be a reason for laxity in waste disposal.

## Conclusion

With the rapid industrialisation process initiated by the expected massive industrial investment in the steel and other sectors, the process of urbanisation of Bellary district will be accelerated. The latter will put heavy pressure on the limited municipal services such as housing, drinking water, sanitation and waste disposal. This calls for advanced planning for the provision of municipal services in adequate quantities. The far sightedness of the municipal and other urban development authorities in this regard is commendable as they have already initiated some action. But the basic lacuna found in their effort is that the pressure coming from industry and the households of the immigrant workers does not seem to have figured in their calculations. If this dimension is added, then the demand for municipal services will be much more than what is captured by these authorities. Keeping this imperative in view, the following suggestions are made for augmenting the municipal services:

1. On housing, there will be a big shortfall. Hence, a major role has to be played by the industrialists and miners by building worker colonies and housing complexes. Government has to step in on a bigger scale by allotting more funds for slum clearance and development. Karnataka Housing Board should accelerate its activities with accent on building EWS and LIG houses which will be in greater demand in future. Housing cooperatives should be encouraged.
2. Industrialists should be made responsible for drinking water supply for their worker colonies. KUWSDB should work at a redoubled pace tapping all sources of ground and surface water. The reduced storage capacity of the Tungabhadra reservoir on account of silt accumulation is acting as a constraint against drawing more water from it without affecting the interest of the agriculturists. One view is silting of the reservoir is caused by the mining activity as a result of which dust and soil are carried by rain water to the reservoir. If that is so, a desilting cess should be

collected from the miners and desilting work should commence forthwith. But a point is made by some experts that since desilting is as expensive as constructing a new dam why not a new dam be constructed. Though there is some element of exaggeration in this view, it is worth pursuing the idea of putting up a barrage up stream to store water for industrial use. That will perhaps resolve the trade off problem arising on account of the clash of interests between the farmers and the industrialists.

3. On sanitation and waste disposal, of course, municipalities will have to play a major role by strengthening the waste disposal personnel and improving their efficiency. Considering the proverbial inefficiency of public sector, two other options may be examined viz., partial privatisation of waste disposal and encouragement to informal citizen groups which may be interested in adopting some wards of the city for maintaining them clean and hygienic. The KUWSDB will be expected to cover the remaining portion of the underground drainage at least in Bellary and Hospet cities where the need is more intensively felt.
4. Finally, provision of all these facilities and their maintenance require funds which will impose heavy financial burden on municipalities and urban development bodies. To reduce this burden a bit it is absolutely essential that the users also will be expected to contribute. So, user charges will have to be collected from those who use these services. Incidentally, that is also a way of ensuring that the services are used more carefully and efficiently because anything that is made freely available is likely to be misused and wasted.

## NOTES

1. It may be reasonable to assume that a norm of 100 LPCPD for city municipal corporations, 80 LPCPD for city municipal councils and 70 LPCPD for town municipal councils may be accepted as the target for achievement.
2. Discussion with the management of Bellary Steels and Alloys Ltd.
3. See KUWSDB, Bellary Division, "Brief Notes on Augmentation of Water Supply Scheme to Bellary city with High Level canal as Source", Bellary, p. 7.

# 7

# LAND AVAILABILITY, LAND PRICES AND LAND GRABBING

M. VIVEKANANDA

Vijayanagar steel plant in Bellary district was conceived by the State in 60's as a public sector steel plant consequent to the heavy public investment made in the steel sector in northern States and the demand by the southern States including Karnataka that the future public investment in steel should take place in these States for ensuring a balanced regional development. The selection of the district for location of the steel plant was prompted by the availability of rich iron ore deposit in the hill ranges of the district spreading from Hospet to Bellary. Though the central Government sanctioned the Vijayanagar Steel Plant in Bellary district and a foundation stone was laid by the then Prime Minister of India in the early 70's, the dream of the State to have a steel plant did not materialise till Jindal came out to start a plant in the private sector. With the commencement of steel plant construction activity by the Jindal, a few industrial houses have come forward in setting up steel plants in the district. It is estimated that about Rs.13,000 crores is likely to be invested in steel plants in the district by the private sector during the coming decade.

The investment of the order of Rs.13,000 crores in steel plants in one district may affect the land-use pattern of the district as setting up of steel plants requires huge size of land for the plants, ancillary units, and for townships of the plants as well as settlements that are likely to come up around the plants due to the presence of ancillary units and the demand that may come from the service sector. Such demand for land for non-agricultural purposes is likely to affect the agricultural sector in many ways. The likely impact of mega industries on agricultural sector is listed below:

1. Area under cultivation comes down which in turn may bring down the agricultural production.
2. The land-use and cropping pattern may change around the industrial units.
3. The above changes may bring in a change in the occupational pattern of agricultural workers
4. The land prices are likely to go up.
5. The increase in the demand for land along with the increase in land prices may encourage land grabbing.

The impact of the mega industries is not restricted to agricultural land alone; the impact can be found even in urban areas which are close to the mega industries. The land prices in these urban areas as well as house rents are likely to increase due to setting up of mega industries.

In the light of the above an attempt is made in this chapter to study the likely impact of setting up of mega steel plants in the district on land-use pattern, land values of rural and urban areas and the tendency towards land grabbing.

**Land Utilisation in Bellary District**

In an agrarian economy, while transferring land from agriculture to non-agriculture use, care should be taken to minimise the adverse effects on agriculture sector. The adverse effects can be minimised if the productive lands are untouched and only less productive lands are transferred to non-agriculture use. The least productive agriculture lands are those kept as fallow and the less productive agriculture lands are those which are under rain-fed agriculture. The classification of land under various uses is provided by the land utilisation statistics and these statistics for Bellary district by talukas are presented in Table 7.1. The fallow land consisting of cultivable waste and current fallow accounts for 11.5 per cent of the cultivable land in the district which is close to the State figure of 11.8 per cent. Across talukas, the percentage of fallow land as percentage of cultivable land is less than 5 per cent in the talukas of Bellary and Hadagalli. The highest percentage of fallow land is found in Hospet taluka with 24.6 per cent followed by Sandur taluka with 23.4 per cent.

Coming to irrigated area, the district has 29.9 per cent of irrigated area to net sown area as against 21.5 per cent in the State. Canal is the major source of irrigation in the district which accounts for about 64 per cent of irrigated area. The higher percentage of irrigation in the district is the result of the investment made on Tungabhadra dam, canal network and land development. The lands under localised area of Tungabhadra project were developed for irrigated crops and these areas shall not be transferred to non-agricultural purposes as the very purpose of developing these lands will be defeated. Across talukas, Hospet has 53.8 per cent of irrigated area which is the highest among talukas followed by Bellary with 51.3 per cent. The other talukas which have higher proportion of irrigated area are Siruguppa with about 38 per cent and Hagaribommanahalli with about 35 per cent. Sandur has 10.9 per cent of irrigated area which is the least among the talukas. Looking to the land utilisation statistics of fallow land and irrigated area, it appears Sandur taluka is the ideal choice for location of steel projects. Hospet taluka has the highest proportion of fallow land as well as irrigated land which suggest that irrigated land might be concentrated in certain part of the taluka and the other part is rain-fed. Though the taluka level statistics provide certain clues, the choice of sites for steel plants should be based on village level land utilisation statistics.

## Land Requirement for the Proposed Steel Plants

At present there are four private sector mini steel plants existing in the district of Bellary with an investment of Rs. 112.11 crores. Another five private sector steel plants are in various stages of completion with an investment of about Rs. 4954 crores. Out of the five, Jindal Vijayanagar Steel Ltd. is the only mega steel plant with an investment of Rs. 3300 crores. The expansion of M/s Bellary Steels & Alloys Ltd. with an investment of Rs. 657 crores is approved by the Government of Karnataka. The second mega steel plant that is likely to come up in a short period is M/s Mukund Steel Ltd. with an investment of Rs. 2530 crores. There is a proposal for a mini steel plant by M/s Mittal Steels Ltd. at Hagaribommanahalli taluka with an investment of Rs.1310 crores. The eight new industries mentioned above will account for an investment of Rs. 9451 crores.

An attempt is made here to assess the land requirement for the above mentioned industries and the industries that are likely to come to the district during the course of next ten years taking into account the requirements for industrial townships and ancillary units. The discussions with the industrialists reveal that there is no approved norm for land requirement either based on capital investment or production capacity of

**TABLE 7.1: Land-use Pattern in Bellary District—1992-93**

*(in hectares)*

| Taluka | Geographical Area | Forest | Land put to non-agricultural uses | Barren and uncultivable land | Cultivable waste | Current fallow area | Net sown | Irrigated area | (6+7) as % of (6+7+8) | (9) as % of (8) |
|---|---|---|---|---|---|---|---|---|---|---|
| (1) | (2) | (3) | (4) | (5) | (6) | (7) | (8) | (9) | (10) | (11) |
| Bellary | 169027 | 2877 | 7662 | 8483 | 1273 | 6067 | 142309 | 72998 | 4.90 | 51.30 |
| Hadagalli | 94853 | 4738 | 9384 | 2766 | 1747 | 944 | 73058 | 10919 | 3.55 | 14.95 |
| H. G. Halli | 97599 | 4482 | 19980 | 5147 | 3676 | 2890 | 60211 | 21058 | 9.83 | 34.97 |
| H. R. Halli | 143024 | 22230 | 11232 | 6258 | 3224 | 2636 | 95036 | 11439 | 5.81 | 12.04 |
| Hospet | 93374 | 24970 | 6389 | 8546 | 6696 | 6339 | 40020 | 21527 | 24.57 | 53.79 |
| Kudligi | 159706 | 33661 | 11129 | 8159 | 7229 | 7270 | 87813 | 11551 | 14.17 | 13.15 |
| Sandur | 94359 | 24118 | 7170 | 17700 | 1659 | 8971 | 34696 | 3770 | 23.45 | 10.87 |
| Siruguppa | 104278 | 2171 | 6775 | 2664 | 4177 | 13959 | 74189 | 28172 | 19.64 | 37.97 |
| Total | 956220 | 119247 | 79721 | 59723 | 29681 | 49076 | 607332 | 181434 | 11.48 | 29.87 |

*Source:* District Census Handbook, Bellary District, Census of India, 1981.

steel plants. So far only Jindal Vijayanagar Steel Ltd., has obtained allotment of land and taken possession of it in Bellary district. The information on land requirement by three steel plants is furnished in Table 7.2 which includes Jindal Vijayanagar Steel Ltd.

TABLE 7.2: **Investment-Land Ratio for Steel Plants**

| Name of the Steel Plant | Investment (in Crores) | Land requirement (in hectares) | Land Investment ratio |
|---|---|---|---|
| M/s. Mittal Steel Ltd. | 1310 | 485.6 | 0.37 |
| Bellary Steel & Alloys Ltd. (Proposed plant) | 870 | 323.7 | 0.37 |
| Jindal Vijayanagar Steel Ltd. | 3300 | 1598.5 | 0.48 |
| Total | 5480 | 2407.8 | 0.44 |

Table 7.2 shows a close relationship between investment and land requirement of the steel plants. The land-investment ratio of M/s Mittal Steel Ltd., and Bellary Steel & Alloys Ltd., is 0.37 whereas the ratio for Jindal Vijayanagar Steel Ltd., is 0.48 and the average ratio for the three plants is 0.44. The three plants might have included the land requirement for their township in their land requirement exercise. The average ratio can be used as a thumb rule for assessing the land requirement for the steel plants that are likely to come up over the period of ten years. The thumb rule suggests that one crore of rupees investment in steel sector requires 0.44 hectares of land. The anticipated investment of Rs. 13000 crores in steel plants in the district requires about 5.7 thousand hectares of land both for the plants and the townships. It was suggested that another one-tenth of land may be required for the ancillary units. It can be reasonably assumed that another 25 per cent of the land may be required for planned settlements outside the steel plants. So, the total land required for steel plants, townships, ancillary units and for settlements outside the steel plants for Rs. 13000 crores investment in steel plants is about 7.7 thousand hectares.

### Land Availability for Non-agricultural Use

Mass scale transfer of agricultural land to non-agricultural purposes in a region is likely to bring down the agricultural production of that region.

So, the criterion that is to be adopted for identifying land for transferring to non-agricultural purposes should be to minimise the loss to agricultural production in the region by such transfers. This can be achieved by transferring the low productive agricultural lands of the region to non-agricultural purposes. This, however, requires identifying such land in a contiguous belt by looking into the land-use pattern as steel plants require huge area. Further, it is preferable to identify the land for the steel plants near the mining areas to minimise its adverse effects on agriculture. An attempt is made here to identify contiguous belts having low level of irrigation in Bellary, Sandur, and Hospet talukas which are in the heart of the mining area of the district. A close scrutiny of land-use statistics of villages in Bellary, Sandur and Hospet provide two belts satisfying the criterion of low agricultural productivity: one in Sandur taluka and the other in Hospet taluka. The villages under the two belts and their land-use statistics are furnished in Table 7.3. The road connecting Hospet and Bellary (State highway 42) passes through the identified belt in Hospet taluka. This belt has 11 villages with only 0.6 per cent of irrigated area, 13,574 hectares of geographical area, 7,266 hectares of net sown area, 5,272 hectares of forest area and 650 hectares of cultivable waste. The Sandur taluka belt lies south and south-east of Tornagal village. The belt has 16 villages covering a geographical area of 12,282 hectares, 5,054 hectares of net sown area with only 6.4 per cent of irrigated area and 2,566 hectares of forest area. The two belts together account for about 13.3 thousand hectares of cultivable area and if forest area is also included to the cultivable area the area comes to 21.2 thousand hectares. The land requirement that is estimated for the Rs. 13000 crores investment in steel plants is 7.7 thousand hectares. The land that is available in the two belts itself is about 3 times the requirement. Hence, the investment that is likely to come into the district may not adversely affect agriculture if proper identification of the area is done for conversion.

## Status of Land Acquisition

The land acquisition was started for the public sectorVijayanagar Steel Plant in the year 1971 and about 4.9 thousand hectares of land was acquired covering 4.3 thousand hectares of patta land and 0.6 thousand hectares of Government land in six villages in and around Toranagal in Sandur taluka. Compensation was paid to 3.2 thousand hectares of patta land. The compensation fixed for land acquisition was Rs. 1235 to Rs. 6178 per hectare of dry land and Rs. 4448 to Rs. 8043 per hectare of irrigated

TABLE 7.3: **Land-use Pattern in Selected Villages of Hospet and Sandur Talukas**

*(in hectares)*

| Villages | Geographical area | Forest | Net sown area | Irrigated area | Dry area | Cultivable waste | Area not available for cultivation |
|---|---|---|---|---|---|---|---|
| *Hospet Taluka* | | | | | | | |
| 1. Ingaligi | 1708.3 | 881.1 | 681.82 | 0 | 681.82 | 145.38 | 0 |
| 2. Vaddrahalli | 689.13 | 206.42 | 423.82 | 0 | 423.82 | 57.58 | 1.31 |
| 3. Papinayakanahalli | 1871.29 | 1023.19 | 739.18 | 0 | 739.18 | 26.13 | 82.79 |
| 4. Gudlavaddigere | 628.94 | 209.8 | 399.22 | 0 | 399.22 | 10.45 | 9.47 |
| 5. Byluvadigere | 1103.05 | 267.16 | 780.31 | 0 | 780.31 | 0 | 55.58 |
| 6. Kakubal | 1991.9 | 585.58 | 1406.32 | 0 | 1406.32 | 0 | |
| 7. Dharamasagara | 1316.85 | 618.04 | 555.91 | 44.11 | 511.8 | 81.12 | 61.78 |
| 8. Kottiganahalli | 1047.99 | 397.95 | 601.1 | 0 | 601.1 | 30.29 | 18.65 |
| 9. Gadiganur | 1457.79 | 473.53 | 697.23 | 0 | 697.23 | 170.06 | 116.97 |
| 10. Gonalu | 1459.92 | 609.19 | 713.8 | 0 | 713.8 | 103.25 | 33.68 |
| 11. Buvanahalli | 299.01 | 0 | 267.16 | 0 | 267.16 | 26 | 5.85 |
| Total | 13574.17 | 5271.96 | 7265.87 | 44.11 | 7221.76 | 650.26 | 386.08 |

*(Contd.)*

TABLE 7.3 *(Contd.)*

| Villages | Geographical area | Forest | Net sown area | Irrigated area | Dry area | Cultivable waste | Area not available for cultivation |
|---|---|---|---|---|---|---|---|
| *Sandur Taluka* | | | | | | | |
| 1. Joga | 2337.04 | 275.5 | 524.08 | 33.58 | 490.5 | 17 | 1520.46 |
| 2. Nagalapura | 454.13 | 55.1 | 321.33 | 0 | 321.33 | 0 | 77.7 |
| 3. Gangalapura | 352.08 | 112.51 | 216.51 | 12.95 | 203.56 | 0 | 23.06 |
| 4. Gowripura | 235.81 | 66.17 | 94.7 | 0 | 94.7 | 0 | 74.94 |
| 5. Taranagar | 983.67 | 14.37 | 131.29 | 24 | 107.29 | 0 | 838.01 |
| 6. Muraripura | 293.5 | 8.98 | 145.39 | 0 | 145.39 | 21.05 | 118.08 |
| 7. Sankarapura | 100.64 | 0 | 4.7 | 0 | 4.7 | 0 | 95.94 |
| 8. Dowlatpur | 890.95 | 42.33 | 763.02 | 16.19 | 746.83 | 6.07 | 79.53 |
| 9. Krishnanagar | 583.44 | 40.86 | 486.76 | 32.38 | 454.38 | 43.27 | 12.55 |
| 10. Bhujanganagar | 625.94 | 78.5 | 544.38 | 55.04 | 489.34 | 0 | 3.06 |
| 11. Ranjitpur | 209.69 | 47.09 | 120.28 | 0 | 120.28 | 0 | 42.32 |
| 12. Narsinagar | 137.6 | 66.2 | 54.6 | 0 | 54.6 | 10.12 | 6.68 |
| 13. Kodal | 2138.03 | 1528.96 | 559.3 | 82.56 | 476.74 | 0 | 49.77 |
| 14. Chikkanatapura | 1473.37 | 209.49 | 512.35 | 36.02 | 476.33 | 283.29 | 468.24 |
| 15. Yerabanahalli | 1247.78 | 20.28 | 575.53 | 29.54 | 545.99 | 0 | 651.97 |
| 16. Musenayakanahalli | 218.24 | 0 | 0 | 0 | 0 | 0 | 218.24 |
| Total | 12281.91 | 2566.34 | 5054.22 | 322.26 | 4731.96 | 380.8 | 4280.55 |

land. Those farmers who approached the court got better compensation ranging from Rs. 1235 to Rs. 17792 per hectare of dry land and Rs. 14827 to Rs. 32124 per hectare of irrigated land. It appears about 40 cases are still pending in courts for fixation of market value. Those who have not moved the court have to satisfy themselves with the compensation initially fixed by the Government.

As public sector Vijayanagar steel plant did not materialise the land that was acquired by the Government for that steel plant is now available for private sector steel plants. From this acquired land Jindal Vijayanagar Steel Ltd. has obtained 1598 hectares of land from Government at the rate of Rs. 111 thousand per hectare. In addition, Jindal has paid Rs. 12.3 thousand per hectare as ex-gratia to farmers for taking possession of the land. In the entire transaction, the Government has made a profit instead of passing on the benefit to the farmers who lost the land. The role played by the Government appears to be that of a middle man rather than that of a facilitator. It appears that Government is planning for rehabilitation programmes for the poor farmers whose lands were acquired for Vijayanagar steel plant. If the Government had passed on the value of land it got from Jindal to these farmers there may not be any need for the rehabilitation exercise.

At present the Government has 3.3 thousand hectares of land for allotment to the proposed steel plants. In addition, the Government may have to acquire another 2.79 thousand hectares of land to meet the land requirements of the proposed steel plants during the next ten years. In acquiring the land and allotting it to the industries the Government shall play the role of a facilitator by passing on the land value it realises from the industries to the farmers who forgo the land. It can thereby minimise litigation on this account.

## Land Prices

The land prices in the villages along the State Highway 42 from Bellary to Hospet started increasing with the commencement of construction activity by the Jindal Vijayanagar Steel Ltd. The discussions with the local knowledgeable people in the villages (mentioned in Table 7.3) in Hospet taluka which are located along the State Highway revealed that the land price per hectare of dry land about a couple of years ago was about Rs. 49 thousand for the road side lands and Rs. 24.7 thousand for the lands in interior. The construction activity by the Jindal has given confidence to people that steel plants are likely to come to that area and aroused their expectations for higher land prices. The expectations are strengthened by the price paid by Jindal to the Government for the land it obtained and by the continuous enquiries by outsiders about land prices. Recently, people from outside these villages have purchased road side lands in some of these villages by paying Rs. 173 thousand per hectare. All these have created a reserve price for the land which is about Rs. 247 thousand per hectare. Land transactions in these villages have come down because of the reserve price and farmers are eagerly waiting for land transactions at the reserve price.

It appears that farmers will be better off by disposing of land at the reserve price as they are currently obtaining from cultivation on an average (average of four years as the area is drought prone and farmers are likely to get good harvest once in four years) a net income of Rs. 3707 per hectare per year without imputing family labour cost. The farmers may not be getting any income from farm economy if imputed family labour cost is taken into account. Industrialisation of the area may become a boon to the farmers if they could get the reserve price for their lands.

The house site prices in and around Bellary and Hospet towns also increased in recent years by about 6 times as a result of the general expectations of rising land prices in the wake of urban growth generated by the proposed industrialisation. The increase in the price of urban sites may become a transition phenomenon during the construction stage of the plants and become stabilised if the industrial townships are developed in and around the plants.

**Land Grabbing**

Unauthorised occupation of Government lands is common in Bellary district. One of the apparent factors for this is the high percentage of landless agricultural labourers (the phenomenon peculiar to northern Karnataka districts) and the policy of the Government to regularise the unauthorised cultivation of Government lands by landless people by awarding pattas. This might have prompted the landless to occupy most of the Government lands with the fond hope that the land pattas may be awarded to them. The field visit to Hospet taluka revealed that even forest lands are not spared and most of the lands that are suitable for cultivation appears to have come under unauthorised cultivation. Land grabbing already appears to be a common feature in this agricultural region. The situation may not be very much different in the urban areas either.

To sum up, the proposed setting up of steel plants in this district may not adversely affect agricultural production if the industrial sites are selected in the belts where the agricultural productivity is low. Consequent to the move towards industrialisation in the district, the land prices have shown a tendency to increase. The farmers will be better off if they obtain a fair market price for their lands. In acquiring the land and allotting it to the industries, the Government shall play the role of a facilitator by passing on the land value it realises from the industries to the farmers who forgo the land and thereby minimise litigation. The fear that industrialisation brings in land grabbing may be untenable in this district because this phenomenon has already been present in the district even before the industrialisation process has started in a big way.

# 8

# LABOUR SUPPLY, MANPOWER REQUIREMENT AND CONTRACT LABOUR SYSTEM

V.S. SATYAPRIYA and P. THIPPAIAH

The major thrust of this chapter is towards highlighting the manpower requirement (demand) vis-a-vis its supply and the existing arrangements for meeting its demand by the industrial sector, particularly the unskilled labourers characterized by their low bargaining power associated with their skills. A fuller understanding of the supply, demand and contractual arrangements for various categories of labour assumes great significance in the context of the envisaged huge investment in the large and medium industries in the coming five to ten years. Specifically, the attempt in this chapter is in the direction of understanding the demand for various categories of labour by the proposed new large and medium industries and the expected growth in the downstream industries in terms of investment and labour requirement. While doing this, first the existing pattern of employment by sectors is presented. This is followed by an examination of the demand for labour and its supply. The expected demand for labour is based on the existing pattern of employment vis-a-vis the expected volume of investment. It may be mentioned that the present exercise is constrained by the non-availability of detailed information on various aspects. However, an attempt has been made to make the best use of whatever information is gathered from published and unpublished materials and personal visits to the various industrial units and discussions with the knowledgeable people in the field.

### Data Base

Basically reliance is placed on three sets of data regarding the trends in supply and demand of industrial work force in the district. These are (a) Population Census for the years 1981 and 1991, (b) Economic Census of 1980 and 1990, and (c) Publications and records of the Department of Industries and Commerce. These data are supplemented by the relevant information made available by the District Employment Exchange, Labour Department and the Bellary Urban Development Authority. Insights into the various issues made possible by discussions with the various officials, industrialists and others are also made use of in the present exercise.

**Current Status of Labour Force**

Bellary district has a total population of 1.89 million (Population Census 1991) with a participation rate of 45.13 per cent, an increase of 2.42 percentage points from 1981 (42.71 per cent in 1981). In absolute terms the number of workers increased from 6.36 lakhs in 1981 to 8.53 lakhs in 1991, i.e. by 2.17 lakhs or 34.10 per cent against an increase of 26.92 per cent in total population.

Coming to the distribution of workers, sector-wise, agriculture (cultivators + agri-labourers) shared as much as 74.83 per cent, mining and quarrying 1.95 per cent, manufacturing, processing, servicing and repairs 5.58 per cent and the tertiary sector 8.58 per cent (Appendix Table A1). An interesting and all the more relevant aspect is the pattern of growth of workers across sectors. A little over 81 per cent of the increase in total workers was in agriculture. Mining and quarrying, an important economic activity of the district gained barely 0.38 per cent while the tertiary sector accounted for as much as 19 per cent of the increase in the number of workers. The 'Manufacturing, servicing and repairs' sector showed a decline of 1.94 per cent in the total number of workers. However, a further disaggregation of the data reveals that the decline in the number of workers in this sector was contributed by the group 'household industries'; number of workers in non-household industry increased by 16.25 per cent, sharing 2.29 per cent of the increase in the total number of workers though its share in total number of workers declined from 4.67 per cent to 4.06 per cent between 1981 and 1991.

The Population Census data on workers, however, reflects only the magnitude of the stock of labour force and not the actual level of employment. The Economic Census provides information on the number of persons employed under various industrial categories. However, the Economic Census excludes cultivators, agricultural labourers and plantation workers from its purview. These are also presented in Table A1. As can be seen from the Table the number of persons employed showed an increase of nearly 18 per cent (23,012) between 1980 and 1990.

A comparison of the number of workers of the Population Census, representing the supply of labour, and employment data from the Economic Census, representing the demand for labour, reveals that the extent of surplus labour (unemployment) which was 27.13 per cent in 1981 increased to 31.4 per cent in 1991. Sector-wise it rose from 38 per cent to 46 per cent in manufacturing, etc. The mining and quarrying sector however employed only 6.7 per cent and 4.84 per cent of the total number of workers enumerated in the Population Census, respectively for the years 1981 and 1991.

A more relevant feature is the change in the sectoral distribution of employment. Employment in 'mining and quarrying' and 'manufacturing' records a decline between 1980 and 1990 (Economic Census). The decline was 25 per cent in the former and 18.5 per cent in the latter. Increase in employment has come about in trade and commerce (38.8 per cent), transport, storage, etc. (30.73 per cent) and construction (14.66 per cent). Total number of workers (excluding cultivators and agricultural labourers) increased from 171.42 thousand to 214.75 thousand (25.28 per cent) between 1981 and 1991 (Population Census), total employment increased from 124.9 thousand in 1981 to 147.9 thousand in 1991, i.e, by 18.42 per cent or 23 thousand (Table A1). The increase in the total number of workers was much higher than the increase in employment. The additional absorption was only 54 per cent (23 thousand) of the increase of 43 thousand workers. The increase in employment was mainly in the category of 'trade and commerce' and 'others'. Though the manufacturing sector showed a decline in the number of workers (Population Census), as mentioned earlier, the decline was in the household industry sector; the non-household industry sector showed an increase of 16.25 per cent in the number of workers. The Economic Census, however, while covers all categories of industries, does not provide information separately for the household and non-household industry sectors. If one could assume the ratio of workers in these two categories as of the Population Census, then the Economic Census does not show any change in the volume of employment in the non-household sector between 1981 and 1991.

Another source of data on employment is the District Employment Exchange which maintains information on the number of persons employed under various occupational categories. As can be seen from Table A1 total number of persons employed under various occupation categories registered an increase of 7.63 per cent between 1992 and 1995. Excepting construction, under all other categories there was an increase in employment.

Data on employment from the two sources, namely the Economic Census and the Employment Exchange vary considerably. Total employment figures thrown up by the Employment Exchange (1992) is only about 31.86 per cent of the total employment figure given by the Economic Census. Sector-wise also they are not consistent. These wide differences leave one wondering about the coverage and/or reliability of the employment data.

The following broad observations can be made from the preceding discussion:

(a) There was an increase in the work participation rate in the district between 1981 and 1991.
(b) Total number of workers in the district increased by 2.17 lakhs.
(c) Increase in the number of workers (supply) in the non-agricultural sector was of the order of 25 per cent.
(d) Growth in the secondary and tertiary sectors could absorb only 54 per cent of the additional labour force.
(e) The overall excess supply of labour over its demand was of the order of 31 per cent; it was 46 per cent in the manufacturing sector; mining and quarrying employed less than 5 per cent of the total available labour under this category.

**Contract Labour System**

As far as the mining activity in the district is concerned, except one public sector undertaking by the National Mineral Development Corporation (NMDC), the rest, numbering 113, are in the private sector.

The breakup of mines is as follows:

| | | |
|---|---|---|
| (a) Iron Ore | 97 | (including NMDC) |
| (b) Manganese | 11 | |
| (c) Red Oxide | 5 | |

Besides these, there were 54 Quarry lease holders and a few sand and quartz ore lease holders.

These mines are concentrated in Sandur and Hospet taluks. While the NMDC employs about 1500 workers (1035 in the mines and the balance in auxiliary services), total employment in the private mines is around 20 to 25 thousand persons. While the public sector mine is highly mechanized, the private sector mines are semi-mechanized.

The type of labour employed, the ratio of different categories of labour to total labour employed in the mining industry is presented below in Table 8.1.

TABLE 8.1: **Category-wise Employment (ratio) to Total Labour in Mining Industry**

| | |
|---|---|
| (a) NMDC (Public Sector): | |
| (i) Unskilled | 0.0956 |
| (ii) Semi-skilled | 0.2551 |
| (iii) Skilled | 0.6493 |
| (b) Private Sector: | |
| (i) Unskilled | 0.2668 |
| (ii) Semi-skilled | 0.3338 |
| (iii) Skilled | 0.3994 |

(These ratios are used for deriving the expected demand for labour in the mining sector)

Regarding the employment of unskilled and semi-skilled labour, except for the public sector undertaking (NMDC), it is entrusted to the labour contractors and the mines do not employ these categories of labour directly. It is understood that there are 156 such registered labour contractors operating in the area. The wages for the semi-skilled and unskilled workers, for different kinds of jobs, are negotiated with the labour contractors in the light of the minimum wages prescribed. Excepting the public sector undertaking (NMDC) wages for the unskilled and semi-skilled labourers are paid on piece rate basis while the minimum wage is on time rate, which was around Rs. 30 per day. The piece rate for these workers was Rs. 10.15 per tonne and Rs. 1.15 per tonne to the labour contractor. On an average each worker earns about Rs. 50 per day. On the face of it the daily earnings per worker appear to be a little more than the minimum wage prescribed. But in reality this may not be so. This we infer for two reasons: (a) the workers may be overworking to reach their minimum income requirement and (b) given their social and economic status, the extent of collective action by them, they are more than likely to be exploited by the labour contractors. It was also gathered during our field visits that the labour contractors deduct a certain amount from the wages to be paid to the workers. These apart, the workers are denied minimum medical and other facilities like creche. It was reported that women workers constitute about 7 to 10 per cent and children 3 to 4 per cent of the total workers. Female and child labour is engaged mainly in loading and sorting operations of iron ore. The discussions with the Department of Mines and Geology, and the Mine Owner's Association place the number of workers in iron ore mining around 20,000 to 25,000. Regarding the future entrants into this occupation, the discussions with labourers reveal that there may not be any considerable increase in such new entrants into this occupation for reasons like hard physical labour, inadequate basic facilities like housing, health, schooling for children, etc. Also the workers are not inclined to work for any extended period of time. This attitude of the workers towards this occupation appears to be a major factor for the mining companies to depend upon the labour contractors for a stable supply of workers. The Miners Association also indicated that the mining workers work only 60 per cent of their capacity and this has led to a gradual increase in the level of mechanization of the various operations in mining. However, the Department of Mines and Geology visualise an increase of 15 per cent to 20 per cent in the number of workers in mining in the near future due to the massive investment that is likely to take place in the steel sector even with a bias towards capital intensive and labour saving technology.

## Present and Potential Employment Scenario

If we closely observe the developments taking place in the district due to industrialisation, the district would not face shortage of labour force drastically. There are several reasons for this kind of observation.

The district has 20 large and medium scale industries with a capital investment of Rs. 3,51,204 lakhs employing 13,423 persons (Table A2). The number of small scale industries in the district is 6,511 with a capital investment of Rs. 4,755.66 lakhs and employing 31,013 persons. The capital-labour ratio for the existing large and medium industries is Rs. 26.164 lakhs per unit of labour. Assuming the capital-labour ratio of the existing large and medium scale industries, the expected investment of Rs. 13,000 crores would create 49,687 additional jobs. This assumption of unchanged technology, however, may not be fully justified and it over estimates the labour requirement. Based on the information collected during our field visits specifically with reference to the proposed industries in the district, the investment required per unit of labour is Rs. 1.32 crores. On this basis the expected investment of Rs. 13,000 crores would create 9,500 additional jobs. This could be taken as the projected demand for labour when the proposed industries come into full production stage.

Resulting from the setting up of the new industries the estimated number of downstream industrial units that are likely to come up is 136 with a capital investment of Rs. 12,825 lakhs with an employment potential of 5,310. The spin-off effect of the investment of the various industries would be felt on the service, transport and other ancillary industries. According to one estimate the investment arising from the spin-off effect would be of the order of Rs. 2,364 crores. These estimates are more in the nature of guess-work rather than on any firm factual basis. Hence the likely employment generation due to these factors are only indicative. Assuming that indirect employment, i.e. in service, trading, transport and other related activities, would be three times the employment in the mega and downstream industries, the number of additional jobs that are likely to occur is 44,430. It may be necessary to look into the role of the formal/informal sectors where such employment opportunities would arise. If the past performance of these two sectors is any guide, then the increase in employment of the magnitude we have noted above would be mainly in the non-agricultural informal sector. It may be seen from Table A3, that nearly 70 per cent of the growth in employment has occurred in the non-agricultural sector. Such a pattern, if it persists, has certain specific policy implications. These would be particularly in the direction of introducing strict enforcement of wage regulations, provision of basic labour welfare measures, prevention of employment of child labour, more particularly in health hazard occupations. The tendency to employ more of child labour may also become more pronounced in the event of a shortage of labour supply and in the face of rising wage rates for adult labour.

Thus, the total demand for labour under all categories, with the full realization of the expected investment, would be in the order of 59,240. Based on the Population census (1991) the supply of labour (i.e. Total workers minus Cultivators, Agricultural labourers, those engaged in forestry, fishing and mining) is 1,86,539; actual employment given by the Economic Census (1991) is 1,47,916. The difference between these two, 38,623, would give the magnitude of available total labour. The estimated additional demand for labour of all categories is 59,240. Since the projected demand for labour is at the full production stage of the industrial units, which may stretch for a period of 5 to 10 years, the supply of labour has to be inflated accordingly. Assuming the 1981-1991 growth rate of workers, which is 2.6667 per cent per annum, the addition to workers, in the categories we are concerned with here, would be of the order of 50,011 by 2001 AD and the total supply of labour by then would be 2,37,549. Total employment, i.e. existing plus expected, by 2001 AD would be in the order of 2,06,559 giving a surplus of 30,990. Thus, there may not be a deficit of labour supply of any significant order with all the expected investment.

So far we have considered only the aggregate demand and supply of labour. It is, however, essential to examine the demand and supply of labour by category of skills. With whatever scanty/sketchy data that is available an attempt is also made to understand this dimension of the manpower requirement. Table 8.2 presents the estimated demand, supply and surplus or deficit of manpower in the district.

TABLE 8.2: **Supply of and Demand for Labour by Skills**

| Category | Supply | Demand | Surplus/Deficit |
|---|---|---|---|
| Technical | 1251 | 853 | 398 |
| Administrative | 8460 | 1571 | 6889 |
| Skilled | 3847 | 12164 | −8317 |
| Others | 52301 | 44651 | 7650 |
| Total | 65859 | 59240 | 6619 |

*Source*: Manpower supply and demand are based on Table A4 and A5.

As can be seen from the above table while there is an overall surplus of labour, the shortage or deficit appears to be in the supply of skilled manpower. It is likely, that all those skilled persons seeking employment may not have registered in the employment exchanges. Also technical graduates and post-graduates are not registered in the employment exchanges. To that extent the supply of skilled manpower presented above may be an underestimate. Also, the growth in the skilled manpower over the next 5 to 10 years also has to be taken into account since the demand for labour covers up to the full production stage of the industries.

During the construction phase of the industries there would be a considerable demand for mainly unskilled and to a lesser extent skilled and semi-skilled labour. After the construction phase is over, it is likely a section of the labour force will be absorbed in the industry itself.

As mentioned earlier employment in the mining activity is considered separately. There appears to be a great divergence in the data on workers engaged in the mining industry reported in thePopulation Census, Economic Census and the Employment Exchange (Table 8.1). While the Population Census refers to the stock of labour force, the employment data reported by the other two sources appear to be gross under estimates. Even the figures given by the Mine Owners Association, which is in the range of

20,000 to 25,000 appear to be on the higher side. As an alternative, it was attempted to estimate the total employment in iron ore mining using the existing employment in the NMDC and a private sector mining company. The details are given in Table 8.3.

TABLE 8.3: **Production and Employment in Iron Ore Mining (1993)**

| | Ore Production | Employment (Current) (tonnes) | Output/ Worker (No) (tonnes) |
|---|---|---|---|
| Public Sector (NMDC) | 1003200 | 1500 | 669 |
| Private Sector | 344396 | 1063 | 324 |
| All categories | 1347596 | 2563 | 526 |

As can be seen from Table 8.3 the iron ore output per worker ranges between 324 tonnes to 669 tonnes while the average is 526 tonnes. The public sector mine being a highly mechanized one the output-labour ratio is considerably higher, more than twice the private sector mine. Present employment in iron ore mining using the above three output-labour ratios with a total current iron ore production of 4.66 million tonnes is shown in Table 8.4.

TABLE 8.4: **Existing and Projected Employment in Iron Ore Mining**

| | Present Employment | Projected Employment | Net additional Employment |
|---|---|---|---|
| | 1 | 2 | 3 (col. 2—col. 1) |
| (a) NMDC ratio | 6964 | 8971 | 2007 |
| (b) Private Sector ratio | 14377 | 18519 | 4142 |
| (c) All categories ratio | 10107 | 11491 | 1304 |

The total employment derived on the basis of the NMDC data is close to the District Employment Exchange data, though it is much lower relative to the total labour force (16661) in mining reported in the Population Census 1991. (The surplus labour works out 58 per cent). It may also not be justified to assume that all mines are adopting the same high labour saving technology of the NMDC. Alternatively, the other two estimates are much closer to the total labour stock though lower.

The expected total iron ore requirement with the commissioning of the proposed steel units is put at 6 million tonnes. It is not unlikely that the future mining activity would move towards a high technology with a lower human labour component. The projected employment to achieve this level of ore output is also presented above. Looking at the past trends there may not be any considerable addition to the existing mine workers and the total mine labour would barely cross 17000. Even with a *status quo* in the mining technology the demand for mining labour would just match the supply. Thus it appears from an analysis of the data, we have had access to, that the mining industry is not likely to face any shortage in the supply of labour.

While the above may hold good as far as total supply of labour is concerned, shortage in the supply of specific skilled labour may arise. Using the ratio of existing labour use by skills the additional labour required by skills in the mining industry is also worked out. These are presented in Table 8.5.

TABLE 8.5: **Projected Demand for Mining Labour by Skills**

| Norm | Unskilled | Semi-skilled | Skilled | Total |
|---|---|---|---|---|
| 1. NMDC | 192 | 512 | 1303 | 2007 |
| 2. Private sector | 1106 | 1382 | 1654 | 4142 |
| 3. All categories | 215 | 374 | 715 | 1304 |

Thus even after meeting the demand for labour in mining there would still be a surplus. This is when one looks only at the total labour supply and demand. However, skill-wise there could be a shortage of skilled labour. It needs to be mentioned here that the supply of labour refers only to the current status and this needs to be adjusted upward to account for future additions to the skilled labour category particularly. It is more than likely, that the changing industrial environment would induce more entrants into the skill formation training courses. Also the mining industry itself imparts the necessary skills required. In view of these various factors it may not be too much off the mark to expect a balance between the supply of demand for labour with the realization of the proposed huge investment in the steel industry in the district.

## Summing Up

The basic objective of this chapter was to understand the supply of manpower vis-a-vis its demand, the contractual arrangements for labour of various categories in the context of the proposed huge investment in large and medium scale steel industries and the expected growth in the downstream industries in terms of investment and labour requirement. The likely demand for labour due to the spin off effects of these industries is also touched upon. This chapter also examines the demand for labour in iron ore mining which is the basic raw material for the proposed new industries.

This chapter has mainly relied on the available official statistics, published and unpublished. However, the discussions with the officials, industrialists and our own field visits the district has largely helped in drawing meaningful interpretations of the statistical data.

An analysis of the data on labour supply and its employment by sectors revealed the existence of surplus labour which is of a considerable magnitude.

Based on the Population Census, while the number of total workers in the district, between 1981 and 1991, increased by 34 per cent, the increase was 25 per cent in the non-agricultural sector. Growth in the secondary and tertiary sectors could absorb only 54 per cent of the addition to labour force in this sector. The overall excess supply of labour over its demand was of the order of 31 per cent; it was 46 per cent in the manufacturing sector.

In absolute terms the surplus amounts to 38,623 persons, i.e. the size of labour available. To this surplus, the future growth in the labour force by the time the proposed industries go into full production has to be added. A simple arithmetic calculation gives the estimated labour supply as 237,549 by 2001 A.D. Total employment, existing and plus the projected, could be in the order of 206,559. This includes employment in the manufacturing and in the secondary sectors. Therefore, the question of labour shortage with the completion of the industries may not arise.

While this may be true in the context of overall supply of and demand for labour, there may exist shortage of certain categories of labour, particularly the skilled manpower. This, however would depend upon the growth in the skilled manpower required by these industries. (The projection of this aspect is however could not be attempted in this chapter).

Even in the mining sector, our exercise, though a limited one, does not bring out a situation of labour shortage in the near future.

While the analysis does not portray a picture of labour shortage, the sectoral growth in the expected growth in employment needs to be viewed with some seriousness. It is shown in this chapter that the growth in employment in the service and related sectors, which would be in the neighbourhood of three times the employment in the organised industries, would be mainly in the informal non-agricultural sector. Such a pattern, if it persists, has certain specific policy implications. These would be particularly in the direction of introducing strict enforcement of wage regulations, provision of basic labour welfare measures, prevention of employment of child labour, more particularly in health hazard occupations. The tendency to employ more of child labour may also become more pronounced in the event of a shortage of labour supply and in the face of rising wage rates for adult labour.

# APPENDIX

TABLE A1: CLASSIFICATION OF INDUSTRIAL WORK FORCE: BELLARY DISTRICT—RURAL & URBAN

| Category | Workforce (Popn.Census) | | Employment (Economic Census) | | Employment (Emp.Exchange) | |
|---|---|---|---|---|---|---|
| | 1981 | 1991 | 1981 | 1991 | 1992 | 1995 |
| 1. Cultivators | 219269 | 279349 | | | | |
| 2. Agri Labourers | 245415 | 358935 | | | | |
| 3. Livestock, forest, fisheries & others | 7521 | 10552 | 5127 | 4580 | 1860 | 1860 |
| 4. Mining & Quarrying | 15839 | 16661 | 1066 | 807 | 5634 | 6893 |
| 5. Mfg, serv. & repairs | 50198 | 47594 | 31342 | 25545 | 5608 | 6545 |
| (a) Household industry | 20435 | 12995 | | | | |
| (b) Other than Household industry | 29763 | 34599 | | | | |
| 6. Construction | 9233 | 13994 | 1323 | 1517 | 2921 | 2790 |
| 7. Trade & commerce | 34007 | 53756 | 41060 | 55273 | 854 | 967 |
| 8. Transport, storage & communication | 14901 | 19412 | 2571 | 3361 | 4400 | 4475 |
| 9. Others | 39718 | 52781 | 42415 | 56833 | 25859 | 27203 |
| Total | 636100 | 853035 | 124904 | 147916 | 47136 | 50733 |
| Total Population | 1489225 | 1890092 | | | | |

*Source*: Census of India 1981 and 1991, Series-9, General Economic Tables, Part III A & B (i). Economic Census 1980 and 1990; District Employment Exchange, Bellary.

**TABLE A2: EXISTING AND PROPOSED INVESTMENT AND EMPLOYMENT**

*(Rs. in crores)*

| | Large and Medium Industries | | | Small Scale Industries | | |
|---|---|---|---|---|---|---|
| | Units | Employment | Capital | Units | Employment | Capital |
| Existing | 20 | 13423 | 3512.04 | 6511 | 31013 | 47.56 |
| Proposed | 11 | NA | 10146.71 | | | |
| Proposed Downstream Industries | | | | 136 | 5310 | 128.25 |

**TABLE A3: TOTAL EMPLOYMENT IN FORMAL AND INFORMAL SECTORS (RURAL & URBAN) 1980 & 1990**

| Category | 1980 | | | 1990 | | |
|---|---|---|---|---|---|---|
| | Formal | Informal | Total | Formal | Informal | Total |
| Agri Own a/c Enterprises | 10 | 3100 | 3110 | 28 | 2525 | 2553 |
| Agri Establishments | 258 | 1759 | 2017 | 571 | 1456 | 2027 |
| Non Agri Own a/c Enterprises | 1002 | 52076 | 53078 | 772 | 59549 | 60321 |
| Non-Agri Establishments | 36788 | 29911 | 66699 | 44699 | 38316 | 83015 |
| Total | 38058 | 86846 | 124904 | 46070 | 101846 | 147916 |

**TABLE A4: NUMBER OF UNEMPLOYED BY SKILL STATUS**

| | Men | Women | Total |
|---|---|---|---|
| Technical | 1173 | 78 | 1251 |
| Administration | 5871 | 2589 | 8460 |
| Skilled | 3846 | 1 | 3847 |
| Others | 45510 | 6781 | 52301 |
| Total | 56400 | 9459 | 65859 |

*Source*: District Employment Exchanges Bellary and Hospet.

**TABLE A5: NORMS FOR PROJECTING LABOUR DEMAND**

| Norms | Large Scale (Based on 1984-85 data) | Small Scale (Based on 1975 data) |
|---|---|---|
| Technical | 8.98 | — |
| Administration | 16.54 | — |
| Skilled | 42.16 | 16.39 |
| Unskilled | 32.32 | 66.80 |
| Others | — | 16.80 |
| | 100.00 | 100.00 |

# 9

# TRADE UNIONS AND INDUSTRIAL RELATIONS

T.G. VITTAL and YERANNA

## Introduction

Bellary District, being a mineral-rich region in the State, has been attracting massive private investment into its iron and steel sector in the recent past. This is likely to have significant implications for work, working conditions, wage structure, welfare schemes, industrial relations and for trade union activity. The emerging industrial activity, in its initial phases, while generating employment opportunities for a large number of workers also creates a work environment in which the workers will be forced to organise themselves into trade unions. As the workers have to organise afresh, attempts will be made by worker-leaders and local leaders of all denominations to organise the workforce. Therefore, it is expected that while the degree of unionisation will be very high, unions will be highly heterogeneous in terms of their ideological affiliations. It follows from this, that the possibility of union rivalry and worker disunity will be very high creating thereby a high degree of industrial dispute potential. Such an unhealthy climate is likely to hamper industrial growth. Keeping in view the decisive role that industrial peace plays in promoting the interests of both the workers and the employers, it would be desirable to prepare a perspective plan for maintaining industrial harmony in the district. The purpose of this chapter is to assess the present position of unionisation of workers and industrial relations and to project into the future, the prospects regarding aspects covering work, wages and fringe benefits now available. A few case studies are undertaken with a view to assessing the scenario of management-labour relations. Having done that, it is the objective of this chapter also to state some policy recommendations.

## Origin and Evolution of Trade Unionism in Bellary District

The origin of trade union activity in the district can be traced back to the Second World War. During the War, petrol was rationed, and only those who had a fleet of 100 buses were eligible to draw petrol: the eligibility condition induced the bus owners to form themselves into guilds of their own; such unionisation amongst the bus owners drove the crew consisting of drivers, cleaners, conductors and automobile attendants to come together and form a trade union of their own. That is how trade union activity had its birth in the district. The movement so started out of petrol rationing got impetus with the emergence of relatively large scale economic activities such as the management of Tungabhadra Dam through T.B. Board, the Shutter Manufacturing Company (now known as Tungabhadra Steel Products Ltd.,) and Hydro Electricity Generation Schemes. The first ever strike launched by the Central Govt. Employees gave the much needed militancy to the workers' organisation. In Bellary, Mr. Dasan Solomon was one to face such dismissal, and the dismissal made him to take up the responsibility of organising workers into unions. Another milestone in the history of trade union movement goes with the termination of 500 workers by the management of NMDC, a Govt. of India undertaking, in 1969; this sad event led to the formation of NMDC Employees' Union and it was the first union in the mineral-based industries to get registered on 15-01-1969; and the first Engineering Union came into being on 02-01-1970. Thus, the trade union movement, in the strict sense of the term, has a history of only three to three and a half decades in Bellary district.

## Trade Union Potential

Among other factors, trade union activity, and its nature and extent, depend upon the nature and extent of employment that the proposed industrial investment generates. Notwithstanding the capital intensive technology that goes into the core sector, the Iron and Steel sector and its ancillary units are expected to cause phenomenal growth of employment. The manpower requirements for the emerging industrial activity have been estimated keeping the creation of additional capacity, input-output and capital-labour ratios as the bases. So far, the proposals for as many as 10 mega steel plants involving additional capacity amounting to 5.88

million tonnes of steel per annum are cleared by the State.

Presently the NMDC is producing 3 million tonnes and the private mine owners put together are producing 4 million tonnes of iron ore per annum. Hereafter, the production of iron ore needs to be stepped upto 8.8 million tonnes per annum to meet the requirements of the emerging units, of course, keeping the present export quantum in tact.

As it is, over 15,000 workers are engaged in the mining and mineral-based industries in Bellary-Sandur-Hospet belt. The new units are expected to create employment opportunities to about 6,150 workers. The DIC Bellary has identified 136 downstream industries with a job potential of about 12,825. From these estimates, it is obvious that in 4-5 years from now, the iron and steel sector along with its feeder industry and ancillaries would be employing nearly 34,000 workers.

## Unionisation and Industrial Relations: Present Position

In this section, to facilitate deeper insights, the present position is discussed at two levels : at the feeder industry levels, and at the core sector level.

### *Unionisation*

The mining operations in the district present a peculiar blend of direct and contract labour. Estimates vary as to the employment figures. The Mine Owners' Association puts the figure at 25,000, whereas the Employment Exchange puts it at 6,880, and the Provident Fund Office at 9,744. There are about 156 contractors employing about 8,584 workers as of September 1995. These figures do have implications for unionisation and industrial relations. Presently, the union activity has embraced only a portion of the workforce : with 99 mines (both public and private) we have only 21 unions operating covering 19 per cent of the mining industry; and the remaining portion of the industry and its workforce has yet to get into the fold of organised workforce. The emerging industrial activity is sure to attract a large number of workers into the region from the neighbouring districts and States with implications for union activity.

The situation is somewhat different in the mineral-based iron and steel sector. In this segment, the workers are better organised; almost all workers in all the units are under the umbrella of some union or the other. Of course, small scale units do not have any trade unions. As per the records of the Employment Exchange, there are 8 mini steel plants employing over 1,550 workers. The unions are affiliated to CITU and INTUC.

The AITUC and HMS have no base in the iron and steel sector, whereas CITU has no base in the mining sector, but INTUC is present in both the sectors. Further, the AITUC and INTUC dominate the mining sector, by claiming for themselves 6,000 and 3,100 workers respectively, leaving only 200 workers to HMS; in the iron and steel sector, INTUC claims 600, CITU 160 and other 300 workers. It is of interest to note that AITUC is concentrated in the public sector units, whereas others in the private sector units.

The nature and the quality of union leadership in the sectors under study are not qualitatively different from those obtaining in other sectors and in other regions of the country. There are unions with political affiliations, and there are unions which have no such affiliations. In the case of the former, the leaders are chosen/nominated by their respective central trade unions, while in the case of the latter, leadership emerges unilaterally from those who wield money-muscle-political power. The members of the former are relatively sensitised to participate in the political process, whereas the latter, by and large, confine themselves to the narrow spheres of individual interests; they do not hesitate to conspire with the management to curb the activities of the democratically functioning unions, and also in sacrificing the interests of their members for their personal gain. In such a situation, often room is made for the entry of criminal elements into unions, with which the patronage of unscrupulous politicians, criminalises the union activities. The region has the bitter experience in the recent past of using the country-made bombs by the conflicting interest groups to settle scores. In the given circumstances, democratic functioning of the trade unions seems to be a distant cry, specially in the mining sector where illiterate and unskilled labourers predominate. The situation is relatively better in the steel sector.

The aforesaid facts about the creation of additional capacity in the mining sector, iron and steel sector and the resultant impact on ancillary units, enable us to visualise the nature and extent of labour union activity and industrial relations in future. The doubling of workers in the region cannot but give a new dimension to trade union movement and leadership. A nefarious nexus between unscrupulous politicians, businessmen and criminals is likely to emerge in a big way with massive industrialisation.

## The Wage Structure

We observe wide inter-sectoral and intra-sectoral wage differentials in the region. The wages which the workers in the mining sector get are different from those which the workers in the steel sector get. Apart from that, within each sector also we notice wage differentials. Again, the wages which the permanent workers get are different from the wages which the contract labourers get. In the mining sector, the workers employed on permanent basis are paid daily wages as per the provisions of the Minimum Wages Act, whereas those engaged on contract basis are paid wages on the piece-work basis. The contract labourers get Rs. 10 to 35 per tonne for various operations such as sizing, cleaning, stacking and loading depending on the nature of ore. Most of the contract workers earn Rs. 40 to Rs. 80 a day. In the case of loading operations, workers get a higher rate per tonne, but their daily wage does not go beyond Rs. 30 since a part of the earnings (Rs. 1.15 per tonne) goes to the contractor. On the other hand, the permanent workers, based on the Minimum Wages Act, get a daily wage ranging from a minimum of Rs. 31.98 to a maximum of Rs. 57.06 (including variable dearness allowance calculated on the basis of consumer price index once in 6 months—April and October) depending upon skill differentials of the workers (Table 9.1).

TABLE 9.1: **The Minimum Wages Applicable from 1-10-1995 to Various Categories of Workers**

*(in Rs.)*

| Category of workers | For work above ground | | |
|---|---|---|---|
| | Basic | V.D.A * | Total |
| Unskilled | 28.00 | 3.98 | 31.98 |
| Semi-skilled/ Unskilled supervisory | 34.00 | 4.86 | 38.86 |
| Skilled/Clerical | 41.00 | 5.74 | 46.74 |
| Highly skilled | 50.00 | 7.06 | 57.06 |

(* V.D.A: Variable Dearness Allowance calculated on consumer price index every half year—April and October)

*Note*: In respect of mine workers the wages on piece rate vary from mine to mine. And further the rate also depends on the nature of ore. The rates commonly paid are as follows:

(1) Calibrated Ore: Semi-hard, Rs. 25 per tonne. Each mine worker will turn out 3 to 4 tonnes of iron ore every day earning an amount of Rs. 80 to Rs. 100. The size of the ore extracted will be from 10 mm size to 40 mm.

(2) Calibrated soft ore: Rs. 20 per tonne will be paid on each tonne extracted and the worker earns about Rs. 80 per day. The size of the ore remains as mentioned in item No.1 viz., 10 mm to 40 mm.

(3) Fine ore: Rs. 15 per tonne is paid to every worker and because of the very nature of the iron ore, each mine worker would be in a position to earn about Rs. 150 per day extracting approximately 10 tonnes a day

(4) Lump ore: Each worker will be paid Rs. 10 per tonne on the ore extracted and he extracts 4 to 5 tonnes a day. Thus, he earns around Rs. 40 to 50 per day.

The workers in the mini steel plants get relatively higher wages than those in the mining sector, *inter alia*, for the reason that the former are more organised and have relatively greater bargaining strength than the latter.

## Dispute Structure

The field study indicates reasonable harmony between the employers and the workers' organisations in the steel sector, whereas it is not so in the mining sector. The mining sector has its own record of disputes. There were 45 disputes in 1994 and 79 in 1995. Of the total of 124 disputes, 71 arose on account of non-payment of terminal benefits to the workers, 21 in connection with the settlement of charter of demands, 12 pertaining to cases of termination of workers, 9 owing to non-providing of employment, 3 because of lockouts and closures, 5 involving service conditions, and 3 for miscellaneous reasons (Table 9.2).

## Fringe Benefits

The workers in both the sectors enjoy some fringe benefits such as provident fund, bonus, medical benefit, etc. Of the two, the mining sector attracts more benefits than the iron and steel sector in the region. However, in terms of worker coverage of the scheme, the steel sector is better placed than the mining sector.

A perusal of the P.F. records of the mining sector shows that only 42 units out of 99 (42%) and 9,744 workers out of 15,464 workers (63%) are covered under the scheme. Whereas, in the steel sector all the 9 units and all the workers (1,473) excepting the executives, are covered under the scheme.

The workers are eligible for Bonus, and are also paid bonus once in a year. But the workers in the mining sector get different rates of bonus depending upon the mines in which they work; the inquiry reveals that in some of the mines, the workers are paid bonus at 8.33 per cent as provided in the payment of Bonus Act; in some prosperous mining companies the

TABLE 9.2: **Industrial Disputes Raised with Central Labour Department, Bellary in Bellary District**

| * | Total | Charter of Demands | Promotion | Termi-nation | Non-pay-ment of Terminal | Service conditions | Non-proceed-ing of employment | Miscella-neous | Lockout/ Closure |
|---|---|---|---|---|---|---|---|---|---|
| Jan. to Dec. 1994 | 45 | 12 | 1 | 3 | 19 | — | 8 | 2 | — |
| 1995 | 79 | 9 | — | 9 | 52 | 4 | 1 | 1 | 3 |

* During the year 1994: One case was referred to Regional Labour Commissioner, Bangalore. One case is pending, one case was quashed due to non-participation of the petitioner all the rest of the cases were disposed of.

During the year 1995: 6 Cases are pending, rest are settled.

rate of Bonus even touches the maximum of 20 per cent; and in some others the rate of Bonus is determined on the basis of bilateral agreements entered into between the employers and the employees' organisations. In the case of loading workers, the rate of bonus, unlike in other mining activities, is paid on the basis of tonnage loaded; a sum of 0.66 paise per tonne is earmarked by the employer towards bonus component, to be accumulated and payable once in a year. We do not notice differential rates of bonus in the steel sector. All the workers, whether permanent, temporary or on contract, are eligible for bonus as per Bonus Act.

The institutions which extend medical facilities to the two sectors are different. The medical benefit which the workers of the mining sector enjoy come under the administrative purview of labour welfare organisation of the Government of India, whereas the steel sector employees come under the purview of ESI (Employees State Insurance Scheme) of the Government of Karnataka.

There are hospitals at Hospet, Sandur and Bellary exclusively to cater to the medical needs of the mining workers of the region. At Kariganur, one of the oldest mining areas in the district, there is a 25-bed hospital with X-Ray facility. The workers who undergo cataract operation are given Rs. 75 each to buy spectacles. For those who suffer from some of the deadly diseases which cannot be treated in these hospitals, financial assistance is extended; the workers, who are advised to go in for kidney transplantation, are given a grant of Rs. 10,000. Further, the workers who lose attendance owing to illness are given a subsistence allowance of Rs. 200 a month. The members of workers' families are also eligible for the medical facilities.

The employees of the Steel sector are covered by ESI (Employees State Insurance Scheme). All those workers whose monthly income does not exceed Rs.3000 are covered under the scheme. Under this scheme the beneficiaries are expected to pay 1.5 per cent of their gross wages/salaries as contribution towards ESI. In the district, of the nine steel plants, five mills with 1325 workers are covered by ESI scheme. They are B.S. Rolling Mills (156), B.S.A.L (758), Navakarnataka Steels Ltd. (337), Shanti Steels (36) and Chamundeswari Steels (38). Here it is to be pointed out that the scheme is not compulsory for the employers; such of those employers who offer better medical facilities than those offered under the ESI scheme, can remain outside the purview of the ESI Scheme. The SMIORE is the lone example in the district to claim exemption from the scheme by providing better facilities than those offered by the ESI scheme under private sector. The labour welfare organisation, which collects a cess from the mine owners at Re. 1 per tonne of iron ore, Rs. 2 per tonne of manganese ore, and Rs. 4 per tonne of crome ore, provides some other facilities to the mine workers and their families in addition to the medical benefits mentioned.

The workers' children are eligible for scholarship ranging from Rs. 250 to Rs. 3000 per annum to meet their expenses of schooling and collegiate education both for general and technical.

The Labour Welfare Organisation also extends financial assistance to the workers in the form of subsidy at differential rates, for different type of houses to be built by the workers. Type 'A' houses attract 75 per cent subsidy subject to a maximum of Rs. 30,000; Type 'B' houses attract 75 per cent subsidy subject to a maximum of Rs. 20,000; and other type of houses attract Rs. 10,000 interest free loan repayable in 9 years with a subsidy component of Rs. 3000.

The mining workers get some community services on subsidy basis, such as bore wells for labour colonies (50% subsidy) purchase of school bus by employers (Rs. 2.25 lakhs subsidy per bus), Colour T.V. Sets for community centres (Rs. 10,000 per set), purchase of medical ambulance (Rs. 75,000 subsidy per van), drinking water tanks, and grants for family planning operations.

## Case Studies

With the express intention to capture the factual situation of industrial relations, a few case studies are undertaken. Based on the access to reasonably reliable sources of information and data, 5 units are selected—2 from the mining sector, 2 from the steel sector, and one chemical unit; of the five, 2 units are from Hospet Taluka, 2 from Bellary Taluka and one from Sandur Taluka. The units chosen are those where union activity is relatively live.

### *Calcium Carbides*

The Panyam Cement's Calcium Carbide factory situated on Karnataka - Andhra border at Hagari village, which is 14 Kms. away from Bellary presents a peculiar case of criminalisation and politicisation of union activity at the cost of industrial relations which have a bearing on the interests of both the employers and the employees. It is a case where industrial peace is often disturbed, not because of the grievances of the workers but because of the inter-factional rivalries of the union leaders aided and abetted by outside political-criminal elements. A series of reciprocal murders have been committed inside and outside the premises of the factory. *The Indian Express* dated 24.1.96 reports 30 such murders during the last 10 years.

*Bellary Steel and Alloys Ltd.*

The Bellary Steel and Alloys Ltd., Bellary, presents another peculiar case of industrial relations, in which the management publicly claims that it has never resorted to any unfair labour practice as specified in any of the labour enactments. Whereas, the union office bearers contend that the management has been resorting to not only anti-labour practices but also to anti-union activities. The official records show that BSAL employees' Union affiliated to the Centre of Indian Trade Unions, was the first to come into existence on 31.10.90. Another union came into being on 13.6.91 in the name of Bellary Steel & Alloys Employees' Union; it is not affiliated to any central trade union. The office bearers of the first union complained management's inimical attitude towards their union leading to not only rupture of industrial relations but also forcing them to seek judicial remedy instead of bilateral solution as proclaimed in the recent industrial relations policy. It is said that by sensing the militant attitude by the aggrieved workers, the management on the pretext of power cut declared lay off since the 1st week of December 1995. The overall situation does not appear to be conducive for the growth of healthy industrial relations.

*Tungabhadra Minerals Ltd., Taranagar & M/S Baladota, Hospet*

Messrs Mineral Sales Pvt. Ltd., belonging to Baldota Group of Companies and T.M. Ltd., (TML) Taranagar, the two leading mining companies, present yet another peculiar feature of union-management relations. The trade union functioning in the former is affiliated to HMS, whereas the one in TML is affiliated to AITUC. Both the unions are reasonably enlightened enough to assert their rightful claims as and when the occasions demand. It is learnt that identifying the dissatisfaction of the workers about the functioning of their union in Baldotas, AITUC made an attempt to organise the workers under its banner in 1979. However, the attempt was reportedly thwarted by the management by filing a complaint under the relevant sections of IPC and Cr.PC., and a case was filed with the District and Sessions Judge, Bellary. In the second case, it is said that the management declared lockout against the workmen for their alleged demonstration against the Chairman of the company demanding variable dearness allowance that was due to be paid to them. The workers finding it extremely difficult to get the dispute resolved through official machinery, had to approach political functionaries to settle the dispute. And it was settled that way only. It is a case where the workers were forced to seek the redressal of their grievance through political interference.

## SMIORE

SMIORE provides a lone example in the region for reasonably enlightened management approach to industrial relations. It has been consistently maintaining industrial peace and harmony without giving any room either for a strike or lockout. The management's secret of success on the industrial relations front is on account of a few benevolent practices. The workers get relatively better wages when compared to their counterparts in the neighbourhood; probably the medical care that they get is something unique in the sector; more than that, their policy of subsidising the edibles which regularly go into the consumption basket of the workers, has contributed significantly to promote and sustain mutually healthy relations between the management and the workers. The essential items like rice, tur dhal, chillies, jaggery, edible oil, wheat, wheat products and jowar are supplied to the workers virtually at a throw away price; the subsidy component ranges from a minimum of 70 per cent to a maximum of 94 per cent (Table 9.3). The subsidy which each worker enjoys every month comes to Rs. 800. In addition to this, each worker is given Rs.1500 per

TABLE 9.3: **Food Subsidy Scheme in vogue at SM & IO, Sandur**

| Sl. No. | Commodities | Qnty. Kgs/Ltr. | Open Market Price | Subsidy Price |
|---|---|---|---|---|
| 1. | Rice | 25 | 13.00 | 2.00 |
| 2. | Tur Dhal | 3 | 32.00 | 2.20 |
| 3. | Chillies | 1 | 72.00 | 4.60 |
| 4. | Jaggery | 2 | 11.00 | 2.00 |
| 5. | Sweet Oil | 2 | 38.00 | 6.50 |
| 6. | Gram Dhal | 1 | 12.00 | 2.00 |
| 7. | Wheat | 5 | 8.00 | 1.75 |
| 8. | Upma Rava | 2 | 10.00 | 3.00 |
| 9. | White Jowar or | 20 | 7.50 | 1.00 |
| | Hybrid Jowar | 27 | 5.50 | 0.75 |

annum to buy clothing for himself and his family; the amount is not repayable. The company has its own educational institutions—primary to collegiate level. The company claims that the aim of its overall functioning is "skills for employment and improved employability is at the heart of the problem of development and growth with social justice".

**Summary and Conclusions**

The emerging industrial situation in the private sector and the massive investment that flows into it, among other things, has significant implications for work, wage, welfare and industrial relations. An estimated investment of Rs. 15,000 crore in the core sector, Rs. 1,000 crore in the ancillary sector and a few thousand crores in the feeder iron ore industry gives rise to a new structure in terms of ownership; hereafter, private sector will dominate the overall industrial activity; the public sector will get pushed to the secondary position. Despite capital intensive technology that goes into the core sector, the ancillary units and the feeder industry, which are relatively labour intensive, put together, are likely to create additional jobs for about 20,000 persons, in various categories ranging from unskilled to highly skilled. This magnitude of job generation provides ample scope for worker concentration, unionisation and the problems that go with it.

The shadow of industrialisation paves the way for unionisation, especially in the mining and ancillary sectors. With the growth of worker concentration and through the influx of immigrant workers who bring with them their experience and knowledge, the situation may become ripe for asserting workers' rights. The existing unions in the region will swell in membership and some new unions will emerge. The advent of politicians of all hues and cries may in the initial stages lead to fragmentation of workers who may be enticed into their fold. This will give scope for many politicians concentrating on workforce as their fodder and workers getting divided leading to formation of many trade unions (individual and political). Further the competition to grapple more and more workers into their fold begins. The dominant unions come to put up stiffer demands questioning the very nature of the earlier settlements and linking up of their demands with the performance of the company. This may in turn give scope for inter-union rivalry.

There is likelihood of lumpensation of a section of workers aided by the money power of the owners and politicians. The other workers who on their part may have no choice but to militate against such tendencies which in turn may be extended to larger area. This will add political dimension to industrial problems. Yet the unions may have to function with the existing politician-criminal interference at least in the transition period of 5 to 6 years. Some managements may continue to discourage democratic functioning of the unions. As such, the animosity between the managements and the workers' unions may disturb industrial peace, unless both of them change their very philosophy of relationship.

In future, the trade unions will conduct their activities keeping in mind the threat of losing jobs owing to massive automation. The managements will be going in for massive automation with the twin objectives of cost minimisation on the one hand, and minimisation of labour problems on the other. Of the two parties, the managements are likely to have more bargaining strength; they can always use the weapon of automation to contain and control union activities.

With "Jobless growth" phenomenon waiting in the wings, the labour unions are likely to change their attitudes in dealing with the management. They can no more restrict their activity to the charter of economic demands; they have to transcend the boundaries of mere economism to develop industrial relations afresh, not on the notion of confrontation but on the notion of co-operation. The workers' needs will grow along with the prosperity of the private units in which they work. Similarly the attitude of the managements' needs also acquire the same dimension. Specific programmes may have to be structured to educate both the parties, to identify their roles in maintaining industrial harmony in the changing scenario.

The experience of SMIORE has shown that industrial peace of a positive nature can be created and sustained by extending fair wages and a host of welfare schemes to the workers. The emerging units in the core sector, feeder industries and the ancillary sector, and the unions therein may also think of replicating SMIORE's experience of success in maintaining healthy industrial relations. Again based on the bitter experience in some units like the calcium carbide and B.S.A.L they may take every precaution to prevent politicisation and criminalisation of industrial relations; otherwise industrial conflicts may attract the interference of unscrupulous politicians who want both the money of the managements and the votes of the workers.

Given the skill of the manpower now available in the region, a substantial portion of the high-skill jobs in the mega-steel plants may be filled in by outsiders. Such a trend may bring to the surface the spirit of the 'sons-of-the-soil' theory with its unqualified potential for industrial disharmony. In the circumstances, the locals, instead of registering protests and disturbing peace may have to acquire and upgrade their skills to meet the needs of the mega-steel plants. The managements on their part can minimise the negative impact of 'sons-of-the-soil' movement by filling most of the jobs warranting lower skills with the local persons, and also by starting training institutes to train the locals to acquire the skills required to work in their units.

# 10

# INDUSTRIALISATION AND ECOLOGICAL DISASTER

K.G. VASUKI

## Introduction

A massive size of investment is expected to take place in Bellary district following the establishment of steel mills and along with them when several downstream industries are going to be started. As the steel mills are mineral based, mining of minerals, especially iron ore, will be accelerated. Though the district is apparently going to be benefited by such an industrialisation process, the latter will create some negative externalities. One such externality is the ecological disturbance. It is proposed in this chapter to examine the negative externalities of the proposed industrialisation of the district and to indicate how these externalities should be internalised.

## Physical Features of the District

Bellary district is situated almost in the centre of the State. The district is elongated in the South West-North East direction. Physiographically, Bellary district has been divided into eastern and western blocks. The Sandur hills which run North West-South East directions divide eastern and western blocks. It is important to note that the eastern division is a flat terrain. But it has small clusters of hills. The elevation of these hills ranges from 355 metres to 586 metres above MSL. But the western division forms largely a rugged hilly terrain. Its elevation ranges from 508 meters to 1099 meters. Bellary district has Tungabhadra, Hagari and Chikkahagari and other tributaries as rivers.

The Sandur hills which include Kumaraswamy hill (1036 m), copper Mountain range (1001 m) which has Mallappana Gudda range including Mallappanabetta (968 m) and Kullahalli range which includes Kallahalli peak and Kudligi hills which is also called Kailasa Konda are the important hill ranges of Bellary district. Apart from this, the hilly clusters like Daroji, Kampli, Kurgodu and Bellary also form important hill ranges.

The rainfall of the district is 639 mm (average annual rainfall—July to November) which is very low compared to the State average. The slopes of the Sandur hills account for some vegetational cover in the district. It has valuable flora-fauna, which are in danger because of the mining activity. The hill range and the plain terrain have red and black cotton soil caps which are high in nutrients for crop cultivation.

After presenting the physiography of Bellary district, it is important to take note of the available mineral resources in the district. The mineral resources that are available can be divided into metallic, non-metallic and minor minerals. The metallic minerals are iron ore, manganese ore, red oxide, gold, copper and lead, the non-metallic minerals are andalessite, asbestos, corundum, clay, dolomite, gypsum, limestone, lime kankar moulding sand, quartz, soap stone and red ochre, and the minor minerals are ornamental pink and grey granite, granite building stone and sand.

## Impact on Ecology

The massive industrialisation that is taking place in Bellary district is a part of the globalisation process. The type of industries which are coming up here are mostly based on minerals. The existing industries in the district are also dependent on mineral resources. There are many Iron and Steel plants which are mainly processing iron ore. An iron and steel plant is a potential source of environmental pollution. The pollutants in the form of solids, liquids and gases are generated vastly in any iron and steel industry. These pollutants have a hazardous effect on the environment especially on the flora and fauna. The air pollutants in a steel plant are mainly dust and gases such as sulphur dioxide, carbon monoxide and nitrogen oxide. Air, in and over the plant area and beyond its boundaries, gets polluted with gases, fumes and dust particles emanating from the industries. Sulphur dioxide is formed in considerable quantity when coal, coke or certain fuel oils are burnt. Sulphur dioxide can cause greater damage if it is emitted in greater quantity. From a consideration of atomic weights it is seen that a molecule of sulphur dioxide weighs twice as much as an atom of sulphur. So, for each tonne of sulphur in the fuel there are nearly two tonnes of sulphur dioxide in the fuel gases and it is estimated that an average of nearly three tonnes of sulphur dioxide is emitted from every hundred tonnes of coal or coke burnt. The gas is responsible for acid rain. A record of industries in Bellary district and the amount of gas emitted per day by them has to be maintained to understand the damage caused by these industries. As part the of the field work when the present writer went to some of the industries it was noticed that not even a single industry was seen with any measure to prevent atmospheric pollution. Apart from this, these industries also cause a lot of water and noise pollution. The waste material from these industries are very hazardous. A visit to three hospitals in Hospet, Kariganur and Bellary revealed that more number of patients are suffering now from chronic bronchitis, tuberculosis and waterborne diseases. This fact is a clear indication of the air quality and air pollution. A regular air quality assessment is necessary and called for.

The Pollution Control Board data shows that there are some 16 large-scale industries which have an investment of more than Rupees fifteen thousand crores. Almost all these industries are iron and steel processing units which are a source of air pollution. The moulding sand dump is increasing day by day and has a genuine cause for concern.

As stated earlier, many industries are coming up in Bellary district and according to an analysis the mining activity will increase by three fold in course of time. The open cast mining is a threat to environment The miners blast the earth with explosives and take out iron ore. In this process, the blast and the debris or dust cause a lot of pollution. As per a reliable source, one tonne of iron ore produces three tonnes of dust and debris. The wind blowing South-east blows the dust and spreads it to a radius of nearly 30 Km from the mining area. The dust storm which does not settle down is a nuisance to atmosphere and it is a major source of health problem. Hospet, Toranagal, Sandur, part of Bellary and many small villages are facing the problem of dust and the consequent ailments like bronchitis, tuberculosis and breathing disorders. The ecological degradation caused by the mining activity leads to undesirable change in temperature, rain pattern, humidity, top soil loss, increase in erosion and siltation.

We cannot imagine Bellary district without the river Tungabhadra. As per the available statistics, because of the mining siltation the dam water storage capacity has come down by 25 per cent. This is an alarming development. The tanks in Kamalapur, Daroji and other canals are filled with the mining debris which has reduced the water storing capacity and is causing health hazard to people and bovine population. One can see the red water flowing everywhere in Bellary district which is mainly because the mining dust and siltation are carried by it. As mentioned earlier, top soil forms within several feet. Once the top soil goes, the soil becomes dead, loses its fertility and leads to erratic temperature. Bellary always witnessed a variation in temperature—either it touches the highest or the lowest level. The soil loses its characteristic of absorbing heat or chill. This is one of the major factors leading to the ecological disaster in Bellary district. The debris and the dust are a great threat to the flora and fauna. This is evident from the present status of the Sandur belt which once had a thick forest cover but now because of mining activity it has lost all its vegetational cover leading to ecological degradation. As stated earlier, siltation is causing a great danger to agriculture. The storage capacities of Tungabhadra dam and other tanks and canals have come down. But both the industrial and agricultural sectors are dependent on river Tungabhadra for their water requirement and this dependence is increasing day by day. This is causing a great pressure on the river.

As one could see from the mining activities, blasting is a major contributor to the ecological degradation. The blast in the open mining is very crude and this leads to noise pollution and dust pollution. According to R. Nijagunappa, Director, Gulbarga University Post Graduate Centre, Nandihalli, the tremors are a great threat to ecology and causing damages to monuments at Hampi (Recent example is the crack developed on the Stone chariot).

The mine blasts are said to be causing tremors as under earthquake conditions. This is evident from the data collected for a three-year period at Gouri Bidanur Seismic Array ; it has recorded thousands and thousands of tremors which are in the magnitude of 4.0 to 5.0 in the richter scale. If the mining activity increases further due to industrial needs certainly we are going to face disasters of greater magnitude.

The Tungabhadra dam is situated very close to the mining range. Just 2 Kms from the dam site one can see intense mining activity going on. With increased demand for ore mining activity close to dam site is likely to increase further. This will certainly have an adverse repercussion. Pressure on the dam is day by day building up as of now. In future the pressure will be more causing damage to the dam itself.

Let us also examine the nature and type of blasts. Each blast is like a bomb exploding. The miners use gelatine sticks, ammonium nitrate, fuse and detonators and diesel for blast. They dig holes which vary from two inch dia to six inch dia. And the depth is around 8 to 15 feet. They mix amonium nitrate with diesel and fill it up in the hole. Then the gelatine sticks are placed in the hole with the detonators. The hole is sealed with ammonium nitrate; with a wick, a man kindles the fire. They also use the electronic devices. In a mine an approximate 3 kg gelatine and 20 kg of ammonium nitrate mixed with 5 litres of diesel are used as explosives for a hole of 4 mm dia and 10 feet deep. They use 60 to 150 blasts per day depending upon the production requirement. More production means more blasts. These blasts as stated above are causing a lot of tremors scaling in between 4 to 5 in Richter scale. This will increase by three fold and the effect will be disastrous.

Taking into consideration the present production of iron ore and other minerals, the deposits will last for only 30 to 35 years. The future is blank. Bellary district will become a desert with red dust flowing all over. People are going to get a lot of diseases which are probably unknown to the health community. The debris or mine slush or the waste is so useless that not even a single tree will grow on that. This is evident from Kudremukh experience. Mangalore University has taken a project of experimenting to give vegetational cover to the mining debris. But even 10 years after that attempt not even a single tree has grown over there. It is evident that vegetation cover is not possible at all on such sites. The same thing would repeat in Bellary district. Imagine the Bellary district map having no vegetation, no natural resources and only full of diseases. A traumatic experience is in store for the people over there.

The damage has already been done. But it is our prime concern that we should protect all the available natural resources from further exploitation. Industrialisation is not an answer to development. As it is, the district portrays a tale of sad picture.The repercussion from the abuse of natural resources is unknown. People should realise the gravity of situation. The participation of the people at local level to understand the local needs and solve the local problems is essential. Rules governing the environment protection are not at all there. Employment generated by these industries will not help even one per cent of the population. But the exploitation of mineral deposits in terms of value is crores and crores of rupees. But the amount of money the district is getting by the so-called developmental activities is to be ascertained by the economists. They should also find out the ecological degradation in relation to the value gained. It is not possible to repair the damage done. But the question now is: Is it not possible to stop further ecological degradation. The amount of industrialisation and the policies of the Government clearly shows that it is not possible to curtail ecological depletion. Bellary district faces the threat of becoming a desert. Therefore, keeping all these repercussions in view a few guidelines may be given for consideration of the policy makers.

1. The mining technology should be updated. In Canada, mining is done without toppling the top soil. The same technology may be used for mining in future.
2. The industrialists who are depending on the mineral resources and the mine owners should be made responsible for the development of the area. They should be made responsible for providing drinking water system, protecting the rivers, maintenance of good hospitals and other related development activities.
3. The Government is getting just Rs. 10 crores per year as royalty. The lease contract rates should be raised by 500 per cent and this may help us to repair the damage wrought by unmindful mining activity.
4. The industries which are involved in iron and steel processing must adhere to the pollution control norms. They should spend 30 per cent of the budget for the pollution control measures.
5. The blasts are a cause of concern. The mining technology should be updated and the technology available in Canada and other countries to minimise the blast should be imported.
6. A seismographic station should be commissioned at Bellary to monitor the tremors and to control the blasts.
7. The industrialists and the mine owners should be made responsible for desilting the Tungabhadra dam. The process should become a pre-condition to the newly coming industries.
8. NGO's should be given free hand to monitor and deal with the industries. As the governmental agencies have failed to implement the norms regarding pollution, NGO's should be allowed to take up this role and it is necessary that a legislation to that effect should be passed.
9. Catchment basins should be located to trap all sediment that might flow from the mine area.
10. Steps should be taken to instal ropeways in place of roads for transportation of the iron ore.
11. Iron and manganese ore fines which are sources of ground water pollution should be utilised after pellatization.
12. A committee of the local people drawn from all walks of life should be constituted to monitor and control the polluting

industries. A legislation in this regard is necessary.

13. Soil conservation measures such as contour ploughing, strip cropping, rotation of crops, planting of cover crops and other methods should be practiced.
14. It is necessary to recall a case filed in the court by the Vice-Chancellor of the Gulbarga University against the mine blasts and noise pollution around the Nandihalli campus. Some such public interest litigations have to be filed wherever ecology is disturbed.
15. Revegetation methods such as planting of trees should be adopted in the mining area.

These are the measures that can be adopted to prevent further ecological degradation in Bellary district. As seen from the practices and the loopholes in the laws we have no positive belief in this regard. Therefore, the NGO's and the local people should protect the ecology of the land by playing a more active role in future.

# 11

# CONSUMERISM, MONEY-LENDING AND LIQUOR TRADE

MANOHAR YADAV

## Introduction

The main purpose of this chapter is to deal with the problems likely to be created by the phenomenon of consumerism which is expected to emerge as a part of the process of industrial development of Bellary District. Although consumerism, on its face, appears to be facilitative in many ways its side effects are not less in number. Sometimes they are diverse, varied and dangerous in nature, capable of causing any number of dismal social consequences. However, an attempt is made here to confine ourselves only to two of its follow-up activities, namely—money-lending and liquor trade.

## Money-lending

The money market has organised and unorganised segments. The organised forms include the commercial and the co-operative banks; and the unorganised forms include registered minor individual or private finance corporations, indigenous financial agencies consisting of money-lenders, pawn-brokers and the chit fund practitioners. The sale of consumer goods involving instalments and other forms of sales promotion schemes can also be regarded as concealed unorganised forms of money-lending.

There are 93 commercial and 80 rural banks presently operating in the district of Bellary. Also there are 23 urban and eight primary land development Banks in the district. To meet the demands of various segments of the society, 24 cooperative societies have been functioning in the district. In Bellary sub-division alone such societies number 528. In proper Bellary township, 14 commercial banks have been functioning. But all these organised financial institutions have not been able to meet the credit needs of all the sections of society all the time. Only about 12 per cent of the credit needs of the general public including the farmers are met by the cooperative credit societies; and the commercial banks have been able to meet only 25 per cent of the credit needs of the district. The remaining 63 per cent of the credit needs are to be met by the money-lenders and other unknown sources of credit. Hence, despite the existence of a large number of commercial and cooperative credit banks, the native financial agencies consisting of money-lenders and indigenous bankers continue to hold a fairly important place in the money-market of Bellary.

So as to regulate their business activities many restrictions have been imposed upon these indigenous money-lenders. But their number is always on the increase. There were 155 registered money-lenders in the sub-divisions of Bellary and Hospet in the year 1985. But the number rose to 301 in the year 1995. This means just over a decade, money-lending business in Bellary and Hospet divisions has almost doubled. This is just a documental evidence. The unregistered money-lenders are countless in number in the district. Their share in the rural credit is also not less significant. Almost 40 per cent of the credit needs of the farmers and landless labourers are met by the indigenous money-lenders.This speaks of their dominance in the rural credit system. Their hold over the urban common mass is still more significant and oppressive in nature. A municipal employee in the Hospet township said that none of his fellow workers was free from the burden of loan taken from the local money lenders and that many of them had lost their valuables in the pawn-brokers shop. Money is usually lent on the time length basis and a loan can be extended on the basis of day's interest, week's interest or of month's interest.

In the urban areas of Hospet, Bellary and Sandur, money lenders mostly finance the street vendors, rickshaw pullers, vegetable vendors, residents of workers' colonies, lower middle class employees, municipal workers and slum dwellers. In an area of "Siddalinga Chowki" of Hospet town a pathan is known to have been financing the rickshaw pullers and vegetable vendors on the day's basis of interest. The rate of interest is 20 per cent. A person who borrows Rs. 10 in the morning will have to return Rs. 12 in the evening. A popular rich man in the Ranipete area of Hospet lends money to the general public only to buy the consumer durables such as TV, tape recorder, refrigerator etc. Some of the slum dwellers in Indira Nagar have got loans from this lender to purchase such goods!

Further there are indigenous unorganised bankers in the district who act as master money-lenders or as bankers to the money lenders. If necessary, money-lenders borrow funds from such indigenous bankers. These bankers usually lend any amount of money to persons of their knowledge and trust. Although they operate in the urban areas, their business flourishes even in the rural areas as they operate through the rich landlords.

Because of their direct personal contacts all the money-lenders have their own area of operation including villages. In Bellary township many of the money-lenders are concentrated in the areas of Kaul Bazaar and Bruspet. Each one of them has a definite area of operation. Some of them choose to operate even in the gambling centres or Clubs of Bellary township where they receive double the amount they pay to the customers. The other areas of Bellary township where money lenders seem to be concentrated are Shrirampur colony, Millerpet, the Railway colony, flower street, etc. Much of the district's money-lending business is carried on by Marwaries, Pathans, Multanies and Shroffs. More than 60 per cent of the credit needs of the district are met by these professional and non-professional money-lenders.

Apart from money-lending business, there are various other forms of informal money transactions taking place in the district such as sale and purchase of consumer goods on instalment basis with interest payments, chit fund operations, benefit schemes. Already many of the townships of Bellary district have become the domain of many such business activities. Naturally complex transactions have also emerged. Illegal operation of sales promotion schemes, instalment-based sale and purchase of goods etc., have been put on the market. For instance, there is a discount benefit scheme for the sale of a motor-bike. A person who becomes a member of this scheme by paying Rs. 975 will get eight tickets, each bearing the value of Rs. 975. He will have to sell all of them to other customers. Only after selling all these tickets, will he get the vehicle. If he fails to sell the tickets, he will get nothing and loses Rs. 975.

According to informants in Bellary too similar sales promotion strategies are followed by two wheeler, furniture and dress sellers. The instalments are many and easy but the sum involved is very large. A lady informant said, if it were to be on the instalment basis, each item they sell is doubly charged and that is how the customers are unknowingly taxed. "Yet, people go to them". This is how interest is extracted in the guise of easy instalments.

The chit fund operators have also started calling shots in the Bellary money-market. There are about five registered chit fund companies operating in the Bellary and Hospet divisions. But this is not even one per cent of the actually operating firms. In almost half of the total wards of Bellary and Hospet, the chit fund operations go on in open. Some of the professionals in ward No. 20-21 and 11 and 12 of Hospet are engaged in chit fund operations. In Bellary, the chit fund business is an open secret in the wards coming under the areas of Bruspet and Gandhinagar police stations.

Each of the chit fund companies consists of 10 to 20 members including the foreman. The members deposit certain amount of money every month and get together to dispose it of by bidding for that month. In the process of bidding, one who bids the highest discount is said to have won in the bidding competition and will get the money back during that month. There can also be a method of picking up the beneficiary out of the subscribers where durable goods and articles are involved in the transaction. The net gainer in all such cases is the foreman.

However, chit fund involves some risks to the subscribers. The foreman who is conducting the chit may run away before completing the chit instalments. There is no security over the deposited money for the non-bidders. There is also a possibility that the public may get cheated by the foremen of the chit funds. Both Bellary and Hospet are replete with such cases of cheated chits. The police have registered some such cases. Gandhinagar Police in Bellary have registered two such cases. In Hospet, the town station has received three complaints of chit fund cheating.

### *Conducive Conditions for Money-lending in Bellary*

There are a variety of reasons for the money-lending business to come up in a society. But the main reason is the need of the borrower and the non-availability of loanable funds on easier and simpler terms in the organised money-market. In Bellary district as on date there are 20 large and medium-scale industries and 103 small-scale industries. The number of employees in these industries add upto 44,152. But this is not all. The entire urban working population of 1,90,564 and the rural working force of 6,62,471 which belongs to the lower classes will need money to meet a variety of contingent circumstances. A mine worker in a GB Camp (MMTC) colony told, "that only because of the money-lender's help that he and his fellow workers could survive under the compelling circumstances". Money-lenders come to the rescue of workers at any moment of need. The leading Marwari traders lend money as also advance consumer goods on instalment basis. Many of the workers in the Kariganur mining camp have obtained consumer items from such Marwari merchants on instalment basis. But the price charged has always been double the actual market price. In certain cases where collection becomes very difficult, the money-lenders hire the Goonda elements to recover the loan amount. In Jindal, it is said, the Goonda elements are already operating.

The over-bridge slum dwellers of Gandhinagar area of Bellary opined that the organised financial institutions were of less use to them and for them there was no way out but to beg at the feet of money-lenders for timely help. But one of the Bank Managers in Bellary gave a different version. He said that there were several schemes of credit for the benefit of the slum dwellers, SC/STs and other backward classes. The Scavengers' Credit Scheme, the Mass Banking Scheme, housing loan scheme, differential rate of interest scheme (with just 4 per cent of interest for the poor), weaker section housing loan scheme, self-employment scheme, etc. But very few knew about these schemes. He also said that the poor were not prompt in repaying loan to the Banks. Hence bankers always are cautious while lending to such classes. Many a time they insist on some kind of a security which the poor cannot provide. Under the circumstance, the poor have no option but to turn towards money-lenders who offer loans on simple and easier terms. The informality of the money-lenders' dealings, direct personal contacts and the ease and readiness with which they lend to these sections to a large extent account for their survival and popularity.

*Money-lending in Future*

With this backdrop of the general reasons leading to the rise of money-lending business, an attempt is made to project the future scenario concerning the growth of money-lending in Bellary District. At the outset, some amount of comparison between Bellary and Hospet with regard to money-lending business would be useful to us to work out roughly the magnitude of money-lending business in Bellary district in the near future. Presently the township of Hospet shows more number of money-lenders than in Bellary town. This is because Hospet is industrially more advanced than Bellary proper and that is why it has got a more fertile ground for money-lenders than Bellary proper does. This is an indication of the fact that industrialisation accompanied by urbanisation and consumerism is sure to increase the number of money-lenders. Hence, it can be roughly surmised that higher the degree of industrialisation the more would be the number of money-lenders.

Now, let us work out how prosperous would be the money-lending business in the near future in the emerging environment of industrialisation, urbanisation and consumerism. This exercise can be carried out in the light of our earlier understanding of the compelling circumstances leading to the growth of money-lending business. In the process of industrial development, Bellary will need all sorts of services including domestic and construction services. In response, workers will come in search of jobs. Builders, hawkers, street vendors, helpers, hamals, skilled and unskilled labourers will all flow into the district making it an asylum of all classes of people. In a short period of time, this influx of population will become the part of the process of industrialization and urbanisation. It will also gradually get into the network of complex consumerism which is bound to emerge along with the other two processes. The increase in the circulation of money, earnings and purchasing power of these people will make them respond to the market-beckons created by the wind of consumerism. These people will also try to adopt the life styles of the affluent sections of the society. They will be very much tempted to buy items like radio, TV, tape recorders, pressure cooker, luna or moped and to take to gambling, drinking, visiting restaurants and so on.

The rising spending spree on luxury consumer goods, services, intoxicants, and recreations may put heavy financial pressure on these groups. But since their earnings will not be adequate to meet such demands, they will instinctively try to find out sources, which may include borrowing from friends, relatives etc. If they fail to get money from friends and relatives, they may opt for help from formal financial institutions. But as we have noted earlier since they will not get credit from the organised financial institutions due to technical difficulties, they will then turn to the informal sector money-lenders.

Though consumerism can be counted to be the main reason for the growth of indigenous money-lending transactions, in the industrial set-up of Bellary district, the other force of circumstances will also have an important say in the matter. In the industrial set-up of a society, the vulnerable sections will have a variety of contingent needs such as marriage expense needs, birth and death celebration needs, festival needs, school or sickness needs or even the needs of procuring basic necessities of life such as food, clothing, shelter or minor medical care. To meet such contingent needs, these sections invariably have to depend entirely upon the money lenders.

This is how a favourable environment will be created for the growth and survival of the money-lenders who, having emerged as a class, will build a money-market for themselves around the industrial belt, charge high interest rates. And to collect the money back they do not hesitate to hire goonda elements and to indulge in questionable practices.

Measures to keep control over money-lenders:

(a) Strict implementation of the provisions of the Karnataka Money Lenders Act.

(b) Impose heavy security deposit, depending upon the amount involved and the nature of money transactions in the money lending business.

(c) Raise the license fees to the maximum level.

(d) Illegal transactions should attract a heavy penalty or serious punishment.

(e) Appointment of a full time Assistant Registrar for overseeing money lending and granting him power to check illegal transactions.

(f) In respect of chit funds, the money should be deposited in the joint accounts of a foreman and Assistant Registrar, and the Assistant Registrar should participate in the process of bidding or disposal of the money or the articles involved in the chit business.

(g) The money-lending supervisory squad should visit the district at least once in a month.

(h) Evolution of a 'single window system' or a 'co-operative union' to meet the credit needs of the common man from cradle to grave.

**Liquor Trade**

Liquor trade is another important follow-up activity of the process of consumerism. It has the most favourable chance of flourishing at a faster rate in the district. Based on the quality, chemical composition, nature of production or disposal liquor has been given some brand names. So also the liquor shops have been given brand names. Beer and IML types of liquor are sold through CL1, CL2, CL4 licensed shops, whereas arrack is sold through the arrack licensed shops. During 1992-93 there were 949 arrack shops in the Bellary district. This number came down to 630 and 475 respectively during 1993-94 and 1994-95. This means that in the recent past the number of arrack shops has come down considerably. But this does not mean that the supply or the demand for arrack has proportionately declined. In fact, from 1985 to 1995 there has been a continuous increase, both in the rate of its consumption and supply. The total quantity of arrack required for the district during 1985-86 was 14,92,663 litres. Today, it is almost double that quantity, that is, 36,66,000 litres. This rise is seven times more than the rate of increase in population. However, there has been a shift in consumption from arrack to better brands of IML liquor. This becomes obvious if we looked at trends of liquor consumption since 1991 to 1995. Compared to the IML liquor consumption rate, the rate of consumption of arrack since 1990-91 to 1994-95 has come down by 21 per cent. During the same period the consumption rate of IML liquor has gone up by 30 per cent. This speaks of the tendency of the common man to ape the life styles of his immediate higher affluent group. The remark of a worker of NMDC, who was an arrack consumer earlier, sums up the situation. He said :

> "Who cares for arrack sir! I have rich friends. I always go to the Bars in their company. It is insulting to drink arrack. They too never allow me to drink arrack. And I too, on my own, now-a-days, hesitate to drink arrack. Hence, if I were to drink, I only go in for the fine type of wines."

During 1992-93, there were 161 IML liquor shops in the district. But as on date, there are 215 CL1, CL2, CL7 IML shops doing business in Beer and IML liquor. This means that within just two years the number of these liquor shops has gone up by 25 per cent. However, the official figures do not capture the real magnitude of the establishments engaged in supplying liquor. There are many liquor or arrack shops illegally run in the district. In every municipal town, it is said, the non-vegetarian hotels supply loose liquor to consumers. Loose liquor is often supplied through illegal bottling or seconds business. There are at present three distilleries in the district. All of them are involved in the distribution of spirit to the illegal operators of liquor trade in the district. As a result, the bottling hazards have become most common in the district. The illegal operators obtain the spirit from the factories, dilute, pocket and sell it through licensed or unlicensed shops. Or, they even transport it to other States, where it is sold at higher rates. This part of the liquor does not come under the State excise accounts. It is said that this type of "black liquor business" has been going on in the district with the support of the excise staff itself! As on 6.11.1995, there were 124 and 79 legal arrack shops in Bellary and Hospet sub-divisions respectively. But there were 33 and 18 illegal arrack shops respectively in the same sub-divisions on that date. These illegal shops are established by the excise contractors with the connivance of the Excise Department staff. The laxity on the part of the Excise Department is one reason why such illegal activities flourish in the district. The objective of the Excise Department is to deal with the production, transportation (including export and import), sale and purchase of liquor and also to control the quality of liquor. None of these functions seems to be performed effectively by the Department. In Bellary, one of the excise officials expressed his anguish as follows:

> "Every municipal town in Bellary district is served by one State excise office. The excise personnel are supposed to check the activities said to be legal or illegal in the matters concerning the manufacture, disposal or sale of liquor through the licensed or unlicensed shops. But none of them performs this task sincerely. Many of them do attend offices very sincerely. But they come to the office regularly, not that they should come, but because they get regularly the booty in what might be called the 'black business' of excise:"

If we looked at the quantity of liquor consumed, Hospet appears to be in the lead. The liquor or arrack consumption rate in Hospet is much higher than in other taluks. In Hospet, during 1994-95, 6,92,000 litres of arrack and 1,09,568 litres of IML liquor was consumed. In Shiraguppa, just 3,71,000 litres of arrack and 41,275 litres of IML was consumed during 1994-95. In the same year 2,71,000 litres of arrack and 29,896 litres of IML liquor was consumed in Sandur. Thus compared to all other taluks Hospet shows a higher rate of liquor consumption. However, the case of Bellary is different. Bellary township being the district headquarters,everyday hundreds of people from different parts of the district come for official or business purpose who incidentally have a drink before going back home. During the month of June 1995, 1,05,000 litres of arrack and 16,308 litres of liquor was consumed in Bellary. For the entire revenue year of 1994-95, 12,82,000 litres of arrack and 2,13,907 litres of IML was consumed in Bellary taluk. For such a high rate of liquor consumption Bellary has no other better reason than being a district Headquarters. However, taking the case of Hospet in comparison with other taluks one may surmise that an industrially developed area will tend to have a higher rate of liquor consumption. For, in an industrial or an urbanised society, people get used to drinking habits for various reasons. For a better understanding of this phenomenon the views of a few liquor consumers may be cited here:

Balakrishna, a slum dweller of Bellary, was a mine worker some time ago. He worked hard to bring up his children. But they did not remain under his control. When they grew up and got married, they started quarrelling amongst themselves. Initially, to manage the day-to-day expenses of the family, the elder son was giving all his earnings to the family. But the younger one was spending his earnings on his wife. When this went on, the elder son's wife did not tolerate this. So the quarrel began over sharing equally the responsibility of family. When this did not materialise, the family was divided. Balakrishna unable to bear this shock, took to drinking.

Neelachandra is a factory worker who earns daily Rs.50. He says, he was not given to drinking earlier. But when he joined the factory, he started developing pains in some parts of his body. To soothe the pains of work once he was induced by his friends to drink. Then onwards daily at least one sip of drink became a must for him. He says that now he can't live without liquor.

People from surrounding villages of every town in Bellary district whenever they come to towns usually do not return home without a drink. This serves as an additional outlet to the liquor traders in the towns. An old man from Kudatini village of Bellary taluk said, "all the youngsters now-a-days visit Bellary town atleast twice a week and they come home always in a drunken state. Sometimes they quarrel amongst themselves or beat their wives". Therefore, it appears that the base for the growth of liquor trade has already been established and that it just needs a push for further growth which is likely to come from industrialisation of the district.

### *Future Prospects*

As stated earlier, during the course of industrial development, as the district becomes an asylum of all classes of people, it will also bring in a large number of habitual drunkards. Then as if they are meant for that itself, they just engage themselves in the spread of liquor culture in the district. In course of time, liquor consumption will become a most popular pastime every time giving rise to a new generation of drunkards. Even the teetotalers are likely to become drunkards because, when it begins with company of friends it will only end in habit formation. Also when people start earning more, not knowing how to spend their earnings, they spend it for enjoyments like liquor, cinema or prostitution. May be the educated and the intelligentia will be able to manage to stay away from such evil habits.

The cultural background of the working class may also induce them to go in for liquor consumption. In the absence of proper accommodation, the immigrant workers choose to live in slums. But along side, they also develop a cultural environment in which they may take to bad habits such as alcoholism, gambling, sex play and other affairs of very low cultural standards. Youngsters staying away from their elders or elders staying away from their families may also force themselves into the culture of alcoholism. This is how the district may create a variety of contextual causes making the people go into the habit of sips of liquor.

To sum up illiteracy, inducement through the company of friends, relatives, or sheer cultural background, family worries, strenuous life, pleasure seeking, attempt to ape higher income group life styles are some of the listed reasons why people in the district may go in for liquor consumption. With rapid industrialisation, the base of such persons is likely to expand. Hence liquor trade will flourish in the years to come.

We have already noted that there has been an exceptionally high rise in the consumption of arrack since 1990. The quantity of liquor including IML, beer and arrack supplied for the district during 1990-91 was 54,52,215 litres, which rose to 55,87,404 litres in 1994-95. By 2000 AD, the district may require 1,00,00,000 litres of liquor to meet the needs of the liquor consumers. Also, because of the difference in the prices of arrack sold through the licensed shops and of its illicit version, there is already a heavy demand for the latter. The chances of "black" liquor picking up as a popular beverage in the district are very high in future.Something should be done to check its growth.

1. To check the illegal and illicit versions of liquor or arrack, a special squad consisting of honest officers should be appointed who should locate the spots and punish the culprits as per the rules of excise department.
2. A district level welfare cell may be established to educate the habitual drunkards about the evil effects of drinking.
3. Steps may be taken to overhaul the Department of Excise. The officials who are involved in supporting the illegal liquor trade should be seriously dealt with and punished as per the Departmental disciplinary norms.

# 12

# NEXUS AMONG POLITICIANS, BUSINESSMEN AND CRIMINALS

N. SIVANNA, C. CHARLES NELSON and B. VIJAYKUMAR

## Introduction

It is a well known fact that large capital investment has a corresponding effect on the emergence of 'groups of interests'. Such investment, as experiences reveal, is not only promotive in placing that area on par with the other industrially developed areas but will also put heavy pressure on the common man's social and economic life. As a follow-up to this, there is a greater possibility of a nexus emerging between various actors like politicians, officials, businessmen, industrialists and criminals to meet their own interests. Theoretically speaking, any kind of nexus can be seen as a by-product of one's own 'interest articulation' and 'interest aggregation'.

Keeping the above framework, this chapter makes an attempt to unfold such nexus that is emerging in Bellary district with the inflow of heavy investment and suggests corrective measures to check this phenomenon. The data for this chapter were collected mainly through discussions and interviews with local politicians, officials of revenue, labour and police departments, local industrialists, businessmen, contractors, trade union leaders and criminals. Wherever possible some documentary evidences have also been collected from the concerned Government offices.

## Nexus between Industrialists, Political Leaders and Mafia Groups

With a large number of steel mills and a larger number of down-stream industries coming to be established in Bellary district, a series of activities will be initiated in the region which may pose problems to authorities. Trade union and liquor-based activities, group-clashes both inside and outside the factory premises, crimes like murder, theft, gambling may spring up creating disturbances in the area. All this is possible only when there is a close nexus between the actors involved. The nexus building act among various interest groups originates as a product of protecting their self interest. The politician is interested in mobilising funds for the party and to have his own followers (a vote bank); the factory management's interest is in curbing union activities in the factory; the business community's interests lie in trafficking licenses and avoiding taxes; the officials' interest lie in opting for higher positions and, making speed money; and the criminals are interested in making easy and quick money. When these interests converge, as they seem to, then a nexus among the various interest groups emerges.

In Bellary district, such a nexus is not a new phenomenon. In fact, it already has made dents in some parts of the district. For illustration, in Hagari, a small hamlet, which lies 14 Km away from the district head-quarters, a Calcium Carbohydrate factory was established in 1976. It provided employment to people belonging to nearby villages. This area, which was peaceful, soon began witnessing group-clashes, goondaism and gambling. With the commissioning of the above factory, group activities became apparent paving way for the emergence of two groups each supported by a State level leader hailing from the area and a leader from the neighbouring State of Andhra Pradesh. The main reason for group clashes was the fact that the factory required an adequate and timely supply of raw materials and this was met by two contractors, who were leading the above two groups. For loading and unloading the raw material, they used to appoint daily-wage workers on low wages. This practice generated disappointment among the workers which made them to form their own groups. Incidentally, as reported, each contractor earned huge amount of money and this motivated and induced the other group leaders to indulge in crime activities like murder and goondaism. As a consequence, so far, as revealed from police files, between the years 1993 and 1995, 56 murder cases (Table 12.1) in Bellary police circle have been reported and attended to by the police. Out of this, in Hagari alone 25 to 30 cases have been registered; this indeed is quite an alarming situation.

It is significant to note from the above case that the criminal activities have been supported by the political groups and the factory management. The target of attack has always been the group leader and his followers.

TABLE 12.1: **Comparative Statement of Crime Statistics, Bellary Circle**

| Offence | Year 1993 | 1994 | 1995 | Total |
|---|---|---|---|---|
| Murder | 22 | 21 | 13 | 56 |
| Dacoity | 5 | 1 | 3 | 9 |
| Robbery | 4 | 7 | 7 | 18 |
| House break & Theft | 196 | 210 | 183 | 589 |
| Group Clashes | 65 | 72 | 42 | 179 |
| Mataka Case | 286 | 266 | 69 | 621 |
| Gambling | 3 | 3 | 20 | 26 |
| Total | 581 | 580 | 337 | 1498 |

*Source*: Compiled from the Crime Statistics, Bellary Circle.

One of the police officers, who worked in this area, commented that "All this happens because of the close connection between the labour contractors, the management and local political leaders. This kind of nexus is strengthening the hands of the contractors and group leaders to indulge in illegitimate activities in and around the factory premises". As a follow-up of this nexus, there are instances of contractors seeking MLA tickets, and in many police cases the culprits of the crimes and guilty persons remain unpunished.

To quote another case, in one of the newly commissioned Steel factories, located near Bellary town, altogether different kinds of group clashes have been noticed. These cases are occurring as a result of the connivance between management, political leaders and mafia groups. The prime reason for such clashes, as reported, has been the non-cooperative attitude of the management in allowing its workers to either form their own union or to join the registered trade unions. The management has been thwarting all the efforts made by its workers to organise themselves into an independent trade union. Instead, it has provided all facilities to one of the strong groups, headed by a mafia leader, to form a union. This leader, with the help of his goonda friends, has been wooing and inducing the workers to join his union which is management-friendly. As a consequence of this, at present, there are two unions, one identifying itself with the management and the other with the registered union supported by one of the 'left' political parties.

The above case is indicative of the fact that the management with the help of mafia groups, who are the 'political agents' of local political leaders, is patronising its own union so that it can control the workers. In order to disintegrate the political party-supported union activities, the management is financing not only mafia groups but also nurturing some militant workers as 'Black Agents' whose sole task is to break the unity of the workers and to prevent them from indulging in anti-management activities. Commenting on the work atmosphere of this factory, the President of a union identified three reasons for the problems :

(i) the management's policy of appointing workers on a temporary basis, most of whom are controlled by the labour contractors having close links with the political leaders, mafia groups and management;
(ii) the management's non-compliance with the labour laws and non-implementation of social welfare measures beneficial to workers; and
(iii) the low wages paid to workers.

An inference which can be drawn from the above analysis is that in future this type of work atmosphere may spread its tentacles into the other newly commissioned factories in and around Bellary and Hospet. As expressed by members of the general public, there are already incidents of militant activities gaining strength with the support of mafia groups sponsored by political groups and industrialists. According to one of the management personnel, the political groups interfere in factory activities with the intention of strengthening their political base (vote bank) and to demand funds for their political activities. And the mafia groups do so with the intentions of making quick money and to disturb the work atmosphere. To counter this, the management, sometimes, take the help of mafia groups to prevent strikes, *hartals* and *gheraos*. However, the management are of the view that "if both police and labour department cooperate with us we would be hardly confronting situations such as above".

**Nexus between Officials, Businessmen and Politicians**

With the increasing mafia operations there has been a corresponding increase in crime in the district at an alarming rate. The following pages make an attempt to analyse the district level crime data especially in

Bellary, Hospet and Sandur taluks. For, in the near future, these taluks would be witnessing criminal activities of the kind described above in a large measure.

One of the striking aspects of the district level crime data is that, in recent years crimes like murder, rioting, dacoity, theft have been reported and attended to by the police. Table 12.2 reveals that in the past ten years 501 murders have been committed, 2196 theft cases have taken place and 3029 cases of rioting have been reported. On an average about 50 murder cases in a year have been registered which is very disturbing to note. However, one can find some solace from the fact that in recent years there is a slight decline in its annual growth rate (–2.61 per cent). Further analysis of the crime statistics indicates that the annual growth rate of crime in the district is of the order of 1.18 per cent. The increasing trend in the annual growth rates of the crimes like house-breaking and theft (2.04 per cent), rioting (0.22 per cent) and robbery (3.42 per cent) would create a fright in the minds of the rich and the middle classes.

By taking some individual crimes like murder, dacoity, robbery, housebreak and theft and rioting, an attempt is made here to compare the trends in crime rate in Bellary district with the State level crime rate. As Table 12.3 reveals, on an average crimes such as murder, dacoity, robbery, housebreak and theft and rioting have been committed at the rate of 3.58, 2.03, 1.48, 3.58 and 3.44 per cent per annum respectively. Further, there has been a mark of consistency in their percentage rate over the years (1992 to 1995). However, seen in absolute figures, especially at the State level, crimes like murder, robbery, rioting have been increasing at an alarming rate. For instance, during the year 1992, the number of murder cases reported and attended to by the police was around 1492 which went up further to 1734 in the year 1995 — an increase of 242 cases. Whereas in Bellary district although the incidence of murders has been decreasing between the years 1994 and 1995, there is possibility that with the growing industrial activities and in-migration of labour force the district level authorities will be under pressure to check the crime rate and to maintain law and order, especially in and around the new industrial establishments. This has been the experience of industrial townships like Visakhapatnam in Andhra Pradesh State. Further analysis of crime rates, in terms of number of persons committing crimes per lakh population, reveals that at the State level, 3.31 per cent of persons commit murder per annum whereas in Bellary district this is lower at 2.69 per cent.

As for taluks, especially in Bellary (Table 12.1) and Hospet (Table 12.4), though the crime rate in the years 1993 and 1994 shows an increasing

TABLE 12.2: **Comparative Statement of Crime Statistics, Bellary District**

| Offence | Year | | | | | | | | | | Annual Rate |
|---|---|---|---|---|---|---|---|---|---|---|---|
| | 1986 | 1987 | 1988 | 1989 | 1990 | 1991 | 1992 | 1993 | 1994 | 1995 | |
| Murder | 56 | 47 | 43 | 47 | 55 | 44 | 51 | 58 | 57 | 43 | –2.61 |
| Dacoity | 11 | 6 | 9 | 7 | 12 | 21 | 3 | 12 | 4 | 8 | –3.13 |
| Robbery | 10 | 14 | 12 | 6 | 13 | 8 | 13 | 19 | 9 | 14 | 3.42 |
| House Break & Theft | 495 | 546 | 549 | 511 | 688 | 616 | 726 | 677 | 645 | 606 | 2.04 |
| Rioting | 270 | 282 | 251 | 281 | 297 | 375 | 342 | 318 | 337 | 276 | 0.22 |
| Total | 842 | 895 | 864 | 852 | 1065 | 1064 | 1135 | 1084 | 1052 | 947 | |

Annual Growth Rate : 1.18

*Source*: Compiled from the Crime Statistics, Bellary District.

TABLE 12.3: **Percentage of Crime Rate (of some Individual Crimes) in Bellary District to the Crime Rate in the State (1992 to 1995)**

| Offence | Year | | | | | | | | Average for Bellary District |
|---|---|---|---|---|---|---|---|---|---|
| | 1992 | | 1993 | | 1994 | | 1995 | | |
| | State | Bellary | State | Bellary | State | Bellary | State | Bellary | |
| Murder | 1492 | 3.42 (51) | 1503 | 3.86 (58) | 1504 | 3.79 (57) | 1734 | 2.48 (43) | 3.38 |
| Dacoity | 519 | 0.58 (3) | 307 | 3.91 (12) | 378 | 1.02 (4) | 307 | 2.61 (8) | 2.03 |
| Robbery | 676 | 1.92 (13) | 988 | 1.92 (19) | 1130 | 0.8 (9) | 1081 | 1.3 (14) | 1.48 |
| House Break & Theft | 19113 | 3.8 (276) | 18123 | 3.74 (677) | 19201 | 3.36 (645) | 18485 | 3.28 (606) | 3.58 |
| Rioting | 10447 | 3.27 (343) | 7886 | 4.03 (318) | 9293 | 3.65 (337) | 9665 | 2.86 (276) | 3.44 |

*Note*: Figures in Parenthesis indicate total number of crimes committed in the district.

*Source*: Compiled from the Crime Statistics, Karnataka State and Bellary District.

trend, there is a sudden decline in the year 1995: in Bellary the crime rate has come down from 581 to 337 cases in 1995 and in Hospet from 470 cases in 1993 to 330 cases in 1995. In Sandur taluk (Table 12.5) the crime cases registered between 1991 (254) and 1992 (273) show an upward trend whereas in the years between 1993 and 1995 the data indicate both decreasing and increasing trends (from 214 cases in 1993 the number has gone up to 239 cases in 1995). However, the annual crime growth rate denotes a decreasing trend at the rate of –1.21 per cent in the above taluk. On the whole, the declining trends in crime rates in the above taluks can be primarily attributed to the strong and effective preventive measures taken by the police, particularly at the higher levels.

However, some of the individual crimes like murder, house-breaking and theft, gambling, group clashes may pose a serious problem to authorities in future. These crimes may increase with the corresponding increase in the industrial and other related activities. As revealed from Tables (12.1, 12.4 and 12.5), between 1993-1995, these crimes have been showing an increasing trend. For instance, in Hospet circle, the murder cases which were only four in 1993 went upto nine in the year 1995. Cases related to house breaks and thefts really make the authorities uncomfortable as their number is quite alarming (589 in Bellary, 533 in Hospet and 261 in Sandur). The main reasons for committing different types of crimes are as follows: Murders have been committed for monetary gains, property related disputes, personal vendetta and enmity, communalism and political reasons; house breaks and thefts mainly for making quick money; rioting

TABLE 12.4: **Comparative Statement of Crime Statistics, Hospet Circle**

| Offence | Year | | | Total |
|---|---|---|---|---|
| | 1993 | 1994 | 1995 | |
| Murder | 4 | 6 | 9 | 19 |
| Dacoity | 2 | 3 | 3 | 8 |
| Robbery | 9 | 5 | 3 | 17 |
| House Break & Theft | 176 | 168 | 189 | 533 |
| Group Clashes | 40 | 32 | 40 | 112 |
| Matka Gambling | 225 | 268 | 63 | 556 |
| Gambling | 14 | 15 | 23 | 52 |
| Total | 470 | 497 | 330 | 1297 |

*Source*: Compiled from the Crime Statistics, Hospet Police Station.

occurs due to industrial, political, student and communal disputes. It is significant to note that the majority of culprits belong to the economically weaker sections.

The 'Matka-gambling', a game monitored from Bombay, although shows a negative trend during recent years, may raise its head once again with the free exchange of easy and quick money. For the white-collar and lower class criminals, this game is a source of extra income. At times, this crime is seen as a prime cause for group clashes. However, its decreasing trend has given some relief to police authorities. In fact, the police officers claim that due to stringent measures taken by the Department the intensity of the game has come down. It is interesting to note from Tables (12.1, 12.4 and 12.5) that the number of cases booked between 1993 and 1994 show an upward trend whereas in the year 1995 the number has come down drastically. One of the reasons attributed by the general public, and shared to some extent by the police, is that as the main operators of the game (in Bombay) are under police observation, the game has halted for the time-being but may start once again in future. The citizens also expressed their views that this game is operated with the connivance of police authorities. In fact, the police stations are said to be deprived of huge amounts given by the sponsors of this game. All this speaks of a clear case of the nexus between the police, the white collar and the lower-class criminals.

A close look at Tables (12.1, 12.4 and 12.5) discloses that the crime activities like street gambling and group clashes have been registered in a good number. For instance, in Hospet circle 52 cases and in Sandur 51 cases have been reported and attended to by the police during the last two to five years. As for group clashes, 17 such cases in Bellary circle and 112 in Hospet circle have been registered pointing out to the disturbed law and order situation prevailing in the region. With increase in the migration of labour force from the neighbouring districts and from other States there is possibility that the group clashes and street gambling may show an increasing trend in future.

A discomfiture of the crime statistics, as revealed from Table 12.5 is that, in Sandur circle, there have been reported cases of atrocities committed against women. During the last five years, crimes such as 3 rape cases, 41 cases of molestation and 11 cases of harassment by husband/relatives have been registered. Over the years, these cases show an increasing trend which is very disturbing. And the situation may aggravate in future with more number of female workers coming as construction workers.

Visits to industrial sites and slums reveal that the poor labourers and

TABLE 12.5: **Comparative Statement of Crime Statistics, Sandur Circle**

| Offence | Year | | | | | |
|---|---|---|---|---|---|---|
| | 1991 | 1992 | 1993 | 1994 | 1995 | Total |
| Murder | 6 | 7 | 5 | 4 | 2 | 24 |
| Dacoity | 0 | 0 | 0 | 2 | 1 | 3 |
| Robbery | 0 | 1 | 3 | 0 | 1 | 5 |
| House Break & Theft | 46 | 64 | 46 | 55 | 50 | 261 |
| Fatal Accidents | 16 | 20 | 23 | 26 | 25 | 110 |
| Non-fatal accidents | 99 | 92 | 84 | 101 | 120 | 496 |
| Matka Gambling | 49 | 70 | 36 | 33 | 7 | 195 |
| Street Gambling | 28 | 6 | 9 | 1 | 7 | 51 |
| *Attrocities against women* | | | | | | |
| Rape | 0 | 0 | 2 | 1 | 0 | 3 |
| Modesty of women | 7 | 11 | 3 | 9 | 12 | 42 |
| Kidnapping of Girls & Women | 0 | 1 | 0 | 0 | 1 | 2 |
| Harassment by Husband/Relatives | 1 | 0 | 3 | 3 | 4 | 11 |
| Dowry Death | 2 | 1 | 0 | 0 | 1 | 4 |
| Immoral Traffic Prevention Act | 0 | 0 | 0 | 4 | 8 | 12 |
| Grand Total | 254 | 273 | 214 | 239 | 239 | 1219 |

Annual Growth Rate: –1.21
*Source*: Compiled from the Crime Statistics, Sandur Police Station.

slum dwellers have been put to lot of pressure by the contractors and mafia groups, who in turn are supported by the political leaders. For instance, as stated by labourers "we have been exploited both by the contractors and middlemen and we are always under pressure to give one-third of our wages". Incidentally, the migrated labourers tend to identify themselves with their native contractors which strengthens the hands of the latter to exercise more control over the workers'. Because of this, there have been well-formed groups led by powerful and resourceful contractors.

The slum dwellers have been forced by the local mafia groups for meeting the latter's ends. At the behest of the political leaders, businessmen, house-owners, the mafia groups use the services of slum dwellers. For politicians, they serve as 'vote banks', for businessmen and house-owners they help in collecting money from the borrowers and in evacuating the houses, respectively. Observing the activities of mafia groups, one of the leading industrialists of Bellary remarked "Emergence of mafia groups is mainly in pockets like contracts for labour supply, transportation, scrap auctions, money-lending, country liquor trade. This usually happens with non-descript persons arriving on the spot and unobtrusively operating their way up, capturing power and money gradually till they attain the mafia-status in the area and exercise a vice-like grip on the activities, rendering the organisation and the authorities helpless". It is quite disturbing to note that the members of these mafia groups are the unemployed educated youths and they have been attracted by easy money which they would get by committing such illegitimate activities.

With the increase in the activities of industries the nexus between the officials of the revenue and labour departments, industrialists, political groups and business groups may spring-up. This is especially for evading taxes, trafficking licenses for illegal trades like illicit trading and land grabbing. To cite an instance in support, the local traders, as reported in press, evaded Rupees two crore sales tax by using bogus sales tax forms for transporting foodgrains and other goods. The officials were found to be hand-in-glove with the local traders in committing this act. A good number of cases have been reported as far as giving licenses to illicit trade, to procure land, to establish small-scale establishments on pavements and for giving agencies. In all this, the policy of 'give and take' has been very much observed. In the words of one of the responsible officers "Usually, it is our experience that the businessmen, industrialists and small-scale entrepreneurs bring political pressures and woo the officials to get their work done. At times, the officials succumb to such pressures. This has been going on in spite of our best efforts to check the speed money in our system".

The foregoing reveals that there have been reported cases of nexus even during the pre-industrial phase. This may gain further strength with the increase of industrial and related activities.Seen in this context, the authorities concerned should gear-up to prevent the possible emergence and spread of such nexus. It is strongly believed that the end result of any nexus, by and large, is to gain in physical, positional and monetary terms.

## Some Corrective Measures

The above description unfolds that Bellary district is already experiencing the negative aspects of industrial development. If this is the situation at present one might wonder what would be the case in the future? If these activities begin to happen on a large scale, in future, what are the preventive and corrective measures one might think of?

Here are some of the corrective measures suggested by the officials, industrialists and knowledgeable citizens of the district. While discussing about the measures a senior police officer of the district expressed the need for strengthening the police force, both at the district and at the taluk levels, to curb illegal, illegitimate anti-social activities, to prevent economic offences and group clashes, and more importantly to maintain law and order. As a step in this direction the Department has already prepared and forwarded a 'perspective plan' to the Government for its approval and implementation.

The proposed plan has provided for the establishment of additional Police Stations at Bellary, Hagari, Toranagal, Hospet; establishment of Traffic Circles at Bellary, Kurugodu and Toranagal circle; and establishment of sub-divisions at Siruguppa and Sandur. A point to be noted here is that with the increase in industrial and mining activities, there is a corresponding increase in the heavy traffic movement. As a result, Bellary, Hospet and Sandur zones are already experiencing road accident deaths and road accident offences. For instance, in Bellary taluk, during the last three years (1993-95), there were 65 road accident deaths and 360 cases of road accident related offences and in Sandur circle 110 fatal accidents and 496 non-fatal accidents (Table 12.5). The heads of the above circles strongly feel the need for the establishment of traffic circles, to give training to traffic police personnel and to improve roads, especially the congested ones. Further, in the light of atrocities committed on women, there is a great demand for establishing 'women police stations'. This offence needs to be tackled on a priority basis as the in-migration of female workers to the industrial centres is expected to take place on a large scale, especially for construction works. There is going to be an increase in the female workforce and the chances of women workers getting exposed to such crimes.

Further, the above plan proposes to have one KSRP (Karnataka State Reserve Police) battalion at Bellary to strengthen district special branch, to strengthen railway police station at Bellary and Hospet and to strengthen district police force. This has become necessary in the light of reported cases of robbery, dacoity and theft. It is interesting to note that the criminals, by utilising the available train services between Guntakal and Hospet, commute as ticketless travellers, commit such crimes and run away from the scene. In view of this, there is a need not only to strengthen the railway police force but also to establish 'police outposts' in the vicinity of railway stations especially at Hospet and Toranagal. More importantly, the plan proposes to create two posts of Additional Superintendent of Police for 'law and order' and 'crime'. It was strongly felt by the police authorities that more emphasis should be given for the effective implementation of 'Goonda Act' to prevent group clashes. In the light of the ongoing criminal activities in the district and possibility of their increase in the future, the proposed plan to strengthen the police force sounds timely and necessary.

While commenting on the corrective measures, one of the leading criminal lawyers in the district referred to the incidence of failures in prosecuting culprits of various crimes. According to him, there have been attempts of suborning and intimidation of key witnesses and more importantly the procedures of prosecutions have been subject to lengthy process. As a consequence, in quite a number of such cases majority of culprits remain unpunished. Therefore, there is a need to strengthen police administration, both crime and law and order, not only in terms of making it highly professional but also in shielding it from political interferences. However, regarding the strengthening of police force in the district some citizens were of the opinion that it is not enough to just increase the number of police stations and the police force. It is equally important to ensure that the police personnel are given proper training, especially in the area of human relations. More importantly, the personnel need to be trained in using sophisticated arms and ammunition so that they would be able to combat the illegal and unlawful activities and situations.

There was a strong plea from the factory management that police, labour and revenue departments have to play a key role to diffuse the increasing disturbances in the district. An owner of a Steel industry suggested that since there is a heavy influx of labourers from the neighbouring districts and States, it is necessary to maintain a register relating to their personal background and past life. This would come in handy for police and management to keep an eye over their activities.

As far as the supportive role to be extended by Labour Department to industries, an industrialist suggested, "The Union elections should be conducted by the Department in the factory premises itself. More importantly, the Labour Department should take the responsibility of conducting orientation courses for workers on issues like labour laws, rules, procedures and code of conduct. In the process, the Department could inculcate 'work ethics' among workers and thereby boost the workers morality and create a 'work-friendly' atmosphere in the factory".

As a consequence to the establishment of Steel and other industries, there is a corresponding growth of private mine-owners in the 'iron-ore belt' stretching almost 40 km. With the help of politicians, the mine owners try to put pressure on the revenue officials to get work contracts and licenses. It is going to be a bee-hive activity in coming years. For this, the revenue authorities have to introduce stringent measures to check and control illegal land acquisition, grabbing and tampering of land records. As reported by the Revenue Officials, in many a case concurrence of the Department was not sought for converting agricultural land into industrial sites. Instances of this nature are going to take place on a larger scale with the establishment of major and auxiliary industries in the district in future.

In the light of the unforeseen developments that would take place in the region there is an immediate need to organise 'awareness camps' to sensitise the public about the nuances of the aftermath of industrial establishment. As a prelude to this, the conscientious public, especially youth, should organise themselves to work as 'watch-dogs' to prevent social, economic and political crimes.

As a welfare measure, the authorities can initiate and implement 'social defence' programmes and necessary economic measures for preventing anti-social and criminal activities, and for treating and rehabilitating the habitual offenders. These programmes should aim at promoting the welfare of prisoners, delinquency control, beggary control, prevention of prostitution, alcoholism, gambling, drug addiction and promoting social and moral hygiene. While carrying out this task both the Government institutions and non-Government Organisations have to work together with proper understanding, cooperation and coordination. Both should take upon themselves this task as a social responsibility.

# 13

# INDUSTRIAL SYSTEM AND GENDER CONCERNS

K.G. GAYATHRI DEVI

## Introduction

Industrialisation is undisputedly, an essential pre-requisite for development in modern societies. However, just as it induces many positive effects it also gives shelter to many negative consequences. These are the inevitable results of a changing society.

Presently there is an increasing awareness and participation by women in the process of development. But an important adverse fallout of industrialisation is the increasing crime against women. Crime against women can take two forms: (i) drawing them into prostitution and (ii) abuse of their personal safety and dignity. Industrialisation provides the necessary shelter for the propagation of prostitution. The poor and the destitute fall an easy prey to the hands of pimps and criminals who invariably use them in the flesh trade. Women are often forced into prostitution or to work as sex workers. The second dimension of the effects of industrialisation on women is concerning the personal safety of women in industrial areas. Exposure to a different culture in industrialised towns and cities poses many challenges to the women who migrate from villages in search of work. Coming from backward areas, the sudden throwing open of opportunities would lead to cultural gaps. Women who hail from conservative families, brought up with traditional norms binding their behaviour, are exposed to modern life styles. They have to survive in the urban atmosphere, not always being protected by their male relatives. Commuting to work place, interaction with male colleagues, managing finances—all these expose them to challenges to their own personal safety.

Degradation of cultural values due to a number of factors like impact of the west, mass media like the television, yellow literature etc., have posed threats to the security of women, particularly in the industrialised towns and cities. While women from the upper and middle classes somehow manage to escape, those from lower classes and poor background face problems of personal security. Rape, criminal assault, theft, kidnapping and other kinds of crime against women increase along with the increasing industrial expansion of the urban areas.

Bellary district is going to experience a huge size of industrial investment. It is not certain that the community in Bellary is ready to face the impact of such massive industrialisation on its people, who are still backward and unexposed to the culture of industrial growth. Its women are more backward, largely illiterate, poor and dependent on agricultural wage for livelihood. Availability of wage work in urban centres draws them towards industries leaving them at the mercy of the urban environment. This chapter attempts to outline the threats of such industrialisation on women. It has the following objectives:

1. To evaluate the existing threats for the safety of women in Bellary district and the dimensions of the institution of prostitution.
2. To understand the status and conditions of these sex workers living in the urban centres in the light of industrialisation.
3. To estimate the growth of this profession in the wake of further industrial growth and its effects on the society.
4. To discuss other aspects of ensuring personal safety and dignity of women in an expanding metropolis,
5. And, to suggest remedial measures to arrest the spread of these evils and to provide safe working and living conditions to the women in Bellary.

**Threats to Safety of Women in Bellary, Landlessness and Migration**

The drought-prone nature of the district has resulted in an increased proportion of the poor and landless workers to be highly migratory in tendency. Despite the Tungabhadra Dam, large tracts of its agricultural lands are still dry or left fallow. Jowar, cotton, chillies are the staple crops which provide only seasonal employment to the dependent labourers. Paddy as a labour intensive crop is grown in small patches of wet land. The supply side of labour is complicated by the fact that during and after the reorganization of the State in 1956, the villages lying on and near the border of the two States (Karnataka and Andhra Pradesh) have continued to be interdependent for socio-cultural and economic reasons. Similar caste and religious groups are distributed in both the States with marital and kinship ties kept alive even after partition. Similar lifestyles are common in these villages, with the State boundary being only a geographical limit. But as is evident, the Andhrites with their enterprise have immigrated in greater numbers to the villages in Bellary district in search of agricultural/ casual labour. These labourers from Andhra generally live in 'camps' which are put up by their masters, and work for weekly wages. Hard work, kinship and the fact that much of the irrigated land is under the ownership of Andhrites have facilitated better employment opportunities to these immigrants than the native labourers.

Secondly, the district has a large percentage of people who are the weaker sections, like Scheduled Castes (SCs) and Muslims. This is true of the Madars, one such Scheduled Caste which enjoys the lowest social status owing to its association, traditionally, with leather work. The other SCs like the Dakkalors, Cheluvadis and Koravas are also numerous here. In addition, the forest and river valley areas around the dam site and Hospet have resulted in the settlement by certain castes like the Kurubas, Kabbers (boatsmen) and Bedas or Valmikis or Nayakas (hunters). Having been displaced from their traditional occupations, the members of these castes are forced to pursue agriculture and wage labour in the villages, competing with the SCs. Traditionally they depended on their caste occupations for survival. But this practice underwent changes with the closing of the *jajmani* system of inter-caste relations and dependence. Some of their occupations based on forests or rivers became non-functional with the growth of urban centres and clearing of forests. The surplus population from these castes which did not get absorbed into the agricultural sector in the villages, was forced into the urban centres for employment.

**Urban Settlement and Problems**

Even in the new place of settlement the displaced workers of the agricultural sector and/or the forest-based tribal families failed to obtain employment in the factories. Absence of skill has been an important handicap. Besides, they lacked in enterprise to forge themselves ahead to take up "new" types of wage work, like construction of roads, buildings for industries, dams and mines. Such jobs demanded hard work irrespective of the seasonal variations like sun or rain, and for continuous hours. The culture of forest-based occupations that gave them independence and freedom to work in an informal atmosphere did not exist here. Thus, a number of unemployed villagers from these castes ended up living in cities working as Hamalis, other types of casual workers and, at worst, as criminals.

The notoriety, courage and physical strength of members of some of these communities encouraged the anti-social elements to use them for their criminal activities. Women from these castes, who used to assist men in their traditional occupations or engage themselves in agricultural/ casual labour, found their lives in a jeopardy upon migration to cities. While the resourceful among them with education or skill managed to get into jobs in factories etc., the illiterate and the very poor had to end up as mine workers. But those who did not succeed in both and in whose case certain traditional practices like Basavi are prevalent, have become an easy prey to such professions as prostitution. The anonymity factor in the urban areas has provided support to it. While prostitution is the extreme form of threat to the safety of women in industrialised areas, there are other forms which are affecting their well-being.

As noted already, industrialisation brings with it many changes in the lives of the people who would have migrated from rural areas. Women are placed under different types of responsibilities in cities, where life revolves around the clock. Working hours and other forms of discipline replace the informality of rural living. Rise in costs of living force women to take up employment. Most of the women living in slums take up jobs like domestic servants, construction labourers, mine workers, petty vendors and so on. The risks of personal assault, rape, abduction are greater for the poor and the helpless women who live in the slums. Abuse of women in work places in terms of over work, under payment, physical beatings and sexual harassment are some of them. Women from illiterate and poor families are more vulnerable to these abuses although the others are not saved either. Often, such cases of exploitation are not reported at home by the lady employees for fear of being taken out of their jobs. Commuting to work, late working hours, absence of sufficient female workers and distance to work place—all these make them an easy prey to the anti-social elements.

### Prostitution and Problems of Personal Safety of Women

Against the above background, let us examine the prospects of endangering the safety of women in Bellary district in the event of massive industrialisation. Out of its eight taluks, Hospet and Bellary are the main urban centres. Sandur, Kudligi, Harapanahalli and Hagaribommanahalli are still not much urbanised since there are no industries around them. Expansion of the city is more in the case of Bellary, the district headquarters, and Hospet. This is due to the starting of industries which led to migration of people from nearby taluks, towns and districts, cutting across State boundaries. The excess population has been accommodated in the residential zones based on its economic status. The working class attached to mines and industries formed colonies nearer to their workplace. Yet, a number of slums catered to the residential needs of poorer masses, who could not afford decent housing facilities. Just as lands from farmers are bought to construct steel plants, land value rose within the jurisdiction of the city. House sites have become scarce, rental values of houses have gone up. All these have created problems to the immigrants, particularly the working class. Information about the incidence of prostitution in Bellary was obtained through formal and informal sources. The formal sources were discussions with officers in the departments of police, municipality, and with social workers, and some important citizens. In Bellary, a few slums have been identified as the main pockets of this activity.

**Slums as Centres of Immoral Traffic**

Taking the two cities—Bellary and Hospet, we find that they have the maximum number of slums in the district compared to other towns. A look at the details about these slums in terms of caste, type of houses and number of residents shows that immigrant population from both the neighbouring taluks, districts and from outside the State are resident here. There is a preponderance of people belonging to the SC and ST communities in these slums for the obvious reasons of landlessness, immigration and wage labour. Huts are more in number and the slums are densely populated. The names of some of the slums are indicative of the caste background of their residents. For example, Bapujinagar, Siddarthanagar, Cheluvadikheri, Harijankheri, Ambedkarnagara, Harijanawada, Janata colony and Indiranagara have the SCs like the Madars and Cheluvadis in the main. Similarly, Koravaraoni has Koravas, Talavarapete has mostly the Nayakas or the Bedas (STs), and Mohammedan block has the Muslims. The preponderance of these castes and communities suggests that they are the people living below the poverty line and are forced to live under such conditions. They constitute the major portion of the migrant labour from rural areas, attracted by the prospects of industrialisation. Indicators of backwardness show them as prominent groups among whom illiteracy, unemployment, ill health, child labour and prostitution are high.

Discussions with some men and women in these slums revealed that none of them is in a salaried job. Having immigrated to Bellary a few decades ago from neighbouring villages of both Bellary and parts of Andhra, the slum dwellers depend on casual labour for their livelihood. The main economic activity in most of the houses is said to be prostitution, at least by the younger women. The houses of the prostitutes are closer to the entrance of the slums to facilitate visits by the customers. They are surrounded by shops selling arrack, snacks, tea, eatables and cigarettes/ beedis. The houses of sex workers are identifiable. They have make-shift kitchens outside the houses, the surroundings are relatively cleaner than the other houses. They are decorated with furniture items and the houses have media for entertainment like transistors and tape recorders.

**Reasons for Preponderance of Prostitution**

Poverty and unemployment of the male head of the household is stated to have driven most of the victims to this heinous profession. Having migrated to the city as unskilled labourers, with no roof on their heads, no food to feed their dependents who range from parents, siblings, children and relatives, these women and their families could not refuse the shelter offered by the '*Bayis*', who have settled down in the profession. The informants denied the existence of any racket of transporting such women/ girls to the red light areas in Bombay or Bangalore. However, this is doubtful and is an expression of their fear about being beaten up by the pimps.

The second reason for women to enter into this profession is that it provides what is described by them as 'easy money'. Lack of resources to lead a decent life, lack of skill, education and prevalence of family tradition by way of prostitution or its near system of Basavi, large families, failure in love affairs, motherhood in an unwed condition, desire for a fashionable lifestyle, social surroundings comprising of people who are criminals, drug addicts, alcoholics, ex-convicts, people who are in liquor trade, gamblers, juvenile delinquents, all these have forced or induced women to work as prostitutes.

**Religious or Cultural Compulsions**

The possibility of the system of Basavi (which is popular in the district and its adjoining region), encouraging the institution of prostitution was discussed with the informants and the sex workers. On our visits to some of the slums in Bellary and Hospet, we were often reassured by the informants that the prevalence of Basavi practice is not resulting in prostitution. The argument was supported by the fact that it is a religious practice recognized by the practicing as well as patron families and that it would not result in the evil practice of immoral traffic in women. Even if some ex-Basavis had illicit relations with men, they did so in the capacity of concubines, often remaining loyal to only one or two men throughout their lives. In other words, majority of informants spoke pessimistically about the possibility of prostitutes emerging from Basavi background. For, the faith in Basavi culture does not allow these women to lead an unclean life of regular prostitutes, who cater to men of all castes, irrespective of auspicious or inauspicious days, unmindful of their religious duties of worship on Tuesdays and Fridays, and such other compulsions which bind the lives of Basavis in the traditional system.

At the same time, the same informants did agree that the attractions of easy money, anonymity in an urban atmosphere, urban values with decreasing religious faiths at least among the younger generation, pressure and threats by the gangs that control the economy of a slum through their gambling dens, liquor shops, drug selling points, prostitutes and pimps, by leaders who control them as vote banks—all these would certainly force the Basavis from villages and in the city slums to turn to working as call girls and prostitutes. Empirical evidence on the existence of Basavi cult in the slums was clear when we came across temples for the deities "Huligamma" in these slums. We could see *jogithis* (women dedicated to goddess Yellamma) aged 8 to 60 years going on their religious begging on Tuesdays and Fridays.

## Other Reasons (Political and Crime Related)

Industrialisation leads to increased labour intake both at skilled and unskilled levels. The workers who live either in the colonies belonging to industry, or in separate areas, usually in the slums, are organized under the name of welfare needs by the union leaders. The nexus between the unions, political parties and political leaders is well known. Union rivalry and other forms of rifts bring in rival gangs who are patronized by the leaders—either union or political or by the owners of industries—for personal gains. Liquor, gambling and women are commonly used in treating the leaders to keep them in good humour or to get their consent for decisions. Prostitutes or call girls are procured by the concerned group, depending on the class of the leader.

The same system of offering call girls or sex workers operates in official circles also. Inspection tours of 'Sahibs' are always suspected to be accompanied by consumption of liquor, non-vegetarian food and accepting call girls. In fact, the inspection bungalows in the urban centres are branded for such activities, that any lady officer who is on duty residing there, faces much embarrassing situations or even risks to her personal modesty if she is alone.

In the recent years, falling moral values in society and increase in commercial or materialistic attitudes of people have led to decreasing status of women. Obscenity in films, commercial advertisements, magazines depicting semi-clad women, yellow literature—all have led to eruption of cheap values. The consequence is an increase in risks of personal safety of women in industrial areas.

## Background of Clientele and Reasons for Patronizing

The clients are men from rural areas, other towns and from the same urban areas i.e., those who come to Bellary on administrative, judicial and business trips. The visitors get attracted to prostitutes for not only reasons of sexual gratification. They also get accommodation and sometimes food and tea in their houses. In fact, some of the slums have women who are regular concubines to such men. Others are so to officials, who are often working in other towns/villages than their own, to political leaders/ workers, to criminals, to agents who mediate to accomplish work in government offices and to even police staff. The location of Hospet nearer to Guntakal in Andhra Pradesh has converted it as a junction for road and rail transport. Traffic has increased over the years on both lines. The drivers, cleaners and agents who bring raw materials to the industrial units, the agents for contract labourers, agents for building construction, workers of all categories and classes who would stay in hotels, rooms or in sheds—all of them form the clientele. The latter stay alone without shifting their family till they settle down. Vulnerability to patronize call girls/ prostitutes would be greater in their case.

## A Futuristic Note on the Probable Threats to Safety of Women

Bellary district is not an exception to the fact that rapid industrialisation results in certain negative effects, prostitution being one of them. The concentration of slums in large numbers in Bellary, Hospet, Kamalapura,

Kampli and Sandur suggest that they are the result of heavy industrial investment. The presence of prostitutes and sex workers in these slums is an indication of the scope for earning easy money that drives women to take up this profession. Some of the slums have this as the primary activity of its residents. Nexus between criminals, gangsters and politicians has kept this practice alive by deriving commissions from pimps and prostitutes for the accommodation they have received to carry on their business. Slums are owned by certain political leaders and landlords. The nexus between the leaders, bureaucrats and rowdy gangs has kept this trade prospering. Efforts by the district administration in the recent months have been foiled. There is a very powerful lobby for encouraging gambling, with the decisions about how much bid being taken in Bombay. The news is sent to all sub-centres including Bellary.

The police officers opine that the existing staff under their control in the district is insufficient even for routine duties. They have no extra personnel to check prostitution and to rehabilitate the prostitutes. They state that no formal training has been imparted to even the senior officers to carry out social reform activities and feel that they are overburdened with too many duties as it is. Even the existing NGOs in the district have not paid enough attention to mitigate the ills like prostitution. One leading organisation with headquarters in Hospet trains ex-Devadasis in tailoring activities as part of a rehabilitation programme. The beneficiaries are women from nearby slums who are ex-Devadasis as well as non-Devadasis.

However, it should be noted that the slums which are in existence in Bellary and other urban centres are directly linked in their origin and continuation to the expansion of the city due to industrialisation and setting up of commercial establishments. The proposed huge investment on industries and allied units will only aggravate the existing problems. Further establishment of industries will apply a heavy pressure on infrastructure facilities like housing, transport, water etc. Land values will increase. Continuous waves of immigration to cities will result in more slums coming into being where anti-social activities thrive under anonymity. Competition for wage and white collar labour will leave many disappointed and unemployed.

Secondly, the underworld activities like crime, gambling and prostitution will increase in proportions encouraged by the expanding metropolis. All these will provide easy money. Often these activities are patronized by leaders, industrialists, bureaucrats and gangsters. Call girls or sex workers will have better income levels due to increase in earnings of their clients and increasing consumerism. Empirical evidence has shown that any further expansion of the city will certainly encourage these evils to become established as economic activities as they have become established in Bombay and other metropolis.

**Conclusions and Recommendations**

Hailed as one of the oldest professions in the world, prostitution is a blot on the status of women in a society. Its speedy removal is as essential for the health of that society as are any other welfare programmes. Industrialisation stimulates its further expansion and growth. Sex workers are harmful for themselves as well as for the family since they breed diseases like STD, AIDS and others. Children in such surroundings get spoilt and turn criminals. Therefore, an integrated approach to solve the problem of prostitution and its evil effects on the society are necessary. In this regard, the following measures may be considered:

1. Prostitutes, call girls, sex workers are forced into the profession out of economic compulsions. As immigrants, or second generation residents they consider this as a viable activity. We need to assume that they have no other alternative means of livelihood. It is therefore necessary that there should be concerted efforts to increase employment opportunities for women of all classes and background. Informal sector plays an important role here. Being largely uneducated and unskilled, the women from the rural areas resort to immoral means of livelihood if they fail to get a decent job. The Urban Basic Services Project (UBSP) of the UNICEF which is being implemented by the city municipalities in Bellary and Hospet is useful in this context. It is a training-cum-employment programme. The municipalities in the two cities have formed what are called the 'Neighbourhood Committees'. For every 25 women dwellers, one woman is chosen as the leader of the group. She conducts training courses for others using the sewing machine or other machinery given by the government for each group. After the training, the women are expected to be independent in their employment on self-efforts.

   The UBSPs are good for popularizing communal unity and self dependence among the poor. They are schemes for poverty alleviation and self-employment. In Bellary, so far, 2340 Ashraya sites have been distributed to women, outside the city. This is part of Municipality's scheme for rehabilitation of the slum dwellers. So far, 28 neighbourhood committees in 13 slums have been formed. These programmes should be popularised. UBSP may not be popular among the prostitutes or among women who have tasted the means of earning easy money. However, efforts by both the government and the voluntary sector are needed in encouraging women and men in their households to avail such benefits.

2. Since migration to urban areas creates the chain of events like formation of slums and anti-social activities, efforts should be made to create gainful employment for the landless in the rural areas. Self-employment schemes should be implemented without faults, gaps, corruption and delays. Strict birth control measures would help in limiting the size of the family. Economic push factors must be kept under control in the villages, so that the attractions of the city such as industrial employment opportunities become the last resort of the ruralite. This helps in delimiting the size and number of slums.
3. More than the women, it is the men who should be blamed for the practice of prostitution. It is their unemployment and habits of crime, laziness, alcoholism and gambling habits which force their women to earn by whatever means they could. Under no conditions a woman prefers to become a prostitute. Exceptions are the call girls who get into the profession for fun and male company. Such cases are in a minority. Economic reasons are basic which need to be solved. The male members of the family of the call girls should consider it a stigma to be called as a pimp or relative of a prostitute. Awareness camps for them, *Kala Jathas* depicting stories or songs on the evils of the practice are useful.
4. There are a number of welfare schemes for the benefit of employment of women. They are implemented through the departments of women and child welfare, and social welfare. State programmes include grants to baby care centres to help working mothers, remarriage of widows and *devadasis*, financial aid to the Development of Women and Children in the Rural Areas (DWCRA), protection to orphans and helpless children, Integrated Child Development Schemes (ICDS), special nutrition programmes for pre-school children, mid-day meals to pre-school children under the special component plan, Integrated Family Welfare Programmes, maternity benefits to women agriculturists and labourers, and appointment of Grama Sevikas and Mukhya

Sevikas. Other schemes which help the household are Mane Belaku , Joint Loan Programmes under Women Development Corporation and KSFC, Training-cum-production programmes which give loans to women, EDP etc. Under educational schemes, scholarships for attendance to rural women, financial aid to children of *devadasis* and other poor women, scholarships to physically handicapped women (both State and central), loan for materials, Seed Money Scheme, *Aadhara*, and incentive to talented handicapped.

The above schemes are highly beneficial to the welfare of rural women, only if they are properly implemented. Official information has shown both satisfactory as well as tardy progress in their implementation. Some schemes like land grants to *devadasis* has picked up over the years, while training and self-employment schemes have shown slow and fluctuating trends. It is possible that the attraction of agricultural land has led to cases where women are owners only in name, while men are the real masters. Or, the land is already sold away to upper castes in the village. Participant Observation in a few villages has shown that *devadasi* rehabilitation schemes are largely on paper and a farce. Livestock sanctioned to them are not brought home. Instead, they are sold away to clear outstanding loans. The male relatives of these women often exploit their own wives or mothers by swindling such grants. In the case of other programmes, either delay in release of grants or vacancies in posts have been causing slow progress.

There is the need to rectify these. Proper implementation of the above schemes will reduce the flow of displaced, unemployed, landless agricultural labourers and marginal farmers to the urban areas. Most of the migrations are not wilfully made. Circumstances have forced them out of the villages. Therefore, one solution to the problem of prostitution is to make life more comfortable in the villages so that emigration is reduced. Women are still valued and respected in the villages here. Although appearing to be rough, the villagers are kind at heart and condemn vice.

5. Having started the industries, the industrialists have to shoulder responsibilities of providing basic infrastructure/civic amenities to their workers, irrespective of the latter's class. Often, health related security measures are waived by them. Pollution control

> measures face the same fate. Narrow business interests of industrialists leads to negligence of workers. Women in particular face the brunt of the problem. Labour Inspectors are not sincere in work. Contractors do not pay minimum wages to workers, specially to innocent women. Exploitation of labour is high. Even trade unions are politicised in their activities and they are no less than others in exploiting the poor. Stringent implementation of regulations may help the poor workers.

At present no concerted effort is being made by any voluntary organization in Bellary to tackle the problem of prostitution and unsafe living and working conditions for women. One or two leading NGOs are based in the urban areas catering to some needy women from the slums. But even the role of these organizations in either creating public awareness about the vices, or to offer remedial measures is limited. One such NGO conducts training classes in tailoring to ex-*devadasis* living in an extension in Hospet town. It complains of problems in obtaining finance from the government to offer sincere service. It appears that those NGOs which depend on the government for funds, and which are small-time organizations, with limited staff, inexperienced, vulnerable for pressure from both the politicians and the goondas, is inefficient in countering such a gigantic problem like prostitution. Bigger organizations like MYRADA may have to enter into the arena. There is an urgent need for the entry of the NGOs to act as facilitators in welfare work undertaken by the government. They should intervene between the government and the people, pose challenges to the law enforcing bodies like the police by keeping vigilance.

# 14

# ROLE OF GOVERNMENT

## Gearing up Law and Order Machinery and Creating Institutional Structures

P.V. SHENOI

### Introduction

We are addressing the issue of securing the proposed industrial development in Bellary district in a socially and economically harmonious manner, which will maximise welfare and incomes as well as minimise misery, injustice and inefficiency. A massive investment is anticipated during the next 5 to 6 years which obviously has conjured visions of paradise for some, plunder for others and strains on government machinery.

One should not yield to a feeling of utter helplessness and impending social disaster; it is possible indeed to accomplish industrialisation with reasonable social and economic harmony, if the lessons of past experience are wisely applied. In many western developed countries, benefits of rapid industrialisation have been realised with minimal disruption of the socio-economic fabric. In fact, the West has developed a framework for creative enjoyment of an unprecedented standard of living. The generation of poison simultaneously with nectar, in "*Samudra-manthan*", is probably unavoidable. We, as social engineers, have to devise systems to maximize the nectar and neutralise the poison. There are adequate lessons of experience to help achieve such a desirable result, provided the people of Bellary, Karnataka and India have the vision and determination to do so.

In this chapter, it is proposed to outline the organizational and policy initiatives to create and develop institutional structures to tackle potential problems on fronts like planning and financing, law and order, physical infrastructure, municipal services and social defence. All these public services will involve substantial additional public costs. Past experience shows that industrialization, while costing the exchequer heavily in terms of additional outlay in public service infrastructure, also generates additional tax revenues for the government to help meet a fair part of additional cost of governance. However, the basic principle is that the industrial unit concerned should bear the cost of economic and social services rendered to its employees, though it may charge its employees for a fair sharing of this burden. One important factor that has emerged is that a large number of public services, including water, sanitation etc., can be entrusted to private contractors on cost-effective basis and further that it is unnecessary to maintain a large army of public employees to render those services.

**Physical Planning**

It is reported that Bellary district has deposits of about 1032 million tonnes of high quality iron ore and 19 million tonnes of manganese ore, mostly concentrated in three taluks in descending order: Sandur (5 clusters), Hospet (8) and Bellary (4). The annual extraction of iron ore ranged between 2.75 to 4.5 million tonnes and of manganese ore 0.13 million to 0.32 million tonnes between 1976 and 1991. In 1995-96, 4.9 million tonnes are expected to be exported (55% by public sector) and 2.4 million tonnes used for internal consumption. Over 25,000 workers are reportedly employed in the mining activity in the district. It is learnt that there are 20 large and medium-scale units in Bellary district, including the mega steel plant, the Jindal Vijayanagar Steel Ltd. (JVSL), under construction; Rs. 1,000 crores are reportedly already invested and Rs. 4,000 crores more are expected to flow into the district in 2-3 years' time. It is thus clear that infrastructural, municipal and social services have to be provided at or near the mines and factories in these three taluks, if the full benefits of the massive investment were to be derived.

Mining of iron ore and manganese as well as production of iron and steel therefrom are activities which are extremely land specific. The commodities in question are bulky; and they are huge consumers of land for mining and processing. Locating townships, housing estates, educational, shopping, entertainment and other plazas as well as transport circulatory systems require extremely careful physical planning in order to economise land and optimise distances from the points of view of industrial pollution and civic amenities.

It is expedient to entrust to the Bellary Urban Development Authority (BUDA) and similar organisations set up in the district, the responsibility to develop infrastructures in the three taluks, if necessary by a law to be passed by the State Legislature. BUDA would take steps to develop areas in the three iron ore taluks of Bellary district. It should expeditiously prepare preliminary land-use plans with the help of competent town and country planners, for making the best use of the natural resources consistent with social objectives. It is difficult to build up expert staff for this purpose in a short period. The task can be entrusted to competent private sector town planners/architects, carefully selected from a field of at least 8 to 10 competent bidders. The preliminary master plans prepared by the selected town planner should be widely publicised; and meetings should be held in all localities by the BUDA and other authorities to explain the proposed plans and invite any claims for its improvement as well as any objections to the features in such plans. These claims and objections should be methodically heard from the affected persons at a pre-notified place and time; and a judicious decision should be publicly delivered within a period of, say, three months of the completion of hearing. There should be an opportunity to appeal against the decision of the Authority to a quasi-judicial body appointed by the State Government; the decision of such body should be final.

Those who wish to set up housing estates, shopping complexes etc., should abide by the Master Plan finalised under the above procedure. It would not be open for any owner of the land included in the Master Plan to use the land for any purpose other than that authorized. Compensation according to law should be provided for the land acquired for public purpose. These plans should form part of District Development Plans under Article 243(ZD) of the Constitution. The companies intending to establish industrial establishments within the jurisdiction of BUDA should be required to submit their land-use plans which should conform to the rational land-use plans finalised by the BUDA. In other words, the iron ore mines, factories, road network, hospitals, shopping centres, schools and playgrounds, housing colonies etc., of the industrial establishment should be laid out in tune with rational land-use norms and industrial policy; in addition, drinking water supply and drainage should also be provided. No licence for iron ore exploitation and other industrial activity should be given till all these pre-requisites for sound socio-economic safeguards are provided and the licensee agrees to meet the full cost thereof. The guidelines specified by the State Pollution Control Board should be followed in this regard. The concerned industrial unit should submit a time-bound programme to implement all these safeguards, in tune with the gradual expansion of the mining and processing activities. The BUDA should set up a Committee for each major establishment to monitor the implementation of these measures within the specified time. Failure of the industrial unit to do so should receive appropriate sanction including closure of the industrial unit.

It is unfortunate that the experience of urban land planning authorities in Karnataka or other States has not been particularly inspiring. It is inevitable that the prices of land would soar; efforts to moderate this by acquisition by the government under the law have proved to be unsuccessful. The owners of land have used political and other influence to escape lawful acquisition of their land. Land acquisition under the law should be kept to the minimum: only for schools, hospitals, roads, parks and other public utilities. Housing estates are best left to the private sector. Large scale acquisition of land by government for public housing estates has often failed; many exceptions had to be made in response to external pressures, with the result that housing development plans have failed to inspire confidence and serve the purpose for which they have been intended. What is wanted in Bellary is a special commitment to answer the urgent needs of the situation, with due regard to the criterion of efficient resource use as well as fair-play to the land owners.

It has been noticed that with urbanization and the consequent upsurge in land values, "land grabbing" or unscrupulous transactions in land, become rampant. Unscrupulous persons deceive owners of land (often recipients of pieces of land from government under land reforms) and get powers of attorney to sell such land, in return for small sums of ready money and under deceit. At times, unscrupulous persons encroach upon government land, create records of possession and even ownership (often with the help of dishonest government officials). Almost always, the "land grabber" acts under a power of attorney of the owner/possessor of urban land. Often the record of lands are altered fraudulently (or even lost) in government offices, at the instance of such unscrupulous persons. These land grabbers are well organized, with support from dishonest officials in government offices. Public interest requires that the genuine owners of land should get the benefit of the upsurge in land values and further that such land should be available on payment of just compensation for use in pursuit of public interest e.g., roads, drains, green space, schools, etc., if logical land-use planning requires it.

There is no easy solution to the problem of land grabbing, excepting vigilance on the part of owners and on the part of related government offices. It is necessary for Revenue officers to hold meetings with the land-owning people about the do's and dont's; powers of attorney should be viewed with suspicion. Public awareness and education as well as swift action against land encroachers and grabbers are the best antidote.

**Law and Order**

The transition from a rural/pastoral to industrial society is accompanied by a change in the crime-pattern, unless strong public spirit and moral forces prevail upon the inhabitants to respect the law. There is likelihood of increases in crimes like dacoity, robbery, house theft, pick-pocketing, criminal breach of trust, rash and negligent driving and crimes under the Excise Act; white collar crimes, relating to banks etc., may also increase. The number of police stations in the three taluks would have to be increased in the light of the increases in population and crimes; and the police force would have to be trained in the prevention, detection and prosecution of crimes common in industrial areas. Similarly, the number of courts as well as the size of jails will also need review.

The police stations as well as the Taluk Police organizations need to be provided with vehicles for greater mobility to prevent traffic crimes. They should be headed by better trained and more senior police officers. A more sophisticated approach will have to be taken by the police to train the citizens for taking due precautions to safeguard their properties and persons and thus reduce the incidence of crime. Police-Public Coordination Committees should be set up and they should play an important role. The management of traffic will need more sophisticated handling. Traffic islands and traffic lights will have to be built. All in all, the law and order organization needs to be considerably strengthened.

There is a need to have police stations manned exclusively by women police to take care of gender-related crimes like eve-teasing, harassment of women, rapes, abduction of women, trafficking in women, prostitution etc. These police stations should be located near slums and market places where the incidence of such crimes is high.

**Physical Infrastructure**

The National Commission on Urbanization (1988) has urged that urban development plans should be comprehensive and compatible with the overall strategy at the State level. Specifically, it has called for factoring into the State Plan the increased demand for power, transport, communication, water, housing, and other services from each urban entity. The Master Plan for the three industrializing taluks in Bellary district should specifically assess the demand for the above services under three demand scenarios: high, medium and low, at different paces of local development. The single most important constraint might be land; and preparation and implementation of master plans for land utilization should solve this problem. The BUDA should secure time bound agreements with different authorities responsible for creating these infrastructural services.

The BUDA should work closely with the different Municipalities and the Panchayats in the three Taluks so that a unified approach is followed by all to facilitate efficient exploitation of mineral resources and creation of the best support services to the industries and the inhabitants of the area. The BUDA should generate resources through loans from the money market and grants from the Government for this purpose.

It is important to note here that the users of all infrastructural services should be adequately charged to recover the full recurring costs, as well as to provide for repayment of loans and for future expansion. For services like water supply, drainage, housing etc., institutional finance is available from HUDCO, banks and other financial agencies on commercial basis; their use should be maximized, since it is unrealistic for the BUDA and local bodies to expect large grants or soft loans from the State or Central Government.

## Municipal Services

The industrial units should be encouraged to build and operate their exclusive townships and provide to them community services like drinking water, drainage, sewerage, roads, street lighting as well as housing services. It would be quite fair for them to charge their employees for these services. There are many steel townships like Tatanagar, Durgapur Steel Township, Bhilai Steel Township etc. which run on the above lines. The BUDA should provide for this in the agreements with major iron and steel businesses in Bellary district. The BUDA should assist the Municipal and Panchayat bodies and industrial townships to plan and operate civic services. While the industrial units are expected to look after all the civic necessities for their employees in their industrial townships, experience has shown that separate townships spring up around the industrial townships to provide several services, which are not supplied by the industrial establishments. The Panchayats in charge of these areas need to be upgraded to Notified Area Authorities so that they can get higher municipal powers and a higher powered Executive Officer to face these difficult problems of urbanization. The single important problem of "emerging areas" is that their citizens are called upon to pay a higher tax needed for larger infrastructural services, even before the latter can take advantage of the newly arrived development.

## Social Welfare and Social Defence

The local authorities like municipalities, notified area authorities and Panchayats in the three talukas should be encouraged to undertake an attack on urban poverty in an integrated manner, emphasising both employment generation and access to basic services involving community level organizations. The Prime Minister's Rozgar Yojana has been introduced to deal with the problem of urban unemployment. Unfortunately, slums do spring up overnight mostly on public lands, unless advance plans are made (a) to evict such squatters and protect such public lands and (b) at the same time, identify areas where housing for the poor can come up. In the latter areas, drinking water, sanitation, roads, schools and social centres should be specifically provided; otherwise, the poor tend to squat on the public land nearest to the places of their avocations/markets and subsequently prevail upon the political leadership to "regularise" their slums. Again, planning for (b) above, very far from the places of avocation of the poor, has failed; there are no short-cuts!

Unfortunately, evils like prostitution, liquor addiction and maltreatment of women and children have been widely observed in newly emerging urban areas. Social defence needs to be strengthened against such evils. These social evils are the result of breakdown of the traditional values of our society when the avaricious forces of capitalism assault it; the rural folk who work in urban areas, often without their families with them, fall a prey to these vices. Use of police force has limited impact; social action, in terms of provision of good housing and recreational amenities, religious and social services etc., can be an antidote to these evils. The industrial establishments should be encouraged to provide better environment through community activities. Non-official/voluntary organizations should also be encouraged to provide these environments and services; and assistance from Central and State Social Welfare Boards or voluntary organizations like SEWA should be secured to build them up.

**Conclusion**

Swift industrialization as planned in Bellary district throws up considerable challenges for the development of imaginatively designed official and non-official organizations to attend to the emerging problems. Fortunately, there are some success stories to light up the path. The State Government and BUDA should prepare films and video tapes of these success stories for exhibition in the cinemas and other public centres for educating the public. Creative participation by the industry as well as the local population of workers and residents is of vital importance. It would not do to depend upon the State Government to contribute all the costs; the beneficiary industry and residents have to make fair financial contributions. In the final analysis, it is the commitment and vision of the latter which will pave the way for a more harmonious life for them in the newly emerging industrial centres of Bellary district.

# 15

# ROLE OF PANCHAYATI RAJ INSTITUTIONS

SUDHIR KRISHNA

## Introduction

The rapid industrialisation ushered in the District of Bellary has got a tremendous bearing on the area and its people. The district taken as a unit would surely be witnessing tremendous growth of its gross domestic product, per capita income and several other such indicators. However, there are various critical dimensions of human development and environmental/ecological factors which are going to be under adverse pressure, arising directly or indirectly out of the industrial activities.

The other papers presented in this workshop have narrated the various dimensions of the possible adverse factors. To recapitulate, they would be as follows:

(a) The physical infrastructure, such as the road network, railways, postal services, telecommunications, industrial water supply, electricity and the industrial layouts—all are getting stretched beyond reasonable limits.

(b) Education and health facilities, being the key infrastructure for human development, too are in the need of big expansion and qualitative improvements.

(c) Basic civic services such as housing, drinking water and sanitation are woefully inadequate even now and would become still worse.

(d) The environmental and ecological balance in the region has suffered enough damage in the past decades and is in urgent need for corrective measures.

(e) Social vices such as liquor trade and crime against women and against other weaker sections are on the rise.

Most of the study reports have recommended for an active participation of the industries themselves, along with the Government and NGOs, in ameliorating these problems. This chapter would highlight the possible role for the Panchayati Raj Institutions (PRIs), namely, the Zilla Panchayat, Taluk Panchayats and the Gram Panchayats in these efforts.

**Why Panchayats should Involve**

The reasons for focussing on the role of the PRIs in this context are conceptual as well as pragmatic. The conceptual factors emanate from the *raison d'etre* of the PRIs, i.e., "to function as institutions of self-government", vide Article 40 and Article 243G of the Constitution. Article 243G specifically expects the State Legislatures to assign powers and responsibilities to the Panchayats of various levels so that they (the Panchayats) function as institutions of self-government in regard to the preparation and implementation of plans and schemes for economic development and social justice.

It should be appreciated that the industries in India are facing stiff global competition, with the liberalised imports of goods and technology. The cost of capital in India is as high as twenty per cent, among the highest in the world! On the other hand, the value of rupee keeps falling vis-a-vis most other currencies. The productivity of labour is also not very high. To cap it all, there is the acute shortage of power, coupled with frequent tripping/failure of power supply. All this has made it extremely difficult for the industry to take upon its shoulder the variety of social infrastructural development projects in the region, however laudable it might appear. This is one of the reasons why the local bodies including the PRIs should join with the industry in these efforts.

The second reason is that the industry should be viewed as a contributor also, and not only a beneficiary, in the process of regional development. They need to be made a part of the team and not just the beasts of burden, even though such burden could have arisen primarily on account of the industry itself. This logic would also lead to the conclusion that the industry, Government, municipalities and the PRIs should jointly invest in and operate the development infrastructure.

Thirdly, the PRIs of the district should feel involved and proud about the arrival of large industries in the district. At the moment, they are largely bystanders and, quite often, either skeptics or seeking largesse from the newly arriving industries. PRIs and other local bodies donning adversarial role in interfacing with industries, is going to be most unfortunate and retrograde situation. We have to create an environment where the local bodies are participants in decision-making in respect of industrialisation of their district/region. As of now, this job is performed by the State Government and other 'higher-level' agencies to the total exclusion of the local bodies. This system has got to be reversed. The State Government should convene a formal interaction with the local bodies at periodic intervals and exchange notes about the industrial development of the region. In this background, let us examine some of the key developmental schemes where the efforts of the PRIs could be fruitfully coupled with non-PRI sources (State Sector etc.) for augmenting the benefits of the region.

**Development of Road Network**

It is seen that the road network of the district is qualitatively inadequate to cope with the carriages carrying weighty goods such as minerals, ores and finished goods like iron and steel. There is an urgent need to widen the roads and make them 'load-worthy'. There is no clear estimation of the quantum of funds required for this upgradation but it would be around Rs. 10 to 15 lakhs per kilometer.

While one can suggest that the industries as well as the government should pump in additional money in the region for road development, it would, in reality, be difficult to bank on these two sources alone. Employment schemes such as the Jawahar Rozgar Yojna and Employment Affirmation Scheme could be dovetailed with the State PWD resources in such a way that the labour component of the cost is charged to the Employment Schemes, whereas the capital costs are met out of the PWD funds. Such an approach would provide an opportunity for financial as well as emotional involvement of the concerned Gram Panchayats and the Zilla Panchayat with the development of this important infrastructure. It will also provide greater employment opportunities to the local people.

While the 1996-97 Budget for Bellary Zilla Panchayat provides a sum of Rs. 13.55 crore under JRY, there is also the usual Plan and Non-Plan Head of Account for Roads and Bridges, under which the following grants are available as shown in the Table.

In addition, funds can be booked from Drought Prone Areas Programme (DPAR), HKADB (Hyderabad-Karnataka Area Development

| Sl. No. | Head of Account | Amount (Rs. in lakh) |
|---|---|---|
| 1. | Master Plan for Rural Roads | 11.00 |
| 2. | Sethu Bandhan | 11.00 |
| 3. | Asphalting of Roads in Village Limits | 11.00 |
| 4. | Formation of Roads in Sugar Factory areas | 5.50 |
| 5. | Halli Heddari (Village Main Roads) | 12.29 |
| 6. | Construction of Roads with People's Participation | 11.00 |
| 7. | Rural Communication | 20.00 |
| 8. | Asphalting District Roads | 20.00 |
| 9. | Other Road Formation | 20.90 |
| 10. | Improvements to existing roads | 9.30 |
| 11. | Formation of other Roads in Sugar Factory areas | 9.06 |
| | Total (PLAN) | 142.05 lakh |
| | Roads and Bridges (NON-PLAN) | 105.79 lakh |
| | TOTAL OF PLAN + NON-PLAN | 247.84 lakh |

Board) Programme and Border Areas Development Programme (BADP), in all of which the Zilla Panchayat has got some say, though to varying degrees.

**Water Supply**

Water is a scarce commodity in whole of the peninsula, more so in Karnataka, and still more so in Bellary district. The district received annually less than 500 mm of rainfall, which includes 'cloud burst' kind of rains, so that the actual useful rainfall is meagre. Subsoil water is getting depleted fast, despite the commendable efforts of the agencies for soil and water conservation and for re-charge of subsoil water.

In this background, the newly arriving industries aspire of tapping water from the Tungabhadra Canals or the dam. Already the tapping of dam water by the JVSL has caused great consternation among the farmers and the people at large. Further such tapping by the industry will surely be objected to by the people strongly.

The water available in the canal network is also oversubscribed already. Besides, water usage and distribution in respect of Tungabhadra Project is covered by an inter-state agreement between the triparian States and therein availability of any surplus water for the new industries is ruled out.

The solution to this problem lies in a synergetic effort of the industry, Panchayati Raj bodies and, wherever possible, urban bodies. The region is interlaced with seasonal rivulets and nallas. On such water courses, check-dams, including the underground bandharas, can be constructed by the joint effort of the beneficiary Panchayats, Industries and others (e.g. municipalities). Such water storage could be maintained also jointly by the same agencies.

For the joint ventures of this type, the funds from the concerned industrial units, municipalities and from the various possible Heads of Account of Zilla Panchayats/TPs/ZPs could be pooled. In respect of PRIs, the possible Heads of Account would be as follows:

(a) JRY/EAS
(b) DPAP
(c) HKADB
(d) DLDB (applicable to Kottur area)
(e) Soil Conservation Programmes
(f) Minor Irrigation

To the extent such combined projects yield to the needs of Departments of Social Forestry and Fisheries, the funds earmarked for these sectors could also be pooled.

**Other Development Programmes**

We have discussed in the foregoing paragraphs the need and scope for involvement of the Panchayati Raj Institutions in development of two key infrastructural facilities, namely road and water supply, needed for industrial development. Similar arrangements are possible, and in fact necessary, in respect of several other sectors without leaving it to be handled largely by the industries. Let us see some other examples in brief and then make concluding remarks.

**Women's Welfare and Protection**

While industries are obliged to make physical and financial provisions for the female work-force, those arrangements can be significantly augmented by the Zilla and Taluk Panchayats, by utilising the schemes of ICDS,

Women's Development Corporation, Formation of Mahila Mandals, DWCRA, DWCUA etc. The ZPs can also be helpful in mobilising State Sector Schemes such as Legal Aid Programme to protect the poor people including women.

**Housing Development**

The Bellary-Hospet Urban Development Authority (BUDA) has got a significant role to play in ensuring proper location of the industry and various other infrastructure and facilities. The State Government must take the BUDA into confidence, in the absence of which the BUDA will be cornered to look at the industry only as a source of securing License Fees or Development Charges. Besides the BUDA, the concerned Gram Panchayats and Taluk Panchayats can also participate in development of proper house sites and layouts, using the schemes of JRY, Ashraya, etc.

**Awareness among the People**

The institutions of Gram Sabhas, as envisaged under the Karnataka Panchayat Raj Act 1993, can be very effectively utilised to bring home the recommendations made in various study reports in respect of worker's rights, women's rights, literacy movement, environment protection, ecological balance, health care and similar other issues. In fact, in the absence of this approach, the Gram Sabhas would become a dissatisfying experience for the people. On the other hand, doing so would make the Gram Sabhas more purposeful and satisfying for the people. Besides, it will bring out integration of development efforts of different programmes at the grass-roots level.

**Concluding Remarks**

Some doubts may be raised about the possible adverse effects of the pooling of Panchayat Funds and on the viability of the Panchayats themselves. It is, however, intended here, by way of concluding remarks, to dispel such doubts. First, the apportionment of funds among the Panchayats should continue to be governed by the Gadgil-type formula introduced by the State Government on 19th December 1986. Within that allocation, the Panchayat should, while planning for the assigned schemes, take note of not only the internalities of the existing problems of the people and the area, but also the externalities of the fall-out of industrialisation. The planning of the various programmes and schemes by the Panchayats should aim at synchronising the same with the schemes of the State sector, industries' contribution and other non-governmental efforts. Such synergetic efforts would enhance the benefits accruing out of those plans and programmes manifolds. It will also make the environment for industrialisation of the district less controversial and more purposive.

# 16

# ROLE OF INDUSTRIALISTS
## Private Enterprise with a Social Perspective

V.M. RAO

Mega projects like the one now in the initial stages of implementation in Bellary-Hospet area, have some common characteristics. They involve huge investments and long gestation periods. They are expected to act like a magnet attracting a host of other industries through forward/backward linkages and transform the area of their location along with its rural hinterland, a transformation imposing severe strains on the local area and communities typically rural-cum-agricultural in their economic organisation and activities. It is also usual for the mega projects to be under considerable compulsion to adopt state-of-art technologies requiring specially trained technical and managerial personnel recruited from outside the area. Frequently, such technologies assume ready and abundant availability of land, water, power and transport and communication facilities which are already under pressure in our economy even with its present modest pace of industrialization.

The other point to be noted about the mega projects is that, while they are located in a particular area, they belong to the national/global networks and do not operate as a component only in the local economy. They have a profound influence on the local area, people and the economy but their perspective and concerns remain focussed on wider issues transcending the area of their location. It is easy for them to merge with larger networks leaving the problems of the areas of their location to local people and organisations with meagre resources and expertise. This gives rise to enclave-like settlements alienated from their neighbours and doing little for the poor cousins surrounding them while drawing on the natural wealth of the areas. Inevitably, there are murmurs of internal colonialism.

However, such an outcome is not unavoidable. With some advance planning and at a modest cost to themselves, the mega projects can play a positive role in helping their hinterland to transform and modernise itself. The mega projects, with their enormous political weight and prestige and command over resources, can be powerful catalysts in activating the development potential of the area and its people. Apart from their own resources even a small part of which could make a dent in the problems of local area, the mega projects could make use of their entrepreneurial and managerial skills to guide the local organisations to augment and effectively pool the funds available for development purposes. Even more critical could be the technical inputs they can provide for infrastructural planning for the emerging future. There are three prerequisites if the mega projects are to play their catalytic role effectively. First, from day one they should establish communication links with the local organisations to become aware of local problems and to have a forum for periodic discussion and review. Second, a conscious policy to win the support of local people would be a valuable asset in maintaining a peaceful and congenial atmosphere for their economic operations. Third, a representative body of all industries in the area would be of help in taking a holistic view of the development needs of the area and to bring together the different agencies to secure coordination and synergy. This body could promote voluntary organisations among the people so that eventually the local people themselves could take a lead in lobbying for funds and using them in a systematic and cost-effective way.

The mega projects would need a well-thought-out plan of action to guide their activities for the local people and area. Distinction would have to be made between problems calling for immediate attention and those which need a phased approach over a fairly long period. Similarly, the activities which are implemented by individual units would stand on a different footing than those to be handled by the representative body. An attempt is made in the brief listing given below to indicate the activities which might be of help to the mega projects to get organised to play their catalytic role in a systematic way.

(a) The individual units could pursue a conscious policy of drawing their workers and subordinate staff as far as possible from the surrounding areas. In the long run, a stable, competent and contented workforce with a significant local component could have a wide-ranging beneficial effect on the local people. There would be greater awareness on their part of the importance of education, health and acquisition of skills. Cultural activities of the unit residential communities could be vehicles to communicate new values, attitudes and perspectives attuned to change. Properly planned, the township of the industrial units could become models for the surrounding communities. For all these effects to occur, the management, staff and workers of the units would have to be ready and willing to integrate themselves with their neighbours rather than remain aloof from them.

(b) The second important front on which the individual units can act is combating the threat of pollution. Industries are commonly perceived as being indifferent to the problem of pollution. They are even believed to use their talents and resources to evade the legislative provisions made to prevent pollution which in any case remain mostly on paper. It would be best for the industrial units to follow a transparent policy of educating the local people about the problems of pollution and seeking their cooperation in tackling them. Often, the search for the solution would have to begin in the research laboratory and its implementation would need continuing consultation and collaboration with local people. The units may be tempted to evade their responsibility for the problems of pollution but, in the long run, the transparent policy would bring them benefits far outweighing the costs. It would lay a strong foundation for building bonds of trust and mutual interdependence between the units and the local people. Again, an area with a pollution-affected economy would hardly provide a congenial setting for vigorous industrial growth and diversification.

(c) There are two other lines of action which the mega projects could pursue collectively i.e., through their consortium operating through a representative body. These are (i) provision of infrastructures and amenities, and (ii) institutional arrangements for training and imparting of skills. As regards the first, the mega projects are likely to bring into the local area for their own use hi-tech facilities for transport, communication and access to energy, water etc. They also usually provide modernised housing, schools, hospitals etc. to their workforce. All-too-often, the township of a mega project would present a sharp contrast to the neighbouring communities living in traditional style with minimal and deteriorating amenities and facilities. While a degree of dualism is inevitable in this respect, it would also offer an opportunity to the mega projects to help in evolving a programme for upgrading the amenities, facilities and infrastructures. The mega projects could come to an understanding to set apart an agreed part of their proceeds to form a fund which could augment the resources allotted to the area by the government and other agencies. More important, the consortium could collaborate with the latter agencies, including the NGOs, to prepare a perspective plan to be implemented in phases in accordance with the availability of funds and priority needs of local area. Given their world-view and technical expertise, the mega projects would be in a position to visualise an optimal feasible programme for amenities, facilities and infrastructures. With the advent of Panchayati Raj institutions, the situation with respect to funds is likely to improve considerably. This, combined with the collaboration-cum-advisory role of the mega projects could lead to substantial improvement in the local area. This is a major front along which the mega projects could play a catalytic role.

(d) Equally important is the contribution the mega projects can make to building up wide spectrum of skills among local people. Owing to the highly sophisticated technology, the direct impact of mega projects in terms of employment they generate would be modest. But the activities emerging as a spin-off of mega projects could bring in their wake large additions to employment. A practice becoming increasingly common is for the mega projects to hand over a number of service functions to specialised agencies. The latter, in turn, would prefer to draw their workers from the local area as the service providers usually operate on a small scale and would not be in a position to set up facilities like housing etc. except for their top management. Secondly, with the growing middle-income population owing to the pickup in the economic activity the demand for a wide range of services would register fast increase and there would be a growing informal sector with rising wages which the local people would find relatively easy to enter. Third, the mega projects create expanding room for self-employed skilled persons engaged as subcontractors, carrying on maintenance and repairs, supplying materials and equipments and processing products ranging from simple to sophisticated. A number of programmes are now in operation to help local people to benefit from growing employment opportunities. A common weakness of these programmes is that the training component of these programmes, particularly for self-employment, fails to equip the people to meet the requirements of emerging opportunities. The consortium of mega projects would have excellent credentials to make informed guesses about the types of skills needed and to devise appropriate training modules for them. The consortium can also give a lead by organising model polytechnics which could later be replicated by local institutions. With the availability of good training facilities and expanding employment opportunities, the loan-cum-subsidy support given by the government programmes is likely to become far more effective than in the past.

The purpose of this note has been to plead for a plan of action which could help the mega projects to make a contribution towards tackling the development problems of local area and people without losing their focus on their principal function of producing hi-tech products and services for the national and global economy. In the long run, development of local area and people would be a positive factor helping the mega projects to grow and gain strength. The plan of action would need a lot of detailed homework and continuing deliberations. Thinking along the activities indicated above could give the mega projects a good start and some relevant targets to fix their sights on. Hopefully, once a steady beginning is made, the response of local people would help the plan of action to acquire its own momentum to move onwards to fresh fields.

The role of industrialists outlined above assumes particular importance in the emerging economic and political changes in India. The new paradigm of promoting rapid growth and industrialisation through structural reforms seeks to provide a level playing field and a congenial policy regime for the industrialists. This, in turn, places the responsibility on the industrialists to help the communities in their areas in adjusting to the radically changed patterns of life necessitated by industrialisation. Further, the recent constitutional amendments to activate Panchayati Raj Institutions, the much larger provisions now being made for infrastructure and amenities and growing political awareness among target groups open up vast scope to improve the living conditions in small towns and villages. The technical expertise and the business acumen of industrialists could help these places in drawing up plans to benefit from the new opportunities. Third, and most important, the industrialists could infuse a new sense of purpose and direction in the programmes for preparing the poor for skill-based occupations which have remained mostly ineffective so far. On the whole, if the industrialists play their part effectively, rapid industrialisation could become a blessing for the backward and the poor instead of being a curse as is apprehended by activists now. Needless to add, in the long run, the industrialists themselves would gain immensely from such a benevolent process of industrialisation. Hence, a bold and generous social perspective would strengthen private enterprise rather than be a burden on it.

# 17

# THE ROLE OF VOLUNTARY ORGANISATIONS

MADHUSHREE SEKHER, B. VIJAYKUMAR and C.K. SHYAMALA

## Introduction

Industrialisation leads to economic growth with a resultant positive impact on both human and physical resources. But concurrently, there could be several adverse fallouts which, if not tackled at the opportune moment, may negate the expected benefits. Corrective strategies in this regard involve two exercises—anticipating the possible ill-effects to gauge their magnitude and then, identifying appropriate agencies and the role which they can play to mitigate the problems (Aziz, 1996). It is the second exercise that is the specific concern of the present chapter.

In this context, this chapter seeks to examine the role which the voluntary sector can play in minimizing the negative impact of the massive industrialisation process expected to take place in Bellary district in the coming decade. Such an exercise acquires significance in the light of the fact that Bellary district is a traditionally backward area of Karnataka. Any development endeavour heie should, therefore, not only result in the improvement and strengthening of its infrastructure and institutions, but also in producing better living conditions for the masses.

The argument in this chapter draws strength from the 'VOICE' concept, as developed by Hirschman (1970). It represents a strategy calling for mobilisation of the locals or affected people and enabling them to 'voice' their needs through appropriate participatory institutions. This could make the society, including the administration, responsive to the people's requirements and, thereby, help in countering to some extent the negative impact of the development process.

The information for this chapter was gathered through discussions with the personnel of different voluntary organisations operating in Bellary district, particularly those working near the industrial centres such as Bellary city, Hospet and Sandur. Local leaders, administrators and the general public were also informally interviewed to get additional insights into the possible future role,of the voluntary organisations in the district. The data thus collected was supplemented by available secondary information on the subject.

The presentation here has been made in four parts. The first section theoretically assigns the role which voluntary organisations are expected to play in any development endeavour aimed at improving the well-being of the people. Against this backdrop of the 'expected role', the second section briefly presents the 'actual role' of the voluntary organisations operating in Bellary district and the type of activities they are presently engaged in. The future role which the voluntary organisations intend to assign to themselves and the activities which they need to undertake to help mitigate the adverse impact of industrialisation in the district has been dealt with in the third section. Finally, in the fourth section, some suggestions are made about the future role the voluntary organisations have to assume in view of the challenges posed by the industrialisation taking place there.

**Expected Role of NGOs**

Generally speaking, industrialisation causes certain negative effects on both the economy and society which can be commonly anticipated. These effects, as noted elsewhere, arise on account of pressure on physical and social infrastructures, municipal services, land, labour and on account of the emergence of consumerism, nexus between politicians, businessmen and criminals, and generation of air and water pollution. If these are the problems that can be expected in Bellary district following its industrialisation, what could be the role of the voluntary sector to help control the situation? Theoretically speaking, the voluntary organisations being location-specific and working with people, have an important role to play in any effort aimed at ameliorating the industrial negative effects. Their 'expected role' in this regard need not be so much as implementing large programmes but rather as providing supportive mechanisms, and complementing the work of the district administrative machinery.

In this sense, voluntary organisations can be expected to play a three-fold role in Bellary district in the coming years:

1. The first type of role could pertain to service delivery (welfarist activities) wherein the organisations could provide direct service to individuals. For instance, they can pressurise for better and adequate municipal amenities or to ensure proper services from different public delivery departments like health, public distribution system, sanitation etc. In this context, they can contribute towards improving living conditions in the slums. They can also maintain local care homes, providing shelter to the old, destitute and the orphan.
2. The voluntary organisations could also take on a role aimed at educating the public and building awareness. In this context, they could conduct skill formation programmes/training for the locals, particularly for the poor with a view to equipping them to avail the employment opportunities thrown up by the industrial activity in the district. They could also undertake programmes aimed at making the public aware about different development schemes of the Government and social welfare activities, so that the latter benefited from such programmes. Above all, these organisations could build public consciousness on issues of social relevance.
3. Third, and most importantly, the voluntary organisations could act as platforms for "social advocacy", helping the citizens, to the extent possible, to secure their rights and to get their grievances redressed. In this pursuit, the voluntary organisations could function as pressure groups and liaison with the authorities, both the administration and the industries. In this sense, their role here could have three broad manifestations : (i) help promote environment protection/pollution control; (ii) ensure justice for the underprivileged and the deprived; and (iii) secure a share of the benefits of industrial development to the locals.

Here it needs to be mentioned that in the present development scenario the goal of enabling the poor to participate in the decision-making processes affecting their lives, is central to the ideology of voluntary organisations. It, therefore, follows that going by the expected ill-effects of industrialisation listed elsewhere, the impact of voluntary organisations as agencies for mitigating the adverse industrial fallouts could be felt most in the social sector and to some extent in regard to environment. With regard to the impacts on existing infrastructure, both physical and municipal, and on certain critical factors of production like land and labour, the voluntary organisations' role could be limited mainly due to the limited resources at their disposal.

**Actual Role of NGOs**

In the light of the arguments presented in the foregoing section, it now becomes imperative to ascertain the 'actual role' of voluntary organisation operating in Bellary district. Here it needs to be clarified that, going by the different types of roles 'expected' of voluntary organisations as vehicles of development and change, no single role-model can be prescribed to the exclusion of other models. A voluntary organisation can execute different types of development activities assuming different types of role—as a means for service delivery, or as a promoter of public consciousness/ awareness, or as an instrument for social advocacy. What could happen is that a voluntary organisation may be particularly engaged in certain types of activities pertaining to one role-model. This may have predominance over the organisation's other types of activities relating to other role-models. In this sense, the voluntary organisation may be identified as having a specific role in the overall development scenario.

An inventory of voluntary organisations operating in Bellary district reveals that not many of them are active here. Focussing mainly on organisations having their base in the industrial centres, we can come across a few bigger and relatively well-established agencies like the Leading Organisation for Rural Development (LORDs), Bellary; the Development Promotion Group of Action Aid, Bellary; Bellary Diocese Development Society; the Working Women's Forum, Bellary Branch; and the Stella Mary Women's Welfare Association, Hospet. Side by side, a few smaller organisations (in terms of organisational size, activities and area of operation) can also be found here such as the Mother Teresa's Institute, Bellary; Mathe Pragati Kendra, Bellary; the Family Counselling Centre, Bellary; Don Bosco Technical School, Hospet; St Anthony's Community Development Project run by St. Anthony's Church, Bellary; and the Bellary Area Comprehensive Rural Development Project run by John Hands Memorial Church, Bellary (presently closed down due to some technical problems). A third set of voluntary organisations, namely, the smaller self-help youth organisations, Citizens Associations and Cooperatives can also be found in the district.

Discussions with the office bearers of these organisations reveals that they are all involved in various development activities. But a critical review of their activities makes it apparent that their interventions are quite limited taking into consideration the various socio-economic development issues that need attention. From Table 17.1 it is obvious that voluntary organisations in Bellary district are essentially playing a two-fold role-service delivery and educational/awareness building. With regard to service delivery, it can be discerned that the organisations have primarily concentrated on giving health care to the poor, in providing assistance (mainly through loan facilities) to the needy, to take up income generating activities, running primary schools and balwadis for poor children and providing shelter to the poor and destitute, including street children. Their activities relating to awareness building range from merely imparting general education to the poor children, to building people's awareness on various issues of public relevance and training them on different income generation activities with the objective of ensuring their economic empowerment.

Thus, although the voluntary organisations in Bellary district are presently engaged in implementing different types of development-related activities, they are not actively involved in social advocacy. This fact could become a weakness for them in their future role in the district. With the industrialisation accelerating there, a number of social issues may arise such as those pertaining to atrocities against women and children, environmental pollution and securing services and benefits for the people not only from the State administration but also from the industries. These may necessitate the involvement of voluntary organisations as pressure groups, calling for (i) policy change, (ii) ensuring that the public is not deprived of some benefit/amenity, and (iii) guaranteeing that injustice does not go unpunished.

Secondly, going by their present activities, the voluntary organisations have limited territorial coverage. For instance, the on-going activities of LORDs, one of the well-established voluntary organisations in the district, are mainly concentrated in 35 villages of Kudligi and Sandur Taluks. Likewise, the Development Promotion Group of Action Aid is presently working in 111 selected villages in the district for implementing its Integrated Rural Water Supply and Sanitation programme. The Bellary Diocese Development Society, having its programmes in the four districts of Bidar, Gulbarga, Raichur and Bellary, has merely 57 self-help credit unions in different villages with a total membership of 1200. This indeed is very limited considering the area covered by the organisation. Stella Mary Women's Welfare Association, another well-established voluntary organisation of Bellary district, is presently working only within Hospet town limits. In course of time, of course, they intend to adopt two villages

TABLE 17.1: **Activities Presently Undertaken by Voluntary Organisations in Bellary District**

*(A Sample)*

| Sl. No. | Name of Voluntary Organisations | Service Delivery | Educational/Awareness Building/Motivational | Social Advocacy |
|---|---|---|---|---|
| | | 1 | 2 | 3 |
| 1 | LORDs | (i) Primary health care: door-step first-aid services<br>(ii) Animal health care services<br>(iii) Supply of livestocks to *devadasis*;<br>(iv) Assisting people is constructing village approach road | (i) Agricultural development programmes (Improved Dry land farming technology);<br>(ii) Extension of development awareness on various Govt. schemes like literacy, health and family welfare, women and child care;<br>(iii) Education;<br>(iv) Environment Development Awareness in rural areas;<br>(v) Formation of self-help village co-operative credit funds;<br>(vi) Training on various income generating programmes like piggery mat weaving, rope making, tailoring, bio-intensive farming and poultry;<br>(vii) Motivating villagers to form self-help groups | (i) Assisting people in mobilising Jantha Housing, old age pensions;<br>(ii) Acting as a forum for anti-dowry, *devadasis* and child marriage system, prohibition of alcoholism protection of the human rights of women |
| 2. | Development Promotion Group | (i) Integrated rural water supply and sanitation programme (Project cost of the water supply part | (i) Building people's awareness about the software components of the watershed management programme | |

| | | | |
|---|---|---|---|
| | of the programmes is free of cost, while for the sanitation part the beneficiaries have to bear 30 per cent of the cost)<br>(ii) Execution of watershed management programme | | |
| 3. Bellary Diocese Development Society | Primary Health Care | (i) Awareness programme in villages on development issues like health, nutrition, savings etc.<br>(ii) Motivating villages to form self-help credit unions | |
| 4. Working Women's Forum (Bellary Branch) | (i) Providing loan facilities to poor women | (i) Training women on income generating activities like tailoring;<br>(ii) Motivating rural women to form self-help credit cooperatives;<br>(iii) Imparting leadership training to women;<br>(iv) Building awareness against *devadasi* system | |
| 5. Stella Mary Women's Welfare Association | (i) Creches and Balvadis for children and shelters for street children;<br>(ii) Watershed management programme at Hadagali Taluk | (i) Awareness building on health, sanitation and hygiene, etc.<br>(ii) Building people's awareness about the software components of the watershed management programme;<br>(iii) Training on income-generating activities for women such as tailoring and typing classes | Campaigning public interest litigations on issues of public relevance like pollution control (compelled a sugar factory in Hospet change its chimney size to control pollution |

*(Contd.)*

TABLE 17.1 *(Contd.)*

| | 1 | 2 | 3 |
|---|---|---|---|
| 6. Mother Teresa's Institute | (i) Shelter for destitute and street children; (ii) Running a charitable hospital; | (i) Education for slum children | — |
| 7. Mathe Pragathi Kendra | (i) Shelter for poor and homeless children; (ii) Counselling to broken homes/families | (i) Free education for poor children; (ii) Awareness building among village women on family planning and nutrition; | — |
| | | (iii) Training to poor women as house-keepers to get better employment. | — |
| 8. Family Counselling Centre | (i) Counselling on family disputes; (ii) Running two balvadis and a lower primary school | — | — |
| 9. Don Bosco Technical School | (i) Working among people affiliated with leprosy—medical support and rehabilitation. | (i) Skill oriented training for the leprosy patients (recovered) according to their physical ability. | — |
| 10. St. Antony's Community Development Project | (i) Scholarship for poor children; (ii) Running a balvadi | (i) Typing and Computer training. | — |
| 11. Bellary Area Comprehensive Rural Development Project | (i) Health services for mother and child | (i) Skill oriented training for income generating activity; | — |
| | | (ii) Motivating villagers to form self-help groups. | — |

for watershed development programme. The Bellary Area Comprehensive Rural Development Project, when it was in operation, covered only 13 villages. If this is the situation under the bigger, better organised voluntary organisations in the district, the geographical coverage under the smaller organisations cannot be expected to be any better. In fact, from what could be discerned during the field visits, the smaller voluntary organisations in the district are extremely localised.

Further, it needs to be stated here that the activities of the voluntary organisations in Bellary district have been essentially targeted towards the rural poor. As such, not many of their activities are targeted for the urban areas (Table 17.1). As on today, the interventions of voluntary organisations in urban areas are mainly of three types; (i) Organisations like the Mother Teresa's Institute, the Maitre Pragati Kendra, the Stella Mary's Women Welfare Association are providing shelter to street children, destitute and running schools for poor children, mainly from the slums; (ii) organisations like the Lions/Rotary Club, Bellary, are providing health facilities for the slum dwellers; and (ii) various sanghas and mandalis in the towns are engaged in imparting training in income generating activities to the urban poor. It can, thus, be said that although the externalities arising due to industrialisation of the district will be felt more by the urban people, the role of voluntary organisations in the urban areas is very negligible as of now.

One important fact that cannot be overlooked here pertains to the Urban Basic Services Programme for the poor, a programme of the UNICEF being implemented in Bellary by the city Municipality. This programme was introduced in the city in 1991 to help the urban poor. Started in Bapuji Nagar Slum of the city and covering a population of 2,180 with a sum of Rs. 3,66,000.00 being spent so far, there are plans of extending the programme to 11 other identified slums in the city. Being executed through self-help neighbourhood committees, this programme can be regarded as one of the important interventions made so far towards urban development. Its significance can be perceived more once the fallout of the industrialisation process starts seeping into the local society.

Notwithstanding the above observations, the voluntary organisations in Bellary district have one very important strength. There is a strong networking among these organisations within the district. In fact, most of the voluntary organisations in the district are members of a district level federation of voluntary agencies called "Seva Sangama". This is a recent development. But it could, in future, become a base for the member organisations to exchange their views, information about their work and also to tap resources (mainly technical and manpower) available with them for better execution of their activities.

**The Future Role**

Given the 'expected role' which voluntary organisations operating in Bellary district need to assign to themselves and the 'actual roles' which they are presently performing, it thus becomes obvious that these bodies need to further strengthen their endeavours so that they become responsive to the demands of the changing times. This could happen in two ways:

(i) by expanding the nature and scope of their on-going activities to take-on issues and problems arising out of the changed societal conditions following the industrialisation process; and
(ii) by expanding the geographical coverage of their work, specifically to the urban centres wherein the impact of the industrialisation could be felt in a greater measure.

Their impact, in this sense, could become more effective if the NGOs highlighted their role as 'social advocators' and worked as pressure groups. However, this is not to undermine their present role and activities in the development of the district. They are undoubtedly tackling the various problems faced by the masses. At the same time, they need to re-examine their present role and activities in the light of the changing environment in the district. What could be their new role/activities in future? Have they already taken up any steps to meet the possible challenges of the industrialisation that is taking place there? It was with these questions in mind that the personnel of some such organisations were spoken to. It may be observed that very few of them had as yet undertaken specific activities pertaining to the changing scenario in the district. In fact, not many of them had given any thought to the expected externalities of industrialisation. Broadly, the voluntary organisations' responses in this regard could be grouped into three categories:

1. Not much awareness about the future industrialisation process in the district and the possible negative impacts: smaller organisations come under this category. However, in course of our discussion some of them, particularly the self-help groups like Mahila Mandalis, felt that in future they could take on the role

of safeguarding the interests of their group members and protecting them against atrocities or injustice by providing "group-strength".

2. Having some awareness, but lacking the initiative and capabilities to plan out future strategies and areas of action. This was either due to inadequate resources or manpower. In certain cases, particularly in the case of religious, charitable institutions, a feeling of religiosity could be observed. This made the members of the organisations' to believe that their future course of action was all "in the hands of God".
3. Having intentions to extend their present activities to cover a wider and varied sections of the public: some of the organisations felt that they could do this by imparting developmental educational training aimed at skill formation, keeping in view the future increase in demand for labour in various sectors following industrialisation. Such a course of action would ensure that the locals benefit from the growing labour market and be gainfully employed. At the same time, organisations like the Development Promotion Group felt that they could extend their present activities to the slums and assist the district administration in setting up low cost houses for the poor. The Stella Mary's Women's Welfare Association felt that they could take on a more active role in public litigation cases, particularly those aimed at pollution control; it thus intends to act as a pressure group.

Notwithstanding this, larger organisations like LORDs and the Bellary Diocese Development Society (BDDS) expressed that they would mainly centre their future activities around people in the villages adjacent to the industries and in urban slums, and motivate them to form self-help groups or credit unions. These groups could be sensitized to the emerging problems and could, in turn, work for meeting their own needs. In this manner, they felt that the people themselves could participate in their own development by tackling their immediate problems such as those relating to housing, sanitation, availability of drinking water, as well as having access to credit.

On the whole, a sense of realism could be observed in the approach of the voluntary organisations towards the expected adverse fallouts of the industrialisation process and the role which they could assume in this situation. It was expressed that voluntary organisations cannot take up development/corrective actions based on certain assumptions only. This amounted to "groping in the dark". The voluntary organisations could perform better if they operate more realistically, responding to the actual needs of the people. Nevertheless, it was generally accepted that the voluntary organisations had a vital role to play in the development of the district in the coming years.

## Some Suggestions

In the final analysis, it becomes imperative to examine whether the voluntary organisations operating in Bellary district have the capability, in terms of resources and manpower, to cope with the demands of the changing situation taking place there, and to live upto the expectations placed on them. It is true that the recruitment of their staff is made by the organisations in accordance to the nature of their programmes, strength of their resources and the extent of the geographical area in which they are working. Nevertheless, the voluntary organisations in the district presently do not have adequate staff except for LORDs and, to some extent, the Development Promotion Group. The former has a total staff of 66 members, which includes qualified full-time as well as part-time workers. Besides, the organisation has community organisers and in each village, where they operate, there is a village health worker and an animator. The Development Promotion Group has about 30 staff members working in different villages where they have their programmes. But this was not the case with most other organisations. The Bellary Area Comprehensive Rural Development Project (which is currently defunct) had a staff strength of 7 members. Often the organisations, however, have only a minimal staff strength. But this is not to overlook the fact that they had problems in recruiting suitable personnel. Nevertheless, some of the organisations tried to resolve this problem by making use of the available qualified personnel (doctors and engineers) on honorary basis.

Secondly, the voluntary organisations operated on different levels of budget. We found that there were voluntary organisations which had Rupees One lakh as annual budget and there were others whose budgets ran into several lakhs of rupees. LORDs for instance, had an annual budget of roughly Rupees 20 lakh while that of the Development Promotion Group was about Rupees 30 lakhs. But, on the whole, most of the organisations expressed that they faced the problem of inadequate resources.

It is against this background that the future role of the voluntary organisations needs to be identified. There, however, is a general lack of perspective in this regard. If the voluntary organisations are to play a significant role in future and help counter the adverse fallouts of the industrialisation process, there is a need for: (i) informing them about the changing circumstances in the district and the expected ill-effects, and (ii) to provide them with some guidance for planning their future strategies. In this context, the ideal thing at the present moment would be for the local administration to call a meeting of the established voluntary organisations operating in the district, and provide them with the necessary information. In the process, an action plan could be prepared specifying (i) the priority areas requiring the contributions of the voluntary sector, (ii) the type of activities they need to undertake, (iii) the agencies whom the organisations could approach for financial support, and (iv) to work out the time frame for their activities. Such a step would not only make the impact of voluntary organisations more effective, but it also could ensure that they work in tandem with the administrative machinery.

It needs to be further emphasised that the overall role of the voluntary organisations should be as catalysts or enablers, working complementarily with the administration and not as competitors. This assumes relevance in the context of the recent government efforts to revitalise the local self-governing institutions through the 73rd and 74th Constitutional Amendment Acts, which have brought issues pertaining to community development under the purview of the panchayats. Accordingly, there is today a need for understanding the functional strength and weaknesses of the local government institutions and the voluntary organisations so that a 'complementary approach' could be identified for tackling the problems of development (Sivanna, 1996).

Based on the above suggestions it is felt that voluntary organisations in Bellary district should assign to themselves the following activities in the coming years.

- — Mass awareness camps on negative impact of industrialisation.
- — Public awareness on mining activity related problems—ill effects on public health; safe drinking water; erosion of top soil and conditions of non-vegetation.
- — Massive forestry programme involving the public.
- — Create a forum for dialogue between NGOs, industrialists and administration.
- — Intensify family counselling, family welfare education programmes.
- — Strengthen the district level network of the NGOs.

— Through the district level network, liaison with State level network, and use this network to work as pressure group on Government.
— Self-help groups may be promoted and links established with financial institutions to avoid problems of money-lending.
— Social safety committees of the public may be commissioned to prevent rowdyism, gangwars etc.

## REFERENCES

Aziz, Abdul (1996), "Industrial Investment: Socio-Economic Implications", *The Hindu Business Line*, Ist January.

Hirschman, A.O. (1970), *Exit, Voice and Loyalty*, Harvard University Press, Cambridge, Mass.

Sivanna, N. (1996), "The Role of NGDOs in Decentralised Governance", (Background Paper prepared for the workshop on ...). Institute for Social and Economic Change, Bangalore (Unpublished).

# 18

# CONCLUSIONS AND RECOMMENDATIONS

SUDHIR KRISHNA

## Introduction

Industrialisation of Bellary district bases primarily on the iron and steel sector, considering the large availability of iron ore. The district also has vast expanse of manganese ore, besides gold, silver and non-metallic ore such as granite, moulding sand, quartz and red oxide: while most part of these ores has been exported, iron ore is in the process of *in-situ* utilisation also due to arrival of several large and medium industries basing on iron ore in the district. While such a large-scale industrial activity brings in vast scope of an all-round development of the district, it also calls for a close scrutiny of the problems associated for full exploitation of the growth prospects. The exercises carried out in this study have brought out many interesting points and also policy recommendations. In this chapter, it is intended to present the findings and recommendations of these exercises in a summary form.

## Physical Infrastructure

Growth of industries in any region depends heavily on the concomitant growth of supporting infrastructure such as the roads, railways, transport vehicles, postal network, telecommunications and above all, electricity and water.

Over the years, Bellary has lagged behind in the relative growth of these infrastructure facilities among the twenty districts of the State. During the years 1976 to 1990, the rank of Bellary district has gone down from eighth to twelfth at the State level.

*Road Network*

The existing industrial activity as well as the prospective industrial development call for a well-knit and strong road network, since heavy loads of raw materials and finished products would move. But, the average road length (per 100 Sq. Km.) in Bellary district is just 49.44 Kms as against the State average of 70.17 Kms (1993-94). The majority of road network of this district is in the category of 'other district roads', in which category the district fares better than the State average. The need, therefore, is to give greater attention to development of road network of higher categories, viz., National Highways, State Highways and Major District Roads.

The load bearing capacity of the existing road network being low, it is unable to carry the heavy loads of ores, machinery, iron and steel. These roads are shared by the industry as well as the general public and now both the industrial as well as the public are suffering due to the poor condition of the road. Therefore, two recommendations are made. One is that more roads should be laid in the category of National Highways, State Highways and Major District Roads. Also there is need to have multi-lane road particularly in the Sandur-Hospet-Koppal sector to facilitate smooth movement of traffic and to avoid road accidents. The second is that greater attention should be given for improvements and better maintenance of the existing road network.

Most of the road network is interlocked with human habitation. As a result, movement of ores, machinery and other goods has been causing dust, noise and smoke nuisance to the people. This necessitates construction of bypass roads or ring roads for major townships such as Hospet and Bellary. Even the remaining habitation require service roads appurtenant to the highway to provide for safety to the people of the adjoining areas. Truck terminals should be developed at important stations such as Bellary, Torangal and Hospet.

*Railways*

Movement of ores and the industrial produce is greatly facilitated by the railway network. Rail network also offers convenience for the other users of these roads (i.e., the general public). The existing railway network for Bellary district is at 3.34 Kms for 100 Sq. Kms as against the State average of 1.59 (1992-93). The number of railway stations in the district (2.73 per

1000 Sq. Kms) is also better than the State average of 1.11. Rail link to the sea port from Bellary is largely only to the Madras Port, which is a circuitous route. Besides, the Madras Port is highly congested too. The need and scope for improvements in respect of the railway network are as follows:

(a) Multi lane rail track is required in identified reaches such as Hospet, Guntakal;
(b) Goods station be separated from passenger station, at Hospet, Tornagal and Sandur.
(c) Rail link to other sea-ports such as Mangalore, Karwar, Goa, Vizag be identified and strengthened.
(d) Railway network for transporting the raw material from neighbouring districts such as limestone from Chitradurga, Shimoga and Dharwar and manganese from Chitradurga and Dharwar needs to be strengthened.
(e) The wagon capacity and availability should be enhanced for faster goods movement.
(f) A systematic linkage between road and rail network is warranted to facilitate 'multi-modal' transport of goods. This would include development of Truck Terminals in the vicinity of goods railway junctions, but bypassing the major towns and cities.
(g) Direct rail links from Bellary to Bombay and Madras needs to be established.

*Communication Network*

In respect of postal network the district with 24.11 post offices per lakh of population is placed favourably as compared to the State average of 19.57. However, the network of speed post and other such specialised services needs to be augmented.

In terms of number of telephone connections per lakh of population, Bellary district with 707.15 is far below the State average of 1016.47 (1993-94). It should be noted that modern day industrial development depends heavily on telecom facilities for the purposes not only of telephoning and STD/ISD, but also of telex, E-mail, Internet, WEB, Fax etc. Therefore, the telecommunication network in the district needs suitable upgradation and development.

*Power (Electricity)*

Iron and steel industry, which is the soul of industrial growth of the district, is a heavy consumer of electrical power. The existing power generating stations at Tungabhadra right bank, Hampi and Munirabad put together generate 99 MW. But the JVSL plant itself would, at its production stage, need 160 MW of power. An estimate of the power needs of all the industrial projects in the district would put the need for power for steel sector alone at 2640 Million KwH.

Though there indeed is a power grid available, the State itself being deficient in power, the grid can be of little help to the district. It is also realised that the State alone cannot provide this huge quantity of power. In the circumstances, the following recommendations are made:

(a) Large industrial units should be forewarned to include 'captive generation of power' in their project proposals.
(b) Smaller units should be encouraged to form a consortium for power generation and use. They should, through the respective consortia, install captive power generation, distribution and supply system.
(c) Bellary, being hot and arid with only scanty rainfall, is ideally suited for tapping solar energy for power generation. A special project for the purpose should be mooted in the lines of Rajasthan.

*Water*

Most of the new industries coming up in the district are dependent on the Tungabhadra water—either from the reservoir or in the river flow. Considering the fact that very little of surplus water is available in this river, novel methods of storing water in check-dams built on minor rivers/rivulets/streams with a carefully designed support system from sub-soil resources, is warranted. Harvesting of rainwater and all types of surface run-offs is also recommended.

*Development of Industrial Estates and Townships*

The growth of large and medium scale industries in the district has opened up avenues for development of ancillary units of secondary and tertiary types on a big scale. These units need to be provided with suitable physical environment for systematic growth. This calls for setting up of a series of industrial estates by the Karnataka Industrial Area Development Board (KIADB) with suitable water, drainage, power, internal roads etc., are provided therein.

Larger conglomeration of such units/estates would need setting up of properly laid industrial townships with necessary support facilities such as schools, shopping complexes, hospitals, housing, recreation. The industry as well as various agencies such as the local bodies and commercial establishments can be involved in creation as well as maintenance of such facilities.

**Human Development**

As it is, Bellary ranks 12th in the State in terms of physical quality of life index. The growth of industry in the district has thrown a challenge to the policy makers in terms of human development, in so much as the latter has to keep pace with the externality of the former. If the people are not 'developed' apace with the industrial growth, it has two fold problems: One is that the industry would have to get manpower from outside, keeping out the people of the district. On the other hand, it would also give a 'no benefit' situation for the people. In totality, therefore, the human development in terms of literacy, education, health and life expectancy and per capita income, all deserve close attention in the context of the rapid industrial development coming up in the district.

*Health Infrastructure*

The health facilities available in the district are far below the State average as indicated by several indices. The Infant Mortality Rate (IMR) in the district was 87 for 1000 live births, which was the highest among all those districts of the State—the State average being 67 (1981). As for the norms of one PHC for 30,000 population and one sub-centre for 500 population, Bellary needs 63 PHCs and 378 sub-centres, as against the existing number of only 52 and 330 respectively. Availability of health personnel is yet another area of concern, with 42.54 per cent of sanctioned posts of Junior Health Assistants (male) lying vacant. High vacancy prevails in the other cadre of health services. Even the Bellary Medical College has got several key faculty positions remaining vacant for years! This situation would become more severely adverse due to the growing pressure of industrialisation.

Industrialisation is also causing newer challenges to emerge in other forms as well, manifested in growing incidence of respiratory and skin diseases, psychiatric disorders, sexually transmitted diseases (STD), premature termination of unwanted pregnancies, various types of fevers, malaria, diarrhoea etc. To meet with the emerging challenges posed primarily due to industrialisation, the strategy for the health sector should keep in view the following recommendations:

(a) Greater attention needs to be given for the health care of women, particularly the expectant and nursing mothers and the children in the age group of 0 to 6 years.
(b) Preventive Health Care and Awareness Programmes should be launched in the industrial townships, particularly for controlling the respiratory diseases, water borne diseases, STD, AIDS and psychiatric problems. Awareness creation among citizens about the new disease structure will be of great help.
(c) Speciality in medical and diagnostic services should be strengthened, especially in the Bellary Medical College Hospital and the Hospet-Torangal-Sandur area.
(d) Industry should be involved in creation and maintenance of health-related infrastructure.

*Education and Literacy*

In terms of educational facility as well as literacy, the district lags behind most other districts of the State. The literacy rate in 1991 was 45.57, putting it at No.17 out of 20 districts (Sl. No. 18, 19 and 20 were Bidar, Gulbarga and Raichur, all four districts being in the Gulbarga division). Dropout rate is high among girl students in the primary level.

In terms of availability of primary schools per lakh of population, Bellary is seventeenth in the State (72.986 vis-a-vis 93.12) in terms of high schools, nineteenth (8.99 vis-a-vis 12.74), in terms of pre-university colleges sixteenth (2.22 vis-a-vis 3.24), seventeenth in terms of general college education (0.90 vis-a-vis 1.37), sixteenth in terms of technical education institutions (0.37 vis-a-vis 0.51). There indeed is a medical college, which is a feather in the cap of the district. However, more than 75 per cent of pre-university colleges do not have science sections at all. There is a Post-Graduate Centre, aimed to focus at earth sciences at Sandur.

The poor literacy rate is going to lead to exploitation of the poor, men and women, particularly in the context of growing industrialisation of the district. Lack of technically qualified youth would mean they would miss the bus of development ushered in by the industrial growth. The syllabi of polytechnics and ITIs of the district need altering to the needs of the industries coming up in the area.

Considering the strengths and weaknesses of the existing educational set-up obtaining with the district and the opportunities and threats heralded by the industrial development the following policy related initiatives are recommended:

(a) Literacy programme (launched as 'Akshara Vijaya" in the district) needs to be intensified and linked to the functional needs of the poor.
(b) The network of educational institutions at all levels—primary upwards—needs to be strengthened and augmented.
(c) Syllabi of technical institutions (polytechnics and ITIs) should be attuned to the needs of the industries coming up in the area. The syllabi of the courses offered by the PG Centre, Sandur needs to be similarly re-tuned.
(d) Similarly, the recently introduced college of Business Management at Bellary also needs to coordinate its course content and methodology to the emerging scenario of the district. The Nandihalli PG Centre should introduce and strengthen the mining and metallurgy courses in consultation with industry.
(e) More science subjects-based Pre-University and degree colleges should be opened.
(f) Industry should sponsor the effort to improve the infrastructure in educational institutions. There should be some form of formal coordination between industry and educational institutions.
(g) The panchayats, DIC and Urban Bodies should reorient their TRYSEM type of Training Programmes to the emerging needs.

## Urban Basic Services

### *Emerging Scenario*

Bellary as a whole is becoming more urban in terms of population. Among the town and cities of the district, Bellary and Hospet are experiencing fastest urbanisation. The urban population of the district, which was 5.65 lakh in 1991, is expected to double by 2011 A.D. Their fast growth in urban population is partly due to natural growth but is accentuated by the rapid industrial development, which is attracting large number of immigrant workers from neighbouring districts as well as from neighbouring State (Andhra Pradesh). Immigrant workers tend to habitate close to the work-place, leading to mushrooming of slums. In terms of slum population, Bellary district ranks third in the State after Bangalore and Raichur districts.

The emerging scenario narrated above has posed serious pressure on the urban basic services, such as roads, drinking water, street lights, sanitation, water-disposal etc. An analysis of the challenges that are posed before urban basic services, leads to the following recommendations.

*Slum Clearance/Improvement*

The Karnataka Slum Clearance Board (KSCB) should enhance its activities in this district. Existing slums should either be cleared by shifting the inhabitants to safer and better layouts under KSCB schemes, or the existing slums should be improved wherever that is feasible and possible.

*Housing*

Schemes of housing and sanitation available under schemes of KSCB, KHB and Nehru Rozgar Yojana (NRY) should be coordinated and implemented with vigour and focus in the district. Government should take up construction of residential quarters for its employees in a bigger way. Housing Financial institutions such as the HDFC, LIC Housing Finances etc., should step in a significant way in this region. Housing cooperative societies should be encouraged to come in a big way.

*Drinking Water Supply*

Since Tungabhadra reservoir is a significant source of water supply even for drinking purposes (out of below silt level storage), its desilting should be taken up. Drinking water supply level, which is currently 60 LPCD (WHO norms for city areas being 70-100 LPCD), will go down to 12 LPCD by 2015, if not augmented. Hence, augmentation of drinking water supply is a must for all major towns and cities of the district. Quality of drinking water supplied needs to be maintained with greater vigilance, especially in the context of rapid growth of slums.

*Sanitation*

The schemes of 'Sulabh Shouchalaya' should be introduced in all the towns and cities to make available neat and clean toilets to one and all at a nominal cost (pay and use basins).

The Municipal Sanitary workers (paurakarmikas) do not seem to be working with expected efficiency and effectiveness. Suitable training programmes and supervisory efforts are required.

Treatment of liquid and solid wastes in an environmental friendly way is required. The Karnataka Compost Development Corporation (KCDC Ltd) should be invited to step in.

Privatisation of waste collection and disposal should be explored.

Informal and formal citizen groups as well as NGOs should be associated in tackling this mammoth task.

The Urban Development Authority should continuously monitor the growth and development in the related areas and prepare schemes suitable for the purpose in coordination with other agencies concerned.

To implement the above suggestions large sums of money are needed. The urban governments need to mobilise resources for the purpose. One way is to resort to 'user charges'. But having imposed user charges, these bodies should have the political will and clout to collect them effectively.

**Scenario for the Land**

The industrialisation of Bellary district is largely basing on the iron and steel industry and its related activities. Such industry requires large extent of lands, estimated to be around 19 thousand acres. Unless carefully planned, diversion of non-industrial lands (say, agricultural lands) the industrial use in a large scale could have several adverse effects such as the fall in agricultural production, impoverishment of the farmers and agricultural labourers, steep escalation in land value and house-rentals and encouragement of haphazard urban growth as well as land grabbing. Accordingly, following policy options are recommended:

(a) Land utilisation statistics of the various taluks of Bellary district suggest that parts of Sandur and Hospet talukas have large pockets of land which have very low agricultural productivity and could be appropriately transferred to non-agricultural uses.

(b) In certain parts of the district, lands are totally rainfed and subject to frequent droughts. Such farmers would be better off by selling away their lands for industrial purposes, if a compensation of around Rs. 1 lakh per acre is paid to them.

(c) Even so, there should be a careful monitoring of the land requirements of each industrial unit. The scheme of 'land audit', proposed by the Government recently, should be seriously implemented.

(d) In acquiring agricultural land for establishment of industries, the State Government should act as a facilitator and should not make any 'profit' out of the process of land acquisition.

(e) The study did not find much evidence to the effect that industrialisation has induced land grabbing. On the other hand, the study noted that unauthorized occupation and/or cultivation of government land is a popular practice in northern Karnataka, including Bellary, with no correlation to the industrialisation process.

(f) The Task Force Committee to prevent land grabbing and unauthorised occupation of land for cultivation or other purposes should be strengthened.

**The Labour Situation**

As of now, almost 75 per cent of the workforce is engaged in agriculture sector, in mining and quarrying about 2 per cent, in manufacturing and service 5.58 per cent and tertiary sector accounting for 8.58 per cent. A little over 81 per cent of the growth in workforce (1981 to 1991) was in agriculture sector, and in non-household industry it was of the order of 16.25 per cent.

There is an overall labour surplus scenario, except in 'skilled workers' category. In respect of mining and quarrying, the trend is to go in for greater mechanisation which reduces the scope for greater employment generation (Jobless growth). On the one hand, the productivity of workers is sub-optional. On the other, workers' statutory needs relating to medical facilities, creche, etc., are usually moderately provided. There are evidences of child labour in hazardous activities. Workers in the organised sectors, such as mini-steel plants, get better wages and better welfare measures than their counterparts in unorganised sectors such as mining. It is often noticed that the legal machinery for redressal of workers' grievances remains inefficient and ineffective. This gives scope for entry of political tensions or unscrupulous elements in the scene. Most often, the workers remain unaware of their rights and responsibilities and the statutory protection etc., meant for their welfare. There is a widespread employment of contract labour. Such labour is highly insecure and susceptible for adverse exploitation. Considering the existing and the emerging trends in the supply-demand and socio-economic environment for the labour force, the following suggestions are made:

(a) Considering the trend towards enhanced mechanisation of various economic activities especially industries, mining and quarrying, skill development programmes for the youth should be taken up extensively. The Departments of Employment and Training, Labour welfare, DIC and Zilla Panchayat can coordinate for this purpose.

(b) Workers' Welfare programmes, as required in the various statutes, should be effectively implemented. These would include payment of minimum wages, provisions of rest-rooms, health/medical care, creche etc.

(c) Employment of children in hazardous industries / activities should be strictly prohibited.

(d) More reliable data-base should be organised and maintained in respect of workers' profile.

(e) Labour welfare departments should be vigilant in enforcing the statutory welfare provisions and in redressing the workers' grievances through statutory means.

(f) Concerted efforts should be made by the government, industry-owners and workers to keep away criminals from the labour welfare/union activities.

(g) Worker education scheme should be vigorously implemented.

(h) Special care should be taken by the Government to ensure that the contract labour system is not abused to the detriment of such workers. In fact, Government should seriously consider abolition of the system of contract labour.

**Ecological Scenario**

The iron and steel industry and also the mining and quarrying activities—all are unfriendly to the environment and ecology of the region. Massive dust raised by mining and quarrying causes health hazard; blasting for mining is equivalent to minor earth tremors causing scare for the protected monuments of Hampi; dust settles down in the water and spreads to silt up the tanks and other reservoirs; mining and quarrying is coupled with deforestation, leading to loss of the fertile top soil; gases from the steel plant are toxic and nuisance to human and animal health.

All this has made the once stable ecology of the district into a very fragile one. To prevent further damage to the flora and fauna of the region on account of unabated growth of industrialisation, following recommendations are made:

(a) Awareness needs to be created among the people at large and among the industrialists of the region about the continued damage to the environment and ecology of the region on account of industrialisation. A benchmark study is needed to assess the extent of environmental degradation.

(b) The Post-graduate Centre for Earth Sciences at Sandur should focus on using safer and more environmental-friendly methods of blasting, quarrying and mining. For this purpose, the academic efforts should be sponsored by the industry.

(c) Applied research activity in respect of qualitatively better, safer and new hygienic mining and quarrying technology going on in developed countries should be identified and adopted with suitable amendments.

(d) Mining debris should be covered with fresh green cover to prevent it from silting up the water courses and sources or from flowing away as dust in the air.

(e) Industry should adopt and undertake a crash programme of desilting of the rivers/rivulets/tanks/ponds/reservoirs.

(f) Rules and regulations governing protection of environment and ecology should be enforced vigorously.

(g) The present lease rentals for mines is abysmally low. It can be raised five-folds.

(h) The Medical college of Bellary should give greater attention to the health and medical problems associated with the emerging industrialisation of the district.

(i) Soil conservation methods should be practised and encouraged extensively.

(j) Special studies should be launched to determine the impact of the industrialisation of different aspects of health of the people and the area, and the preventive/curative measures.

**Urban Credit Needs**

The fast growing consumerism is fanning the fire of credit needs of the people, especially in the urban areas. Besides, there are some traditional occasions for sudden credit need in a family such as birth, death, marriage etc. Cooperative and government sponsored/regulated credit channels such as cooperative institutions and banks are able to provide only about 37 per cent of the credit needs of the people, the rest 63 per cent coming from the money-lenders, chit funds etc. While the indigenous, unauthorised credit institutions provide to the people a channel of credit flow that is simple to access, yet it is highly exploitative in nature. The need is to make the official credit channels more approachable and more publicised. Consumption credit limits should be raised and made more easily available.

Other measures suggested to curb the exploitative character of non-formal credit channels are as follows:

(a) The provisions of Karnataka Money Lenders Act should be strictly implemented.
(b) License Fee and Security deposits for money lenders and Pawn Brokers should be raised substantially.
(c) Illegal transactions should be subjected to heavy penalty.
(d) Full-time Assistant Registrars should be appointed to keep illegal money lending in check.
(e) Operation of Chit Funds should be through a joint account of the foreman and Assistant Registrar.
(f) Vigilance squads should be introduced for frequent surprise checks of the informal money-lending activities.

**Liquor Trade and Consumption**

As a general phenomenon prevalent in all districts, liquor trade and consumption is growing in Bellary district too. However, industrial development, without the concomitant social and human development, is putting the value system of the society to severe strain and encouraging the folks to indulge in liquor consumption in an ever increasing way. Side by side, the illegal trade in liquor, including bootlegging, is thriving in the district. This seems to be happening with the active connivance of the staff of the Excise department.

The present as well as the emerging scenario is causing accelerated decay of the social, moral and familial fabric of the society. To arrest this trend, a set of remedial measures are suggested, which are as follows:

(a) Rules and Regulations of Excise department with regard to quality and procedure in liquor trade should be rigorously enforced.

(b) Training programmes should be organised for the Excise staff to improve their motivation to perform better service to the society.

(c) Social education and awareness programmes should be launched for weaning away the liquor addicts and bringing them back to lead a healthier life.

(d) Better recreational pastime should be provided to the people in the form of community centres, Functional Literacy Programmes, Art and Culture etc.

(e) NGOs and the social service groups working in this field should be encouraged.

(f) Concerted and co-ordinated efforts should be made by the various government agencies such as the PRIs, municipalities, Department of Social Welfare, Women and Child Welfare, Education, Adult literacy, Information and Publicity etc., to bring about great awareness and consciousness among the people about the evils of liquor.

**Trends in Crime**

The industrial development in the district is bringing in lots of money and opportunities for economic activities with little regulation at the social level; there is a free-for-all type of situation prevailing, wherein only the fittest would win. This race is encouraging formation of unholy interest groups and their unethical nexus for mutual gains at the cost of social peace, discipline and order. Even well defined socio-legal set-up such as trade unions are afflicted. All this is leading to nexus of self-interest among the various interest groups such as the politicians, businessmen, bureaucrats and criminals. The sufferer is the poor and the weak, be it slum-dweller or the labourer or the women or the plain and simple common man.

The situation that prevails at the pre-industrialisation phase itself is worrisome enough and needs to be corrected right away to provide a healthy socio-economic environment when the industrial development comes up in full steam. For this purpose, the following recommendations are made:

(a) There should be well defined and transparent method for recruitment of workers—be it temporary, contract or permanent type of employment.

(b) Laws and regulations relating to protection and welfare of the workers should be implemented rigorously.

(c) In particular, minimum wage laws should be well publicised and implemented.

(d) The perspective plan prepared by the Police Department for this district should be given serious and prompt attention.

(e) The strength of police force should be enhanced in the form of more Police Stations, sub-divisions, traffic police, Railway Police and District Armed Reserve. A battalion of State Reserve Police should be stationed at Bellary.

(f) A set of Women's Police Stations should be established in pockets having higher proportion of female workers and where higher incidence of crime against women is prevalent.

(g) The large influx of immigrant workers needs to be appreciated seriously by all the regulatory and welfare departments and agencies, as these workers are highly vulnerable for exploitation by the various self-interest groups.

(h) Orientation courses should be launched for the workers to make them aware of the labour laws and regulations on the one hand and, on the other hand, about inculcating work culture and work ethics among them.

(i) Habitual offenders and criminals should be identified and booked under stringent laws such as the Goonda Act.

(j) Watch dog unit of citizens should be formed to involve the people in maintenance of social and moral hygiene.

(k) All out efforts should be made to create awareness among the people about the nuances of the aftermath of industrial development.

## Problems Faced by Women

Industrialisation has thrown up new economic opportunities to the people of the region. As a result, they migrate from their traditional socio-familial environment into the new world of industrial development. This new world is, at the social plane, ill-organised and has little social or moral fibre. In this new world, the poor and the weak are the most vulnerable. Women being weak in social and physical terms are highly exposed to a variety of hazards at the work-place as well as outside. Traditionally, women of this region too have been home-bound and sheltered by their men-folk. However, the lack of gainful economic opportunities in the native surroundings, coupled with the newer opportunities offered by the industrialisation, have almost forced the women-folk to out migrate to the industrial world. However, only a few of them are educated enough to get decent jobs. A vast majority of them being unskilled with little education, if at all, end up taking up the lowest paid and most insecure jobs such as domestic servants, mine workers, petty vendors, contract workers and casual labourers.

In the above narrated scenario, exploitation of women in the region takes the forms of:

(i) Job insecurity and low wages and
(ii) forcing women into flesh trade. The following recommendations are made to ameliorate the plight of women:

(a) Skill development programmes should be launched for women under different schemes under DIC, ZP, Departments of Vocational/Technical Education etc. TRYSEM is a good model.
(b) The concept of "Neighbourhood Committees", introduced under the Urban Basic Services Project (UBSP), should be encouraged.
(c) Organisation of women in the form of Mahila Mandals should be encouraged.
(d) Self-employment programmes for women should be launched on a wide-spread basis on the lines of DWCRA scheme. Resources could be mobilised from various departments such as that of Women and Child Welfare, DIC, KSFC, PRI, Municipalities, Women's Development, Cooperation, IRDP, World Food Programmes, etc.
(e) Adult Literacy Programmes for the Women should be given greater thrust and coverage.
(f) Ashraya and similar housing schemes should be utilised to rehabilitate the slum dwellers into hygienic layouts. Pattas should be in the name of women.
(g) Family Welfare programmes should be intensified, with focus tuned to women's welfare.
(h) Other women's welfare programmes such as the ICDS, MNP, SNP etc., should be popularised.
(i) Programmes to reduce dropout rate among female students in primary education should be intensified.
(j) Awareness programmes should be taken up to let people

realise the scope of the problem and its solutions e.g., Kala Jatha, Radio Talks, Peripatetic Documentary Films, Exhibitions etc.

(k) Special police stations for women should be created in identified pockets.

(l) NGOs should be activated to take up women's welfare and development activities.

# INDEX